LIVE & WORK in...

HONG KONG

Visit our How To website at www.howto.co.uk

At **www.howto.co.uk** you can engage in conversation with our authors - all of whom have 'been there and done that' in their specialist fields. You can get access to special offers and additional content but most importantly you will be able to engage with, and become a part of, a wide and growing community of people just like yourself.

At **www.howto.co.uk** you'll be able to talk and share tips with people who have similar interests and are facing similar challenges in their lives. People who, just like you, have the desire to change their lives for the better - be it through moving to a new country, starting a new business, growing their own vegetables, or writing a novel.

At **www.howto.co.uk** you'll find the support and encouragement you need to help make your aspirations a reality.

You can go direct to www.live-and-work-in-hongkong.co.uk which is part of the main How To site.

How To Books strives to present authentic, inspiring, practical information in their books. Now, when you buy a title from **How To Books**, you get even more than words on a page.

LIVE & WORK in...

HONG KONG

**Comprehensive,
up-to-date,
practical
information about
everyday life**

RACHEL WRIGHT

howto books

Published by How To Books Ltd,

Spring Hill House, Spring Hill Road, Begbrooke
Oxford OX5 1RX. United Kingdom.
Tel: (01865) 375794. Fax: (01865) 379162
info@howtobooks.co.uk
www.howtobooks.co.uk

First published 2005
Second edition 2007
Third edition 2011

British Library Cataloguing in Publication Data.
A catalogue record for this book is available from the British Library.

ISBN 978 1 84528 429 9

Produced for How To Books by Deer Park Productions, Tavistock
Cover design by Baseline Arts, Oxford
Typesetting and design by Sparks – www.sparkspublishing.com
Printed and bound in Great Britain by Bell & Bain Ltd, Glasgow

NOTE: The material contained in this book is set out in good faith for general guidance and
no liability can be accepted for loss or expense incurred as a result of relying in particular
circumstances on statements made in this book. Laws and regulations are complex and liable
to change, and readers should check the current position with the relevant authorities before
making personal arrangements.

Contents

Notes

Unlike in mainland China, there is no standard Romanization (or 'pinyin') of Chinese words in Hong Kong; some variety of spellings and forms, such as 'Wanchai' and 'Wan Chai', exist side by side. In this book I have tried to use the most common forms.

Confusingly, the English names of streets and places in Hong Kong are rendered in different ways:

- some are a direct translation from the Chinese, such as Central, North Point and so on;
- some are transliterated to achieve an approximation in English, such as Sheung Wan or Mongkok; and
- some English names have no apparent connection with the Chinese name in sound or meaning, such as Admiralty or Happy Valley.

All figures are expressed in Hong Kong dollars unless otherwise stated. The exchange rate is roughly $12 to the £.

The international dialling code for Hong Kong is 852.

Acknowledgements

A great many people have contributed to this book, some unknowingly and some who were reminded of the fact all too frequently. I would like to thank everybody who provided information, contacts or personal experience that informed the writing of this book, as well as those who were kind enough to read sections for me and offer insightful and practical comments. These include Sue Dockstader, ex-President of the Women in Publishing Society, and all the women from the Society who shared their tips and suggestions with me, including Kavita Jindal and Carol Dyer.

Special thanks goes to Stanley Ng, who designed the street maps and contributed many of the photographs. Thanks also to Johann Steenkamp (a muse in this life as in many others), Melanie Nutbeam, Jacquelyn Anderson, Gwilym Box, Shiona Mackenzie, Vessela Dimitrova, Mimi Mori, Adrian Wright, Peter and Jeanette Wright, Theresa Neumann, Shelagh and Ethan Heath, Diana Cox, Kate Allert, Ken Deayton, Sharon Russell, Anita Chan, Helen Ko, Leonard Wong, the Community Advice Bureau, www.geobaby.com, Jean Nicol, Victor Yuen at Knight Frank, and Edina Wong and Simon Smith at FPD Savills (Hong Kong).

In addition, Mandy Petty, Jasmina Gasper, Mary Bodomo, Simon Scott, Andrew Eden, Dr Trevor Lane and several others who wish to remain anonymous.

1. Bishop's Palace, Wyndham Street
Photograph taken by Stanley Ng

Preface

Since the first edition of this book was published in 2005, Hong Kong remains a highly attractive destination for expatriates and their families. Views on the livability of the city remain much what they were five years ago – it is generally regarded as an exciting, dynamic city in which it is reasonably easy to grow wealth because of the low tax structure and continuing demand for foreign expertise. Obtaining information in English is even easier than it was five years ago, as the government has since revamped its website for English speakers, putting most government-sponsored services and official documents at your fingertips.

This new edition reviews recent political, business and immigration developments of relevance to expatriates, includes quotes from new interviews with current residents and updates all information with regard to websites and contact details for restaurants, shops, leisure facilities, schools and associations previously featured, as well as tips on how to find the latest up-to-date information once you arrive in Hong Kong.

Rachel Wright

2. Village along the Lung Yuek Tau Heritage Trail *Photograph taken by Stanley Ng*

Introduction:
Why Come to Hong Kong?

Hong Kong profile
Population: 94.9% Chinese, 2.1% Filipino, 0.8% Indonesian, 2.2% all
other ethnic groups.
Languages spoken: Cantonese (mother tongue), English and Putonghua
(Mandarin).

An ex-colony, a nation of shoppers, a gourmet's paradise, a cultural desert,
the altar of Mammon. The Fragrant Harbour's reputation always precedes it.

New arrivals immediately pick up on the flagrant incongruities everywhere.
In the searing heat of the midday sun an old woman, dressed in black shirt
and cropped black pantaloons, laboriously pushes a greasy old bamboo
basket along the road. The basket is as big as she is and full of dirty paper
for recycling. It's tricky to steer. The edge of her trolley just misses snagging
the sparkling glass frontage of the Armani flagship store downtown. Inside,
expensively understated elegance is wafted about by unobtrusive air condi-
tioning. Like a spectacular lotus in a muddy pond, beauty flowers above true
grit in this city of 7.01 million souls.

Hong Kong is a densely populated city and, in places, it is squalid and make-
shift. Most people work and live in a fraction of the 1,100 square kilometres
that make up the territory: more than 900 square kilometres are undeveloped
lands and 40% of Hong Kong is designated country park or conservation sites.
It's a jagged mixture of pale rural townships mushrooming in the mountains;
quiet back alleys festooned with drying underwear, songbirds in cages and
spider plants; prize-winning übermodern architectural displays in glass and
light; and old-fashioned trams and colonial trimmings. It's a city with 17 public
holidays, most of them with cultural and religious significance still celebrated

3. Wanchai street
Photograph taken by Stanley Ng

publicly in a traditional manner, such as the lanterns in Victoria Park, the fire dragon in Tin Hau or the towering bun festival on Cheung Chau Island.

It is a city constantly remaking itself, updating its image, exploring, questioning and celebrating its identity. The 'barren rock' has shown that it can hold its own in an evolving global economy, benefitting not only from its willingness to embrace foreign expertise and culture, but also from its interdependence with the powerful neighbour across the border. Hong Kong has made the successful transition from a Crown colony to a city of China, without sacrificing its *joie de vivre* or its commercial success. It has faced financial crises and 'flu epidemics and come out fighting. And the fight goes on to remain value-added, the place international companies will want to base their operations in Asia. In that respect, Hong Kong is still winning out over China because it has something the rest of China lacks – the rule of law and the enforceability of contract.

Immigrants from China and all round the world come here in search of better opportunities and a better standard of living. Money is the ultimate status symbol and respect is reserved for those who've got a lot of it. Making money is a something of a jack-of-all-trades skill in Hong Kong. Take Cantopop stars, for example: not only do they sing, but they also star in movies, dance, model, host TV programmes and endorse everything from the English language and electrical equipment to slimming tea and being polite to tourists. Whilst making a buck seems bred in the blood here, and private enterprise a given, the hugely expensive bureaucracy is becoming a liability. The government has recently decided a diet regime is just what the doctor ordered. The high civil service salaries and perks inherited from the British have increasingly been phased out.

Politically, Hong Kong is also experiencing an awakening of sorts. It was 'people power' that threw out a proposed amendment to a 2003 National Security Bill designed to curb freedom of association and, potentially, the press. It was also low popularity that got rid of the 'figurehead' first Chief Executive for the current Chief, a career civil servant trained by the British. Democratic legislators have had to work against fearful odds because of the power of veto possessed by the Chinese Government, but that hasn't meant they've thrown in the towel regarding obtaining universal suffrage within the next decade. In 2010, five Democrats thumbed their nose at the political rule book by resigning from the Legislative Council expressly

Kong's nightly celebration of itself and its wealth-producing skyscrapers (a show reputed to cost the government around HK$44 million per year).

Hong Kong is praised for its economic freedoms, entrepreneurship, openness, financial solvency, rule of law and anti-corruption regime, and it is still the safest place in China to keep your money. However, many Hong Kong companies – as is the case with companies worldwide seeking a cheap labour market – have already moved their manufacturing and assembling plants to the mainland, and are increasingly shifting back office operations there to take advantage of a well-educated workforce. It's a challenging time for Hong Kong, but it is a time of opportunity, too, as the government looks to private enterprise and entrepreneurship to take the initiative.

EXPATRIATE LIFESTYLES

Foreign talent and expertise are still in demand by Western companies with regional offices in Hong Kong, even as more mainland Chinese professionals are being lured to the territory with lucrative jobs. The salary, accommodation and perks will obviously vary according to individual companies, the most favourable terms being negotiated in home countries rather than in Hong Kong itself.

Middle managers, or foreigners employed locally, are increasingly being offered 'local' contracts that may, however, still include relocation allowances, flights and other benefits not offered to Cantonese staff. Obviously income determines the kind of lifestyle you can enjoy in Hong Kong to a large extent. Factors that make it easier for people to increase their net worth include:

- the low income tax – up to 17% for 2009–2010;
- high salaries, especially when compared to how similar jobs are paid in Europe, Australia and New Zealand; and
- a buoyant job market for those fluent in English and Cantonese or Putonghua.

Hong Kong continues to be an alluring Asian location for expats and most are upbeat about their experience of living and working here. People like the city's vibrant cultural mix, excellent food, outstanding natural and constructed beauty, the international lifestyle, and the many opportunities on offer to broaden your horizons – professionally, culturally and socially – in a climate of personal safety. Asians and Westerners alike appreciate the easy access to a global marketplace and the ease of sustaining a Western or Asian lifestyle:

Chapter One

Living as a Hong Konger

'Hong Kong is generally a very safe and easy place to live, on sunny days it's very beautiful, it's bureaucratically uncomplicated, has great public transport, pretty good food choices and it can be amusingly schizophrenic ... very western but very Chinese.' British expat of ten years

For English speakers, Hong Kong is still the best city in the region in terms of English-speaking service providers, work opportunities and demand for foreign expertise. The government recently revamped its English language web pages at www.gov.hk to stream-line business, leisure and residential information and advice, by-passing the need for virtually any face-to-face contact with a staff representative. New tourism brochures, promoting Hong Kong's cultural and historic past, are being printed for the first time in 2010 to complement the existing substantial amount of information on the Tourism Board's website.

CHALLENGES AND OPPORTUNITIES FOR HONG KONG

China's entry into the World Trade Organization (WTO) has demanded some serious thinking on how Hong Kong can maintain its successful role in the region as a free trade *entrepôt* and create value-added services in its traditional strongholds of logistics and finance. Given that a) direct trade is increasingly permitted between Taiwan and China, reducing the through-flow of business in Hong Kong, and b) Shanghai wants to take over as China's shipping, trade and financial centre, Hong Kong needs to manage and benefit from its relationship with China in order to establish its usefulness and competitiveness in the region. The mandarins in Beijing have a plan for Hong Kong. They want to turn it into the capital of a southern megalopolis of 70 million people, stretching all the way to Guangzhou and Macau. The alternative, for Hong Kong, is unthinkable – obscurity as just another Chinese city. Hong Kong is not going to go quietly into that last good night, despite everything Shanghai can do to steal its thunder. Witness 'The World's Largest Permanent Light and Sound Show' – Hong

5. View of Hong Kong Island north side
Photograph taken by the author

Part One

Living in Hong Kong

to trigger a by-election which they touted as a de facto referendum on direct elections.

The march against the National Security Bill was the turning point for one American expat when it came to how she viewed Hong Kong. Laura, a resident since 1997, commented, 'that was the first time I really felt like "a Hong Kong person". It made me realise that there were many different types of people in the city and even the local Chinese population was composed of people of many different walks of life and ideologies, all literally under different banners at the protest. All of us, however, were there marching for a common goal and all just trying to make a life for ourselves here.'

Other expats find much to admire in traditional Asian values. Long-time resident, lawyer Simon Scott, commented, 'I have grown to like the Asian values of executive-led government, respect, and absence of a welfare state. These characteristics have become more appealing when compared with the relative social degeneration of the Western world during the last 30 years. In other words, Hong Kong's (and Singapore's) values are probably more similar to those of my parents and my youth than the values and attitudes and "human rights" now prevalent in the UK and Western Europe. However, such characteristics should be matched by tolerance and an absence of censorship, which is sadly lacking in most of Asia, although Hong Kong is probably the least censored place in Asia.'

There are around 340,000 expatriates in Hong Kong. Many settle, marry, divorce, put their kids through school and retire here, seduced by the good life. And every year, between one and two thousand decide they are never going back, preferring to renounce their nationality and adopt Chinese citizenship instead.

4. *Over the page:* A seafood seller
Photograph taken by the author

- supermarkets stocking most Western and Asian foods;
- clubs and support groups for expat spouses;
- international schools;
- excellent restaurants and atmospheric bars; and
- a wide variety of entertainment and leisure options, catering to all tastes.

The international part of Hong Kong is very small: Tsim Sha Tsui (TST), Central, Mid-Levels, Soho and Wanchai contain the main shops, cinemas, dining venues and bars patronized by expatriates. This means that it is not unusual to run into friends whilst out shopping or eating. In this respect, it retains a community feel, despite having many of the trappings of a much larger city.

PICK A LIFESTYLE

Hong Kong's foreign community is large enough to support numerous circles, largely determined by work type and income. Although it is an expensive place to live, there is a certain amount of flexibility that enables you to save money – this is important if you are on a local contract and not enjoying a generous company package.

Choosing where to live

The main expenditure is housing and there is a vast range of housing types to accommodate different budgets. One of the best things about Hong Kong is that you have quite a lot of choice over the sort of lifestyle you want to create for yourself. If you enjoy hanging out with friends after work and frequently have to grab a cab to the office in the morning, there is plenty of studio-type accommodation downtown –**Mid-Levels** or **Happy Valley** are preferred spots.

If you're into the club scene, the **Soho** area combines bars, restaurants, gay and straight clubs, and fitness centres. If you want a more laid-back lifestyle, you can live on one of Hong Kong's several inhabited islands in a village house with a garden, where you can keep dogs and let your children play in the street – no cars are allowed on most islands. You can grow your own organic vegetables and watch the sun go down from your roof while you drink a glass of white wine after taking a dip in the sea at your local beach. Walk around in a sarong and sandals and nobody will give you a second glance.

There are also in-between arrangements: bachelor flats conveniently located for commuting, but also close to the sea for those stunning night skylines, or in the heart of neighbourhoods that have a traditional Chinese feel. There are many apartment complexes in different price ranges that cater to families with young children and are conveniently close to shopping and restaurant complexes, fitness facilities and activity centres for kids. Examples include lower-end South Horizons in Ap Lei Chau and high-end Repulse Bay. Meanwhile, the strong-hearted and linguistically gifted can go completely native and strike out for urban Mongkok or rural Tai Wai.

If you want to stick together with your clan, certain neighbourhoods provide shelter to a large proportion of expat nationals from the same country. For example, Americans are found in Repulse Bay and Tai Tam, British in Pokfulam, Japanese and Koreans in Taikoo Shing, while a large mainland Chinese community is in North Point.

More information on residential locations is given in Chapter Five, 'Accommodation'.

UNEMPLOYED OR 'TRAILING' SPOUSES OR PARTNERS

Hong Kong is often touted as a mecca for rich, idle expat women who accompany their husbands or partners on a megabucks package. Whilst their husbands are out slaving away to bring home the bacon, the wives employ a small army of domestic workers to clean the flat, walk the poodle, mind the kids, cook the dinner and generally relieve them of every sort of chore.

What do these women do all day? Get bored, is probably the answer. I don't know; I haven't met any women in Hong Kong who fall into that category. But I do know women such as my Aunty Jeanette, who lives in a luxurious apartment, does not work and has to occupy herself for most of the week whilst my uncle is working or out of town. My two cousins are grown up and live in Australia. The decision to come to Hong Kong was, for her, not a straightforward one:

> Hong Kong is much better than I'd expected. I was brought out here kicking and screaming, because I didn't know how I would be able to make friends if I didn't have the kids around me. In the past, that's always how I'd made friends, by meeting other mums. But when I arrived in Hong Kong I found there's such a wealth of organizations designed to pick you up and help send you on your way, that it isn't a problem.

Getting involved in expat groups

Jeanette found that the **American Women's Association** (AWA) was the best at making new arrivals feel welcome. Other groups she joined included the **YWCA English Speaking Members Department** and **Friends of the Art Museum**, which organizes classes in Chinese history and arts and trips in Asia. Details of these clubs are given in Chapter Twenty, 'Interest Groups'.

Jeanette also joined a Ladies Investment Club, a group of about 12 women of all nationalities who get together once a fortnight to pool money, research stocks and try to make a profit. That's the international part Jeanette enjoys about Hong Kong.

She does know some expat women who are unhappy. One Australian woman in her apartment block is depressed and hates living here. Jeanette's explanation is:

> *She makes no effort. I mean, 9:30 is too early for her to be doing aqua-aerobics downstairs in the pool. But I think it's mainly a question of focus. Her kids are at school in Australia so her focus is in Australia. She comes to Hong Kong for two months at a time, then goes back home. What really helped me to get to know the community is doing volunteer work. Doing one afternoon a week English conversation, or helping with riding for the disabled – my next plan. Otherwise your experience is too transient. Then you don't belong in Hong Kong. If you don't make the effort then it's just a busy town.*

An alternative to working

But what about men and women who accompany their partners to Hong Kong and have always worked but suddenly can't? Either the right openings are not available to them or their visa does not permit them to work. Currently, dependents of people admitted for employment or capital investment may take up employment.

According to Rehana Sheikh, a bright-eyed, chatty, motherly figure who advises clients on relocating to Hong Kong, groups like the AWA's **CHAT** (Come Have A Talk) are vital. Newcomers can orient themselves, network and seek advice.

> *Unless they're the much older age group, most women have skills: either they're lawyers, accountants, in communications or teaching or nursing,*

or whatever – they've all got skills. They bring all their skills to this organization, and through it, people can network and find things to do.

Yes, it is possible to be here with a partner or a spouse and not work. It's very interesting. I've met some (married) women who've come here, got jobs, didn't like the jobs, didn't like the work environment, somehow couldn't relate to the work ethics, stopped working, and they say, 'OK, it's only two years, I'm going to travel, do volunteer work, there's no pressure.' You're enjoying it, you're with friends, you make a difference in the community, you're contributing, you're still being very productive. Instead of feeling sorry for yourself and saying, 'Gosh, I don't like this job', or 'I'm not used to sitting at home doing nothing, I've always earned my own living', they're sort of redefining themselves – or maybe having to do it. Some deliberately, some being pushed into it, and some just reluctantly taking it on and then just loving it after that – and I see that a lot. They find they feel a sense of growth, a sense of awareness, learn about another culture, another region. This is very valuable.

More information on volunteer organizations can be found in Chapter Seventeen, 'Volunteering'.

A new career?

Other options include starting your own business (see Chapter Thirteen, 'Work') or taking time out to re-evaluate your career, which is what Fiona O'Donovan did. Back in the UK, she was the marketing director for a software company, but she left her job to accompany her husband to Hong Kong. She started looking for work and was offered a few opportunities in the marketing field but nothing special. Recruitment agencies were unhelpful: she mentions the language barrier, being branded an expat wife – 'they think you're inflexible because you're dependent on your husband' – and the instigation of Putonghua and Cantonese proficiency requirements by HR departments:

I didn't try as hard as I could have. I'd lost my hunger – it was more of a job for me to find out exactly what I wanted to do.

She realized that she'd always been interested in the fitness industry and decided to take courses in Pilates instruction and sports nutrition. She joined

Isofit and is finding her courses very rewarding. Friends and mentors in the industry have been very encouraging:

> *I was told before I came that Hong Kong is a great place to reinvent yourself. There are quite a few courses available and the qualifications I'm taking are internationally recognized, so they can travel with me.*

More information on retraining is provided in Chapter Sixteen, 'Developing yourself Professionally'.

Chapter Two

Managing Costs

'Hong Kong. Live it! Love it! – the slogan used by the Hong Kong Tourism Board – isn't practical if you're living on the breadline, and the pleasures of dining out, drinking and dancing don't come cheap. Obviously it's easier if you're here with a partner and both of you are earning or pooling resources: singles should aim to earn at least $30,000–35,000 a month before tax to live in reasonable comfort and have some disposable income. Families with children may need to factor in the high cost of international schooling.

MAIN COSTS

If you are paying for everything yourself, you will probably find that your main costs are:

- accommodation;
- education for children;
- entertainment, dining out and drinking; and
- travel.

More information on these main cost areas is provided in the relevant chapters.

OTHER COSTS

Salary tax

Salary tax in 2009–2010 was 17%, significantly lower than in Europe and the US, and is not deducted at source. A government-instated Mandatory Provident Fund (that is, a pension fund) creams off roughly another 5% of your salary unless you have a private pension scheme. More information on this and other taxes is included in Chapters Ten ('Money') and Thirteen ('Work').

Monthly and quarterly bills

Other costs to bear in mind include utilities. IDD/Internet usage rates are extremely competitive, but there are also water, gas/electricity and landline phone connection charges to factor into your monthly expenditure. Cable

6. Admiralty view
Photograph taken by the author

and satellite TV are also available. More information on these services is provided in Chapter Five, 'Accommodation'.

Public transport

Getting to and from work and around town is cheap by international standards, but a necessary daily expense unless you have a car. Those living out in the New Territories or on an Outlying Island will find it adds one or two thousand dollars per person to their monthly bills. For more information, refer to Chapter Four, 'Getting Around'.

Cars

Cars are not really necessary in Hong Kong, although they are obviously useful if you need to ferry children around. For more information on the costs associated with running a car, please refer to Chapter Four, 'Getting Around'.

Wardrobe

Clothing may also make a sizeable dent in your wallet. Whilst local-brand casual clothes are cheap, fashionable and well-made, if you wear suits on a regular basis and are larger than a UK size 12 you will probably need to shop at designer stores to find the quality and size you need, or have your clothes made. More information on shops stocking larger clothes and where to find tailors is included in Chapter Seven, 'Shopping'.

Orientation

Your outgoings will also depend on how you orient yourself in Hong Kong. Expat-oriented products and services are expensive – you pay more and you don't necessarily get more. As one Hong Kong savant who has experienced the highs and lows of Hong Kong comments:

> It's from the time of plenty. As an expat, you can get along in the real world – you *so* can do it.

7. Sai Kung Food Alley
Photograph taken by the author

Chapter Three

Arriving at the Airport

Hong Kong's light, spacious and ultra-modern international airport is located 39 km from the city centre on reclaimed Chek Lap Kok island. Smoking is not allowed inside the passenger terminal except in designated smoking rooms. An online itinerary planner allows transport and accommodation booking to connecting destinations around China (www.hongkongairport.com)

VISITOR INFORMATION AND HELP

A **Hong Kong Tourism Board Visitor Information & Services Centre** is located in the Buffer Halls and in Transfer Area E2. Assistance is available between 7:00 am and 11:00 pm daily. Airport Authority **24-hour Help Phones** are located throughout the terminal. Phonecard vending machines are located throughout the Passenger Terminal for using public phones.

MONEY

An **HSBC** ATM cashpoint is located at Level 7 Check-in Hall Aisle G and a **Standard Chartered Bank** ATM is located in Arrival Hall B. A number of money exchangers can be found in the Arrivals Hall, which is open between 5:30 am and midnight.

SHOPS AND RESTAURANTS

A number of cafés and restaurants are located on the same floor as the Arrivals Hall, including McDonalds and Oliver's Super Sandwiches. A 7-Eleven convenience store is open 24 hours; Watsons chemist is open between 7:00 am and 11:30 pm. A branch of Café Deco is located in Departures East Hall (Level 7).

LUGGAGE

A left luggage service (tel. 2261 0110) is available in the Arrivals Hall from 5:30 am to 1:30 am daily. Rates are:

8. Hong Kong view
Photograph taken by the author

- ▪ $35 for up to three hours;
- ▪ $50 for 3–24 hours; and
- ▪ $120 for 24–48 hours.

ACCOMMODATION

Hong Kong Hotels Association information counters are open between 6:00 am and midnight. The **Regal Airport Hotel** is the closest hotel to the airport (tel. 2286 8888).

MEDICAL

The **Airport Medical Centre** (tel. 2261 2626) is at Landside Level 6, Room 6T009 and is open daily from 7:00 am to midnight.

WASHROOM AND NURSING FACILITIES

Nursing rooms for babies and public washroom facilities are located around the airport, including in the Arrivals Hall.

OTHER FACILITIES

Airline lounges, courtesy phones, photo kiosks, beauty spa services and business facilities are also available in the terminal building. For more information, visit **www.hongkongairport.com**.

TRANSPORT CONNECTIONS

Most visitors who fly into Hong Kong use the **Airport Express** train to go downtown – the fastest way to travel. Other options include boarding an airport bus or taking a taxi.

AIRPORT EXPRESS TRAINS

You can buy tickets from the machines opposite the Arrivals Hall or from the Airport Express Customer Service Centre. The train platform is at the same level as the Arrivals Hall. Trains run every 12 minutes: the first train from the airport leaves at 5:50 am, the last train leaves at 01:15 am. As a free service, porters will help you load luggage on and off trains.

The other station on this line is **Tsing Yi.** Children under three travel free and concessions are half the adult fare.

Tickets (sample prices)
- Adult single to Hong Kong station (terminus): $100.
- Adult same-day return to Hong Kong station: $100.
- Adult round-trip (valid for one month) to Hong Kong station: $180.
- Adult single to Kowloon station: $90.
- Adult same-day return to Kowloon station: $90.
- Adult round-trip (valid for one month) to Kowloon station: $160.

Order tickets online and earn Asia Miles (www.mtr.com.hk).

Journey time
- Airport to Hong Kong station: 23 minutes.
- Airport to Kowloon station: 20 minutes.

Free shuttle bus
Train passengers can board a free **Airport Express shuttle bus** from Kowloon and Hong Kong stations to all major hotels. The buses run every 12 or 24 minutes. Taxis are also available.

AIRPORT BUSES

Follow the signs in the Arrivals Hall for airport buses. A number of buses ferry passengers between the airport and the rest of Hong Kong, starting around 6:00 am. Overnight buses operate different hours. Fares range from $20 to $45. Visit www.hongkongairport.com/eng/aguide/bus.html for exact information on routes.

Popular routes include the **A11** to **North Point Ferry Pier** running along the north of Hong Kong Island and the **N21** to **TST Star Ferry Pier**, a night bus operating between 12:20 and 5:00 am.

TAXIS

Follow the signs from the Arrivals Hall to take a taxi. The average fare is

$335 to Central or $270 to TST. The approximate journey time is an hour. Red taxis serve Hong Kong Island, green taxis serve the New Territories and blue taxis serve Lantau Island.

LIMOUSINES

Limousine hire counters are located in the Arrivals Hall and are open between 5:30 am and midnight. The cost of hiring a limousine to Central is about $600.

FERRIES

Details of ferries from the airport to Chinese cities are provided in Chapter Twenty-Four, 'Travel': Chinese travel.

HKIA Frequent Visitor Card

Passengers who have visited Hong Kong via the airport three times or more in the preceding 12 months can apply for a 'Frequent Visitor Card' to facilitate their passage through the airport (apply online at **www. hongkongairport.com/eng/aguide/fvc.html**).

USEFUL PHONE NUMBER

Airport Enquiry Hotline (tel. 2181 8888)

9. New Territories town
Photograph taken by the author

Chapter Four

Getting Around

Essential information

A must-buy: The first thing you need to buy when you get to Hong Kong is the indispensable *Hong Kong Guidebook* (Universal Publications), a bilingual A–Z that also has a public transport guide insert. Although websites such as **www.yp.com.hk** and **www.centamap.com** provide maps that can be printed out, the *Guidebook* is still the most convenient format for everyday use. Updated yearly, you can buy it from most bookshops for about $62.

The language of signs: Hong Kong's road signs and street names are all printed in English and Chinese. Sometimes the English names of city areas are a direct translation from the Chinese (e.g. Central); at other times they bear no resemblance to the Chinese meaning (e.g. Happy Valley); and frequently a Chinese name is transliterated approximately into English (e.g. TST, Mongkok, etc.).

TRAINS

The Mass Transit Railway System

The Mass Transit Railway System (MTR) is the fastest way to get around Hong Kong and trains are clean, well-run and reliable. The service operates between 6:00 am and 1:00 am and has 82 stations along its 9 lines:

- the **Island Line**, running along the north of Hong Kong Island;
- the **Tsuen Wan Line**, which runs north/north-west from Central to Kowloon;
- the **Kwun Tong** and **Tseung Kwan O Lines**, which run to east Kowloon and connect with North Point on east Hong Kong Island;
- the **Tung Chung Line and Disneyland Resort line**, which run out to Lantau; and
- the **East Rail**, **West Rail** and **Ma On Shan** lines, covering much of the New Territories.

10. Fishing boats
Photograph taken by the author

The MTR is used on a daily basis by over two million passengers and is crowded at peak hours 7:30–9:00 am and 4:00–8:00 pm. During the rush hour, trains run every two to three minutes.

Adult fares range from $4 to $26, depending on the distance travelled (see Journey Planner at www.mtr.com.hk). Concessionary fares for senior citizens, children and Hong Kong students range from $3 to $13. The **Octopus card**, an electronic stored-value smart card, is the most convenient way to pay for travel on the MTR, and can also be used on ferries, Kowloon–Canton Railway (KCR) trains and buses, and in parking meters, ParknShop supermarkets and some fast food restaurants. You can buy one at any MTR Customer Service Centre: the price includes a $50 deposit, redeemable when you return the card.

To use your Octopus card on trains, simply swipe the card against an electronic reader at the station barriers and again when you emerge at your destination station. The correct amount will be automatically deducted from your card. Make sure you don't store two cards in the same wallet, or money may be deducted from both at the same time. Cards can be charged up in MTR stations and 7-Eleven stores by adding cash or transferring money from your EPS (Electronic Point of Sale) card. For more information, call the **Octopus Hotline** on 2266 2266.

Single tickets, a tourist MTR 1-Day Pass costing $50 and a 3-Day Hong Kong Transport Pass that includes one or two Airport Express train single journeys (see below) are all available to buy. For other information on fares and routes, visit **www.mtr.com.hk** or call the 24-hour Passenger Hotline on 2881 8888.

Intercity Passenger Services
The MTR runs trains to Beijing (23.5 hours), Shanghai (18.5 hours) and stations in Guangdong province, departing from Hung Hom station in Kowloon.

Airport Express
The Airport Express service runs every 12 minutes all day between Hong Kong station (linked by walkways to Central MTR station) and the airport. The journey takes about 23 minutes, and trains run from 5:50 am to 01:15 am. Passengers can check their luggage in at Kowloon or Hong Kong stations. Some airlines, including Dragon Air and Cathay Pacific, permit check-in the day before departure. Individual airlines have different schedules for check-in, so call them beforehand to check the earliest and latest times for check-in.

Airport Express passengers using Octopus cards can enjoy free MTR connections to or from Airport Express stations if their cards have usable value and their travel on the MTR and Airport Express is within one hour of each other. Passengers who take the Airport Express can board a free Airport Express Shuttle Bus service between Hong Kong and Kowloon stations and major hotels and transport interchanges (buses run every 12 or 24 minutes).

Parking is also available at Airport Express stations. For more information, visit www.mtr.com.hk.

Facilities for disabled passengers

Special facilities for disabled passengers include tactile guide paths, audible devices, a Braille station layout map, Braille plates, a flashing system map and bidirectional wide gates. Wheelchair aid with staff assistance is provided at some stations, wide public lifts at most others.

Services in stations

Besides food shops, convenience shops, heel bars and passport photo booths, MTR stations also provide ATM services, post boxes and public payphones that accept coins and phone cards. Some stations, including Central, Kowloon Tong and Wanchai, are equipped with **iCentres** – computer terminals with free Internet access.

Passengers using the Airport Express can use wireless broadband services to access the Internet and download offline news and e-mail to Palm and Pocket PCs. Access points are located at Hong Kong, Kowloon, Tsing Yi and Airport stations.

The East Rail Line

The East Rail line is the most heavily used as it runs past Shatin, University (Chinese University), Taipo, Shatin Racetrack and all the way to Lowu at the mainland China Shenzhen border. The service gets crowded during rush hours (7:30–9:00 am and 5:00–7:00 pm) and is busy all day at the weekends. It's worth paying double to travel in First Class to ensure you have a seat, especially if you join the train at Kowloon Tong and are going all the way to Lowu. Swipe your Octopus card against the First Class electronic reader on the platform before you get on the train. Paying for your fare with an Octopus card works out slightly cheaper than buying standard price single tickets.

LIGHT RAIL AND BUS SERVICES

A Light Rail service serves expanding communities in the New Territories not covered by the West Rail. Feeder buses run between MTR stations and housing estates.

Public buses

Public buses are currently franchised to a few different companies and their subsidiaries. Journeys cost anywhere from $2.50 on Hong Kong Island to $45 for airport bus services. Senior citizen rates for those over 60, or sometimes 65, apply on some routes. Children under 12 years old are entitled to a half-fare. Have the exact change ready, or pay by swiping your Octopus card when you get on.

Some buses running to Stanley (6, 6A, 6X, 61 and 260) have two-way sectional fares, which means that you need to swipe your Octopus card when you get on and again when you get off, so that the fare deducted matches precisely the length of the journey travelled.

Bus-to-bus interchange schemes give Octopus users concessions when they interchange from one specific bus route to another. Many buses are now fitted with Roadshow video advertising and some programming, although the volume is usually turned down to avoid irritating passengers.

Citybus is one of the major franchised companies, running services on Hong Kong Island, cross-harbour buses and airport buses. A full list of routes served by Citybus and its subsidiary, New World First Bus, is on the website **www. nwstbus.com.hk**, as is a point-to-point search for bus routes and details of days out. Citybus's Enquiries Hotline is 2873 0818. The **Kowloon Motor Bus** company runs services in Kowloon and the New Territories; a route search facility, including a PDA version, is available at **www.kmb.hk**. Other companies operate Lantau routes.

Minibuses (Public Light Buses)

There are thousands of 16-seater cream minibuses that ply the routes not served by the public bus companies. The green-roofed buses operate on fixed routes at fixed fares; the red-roofed buses are free to operate anywhere, except where special prohibitions apply, with unregulated routes or fares. Operating times vary. Minibus drivers have a reputation for being fast and furious drivers, but nothing beats being able to flag down a minibus for convenience.

Green minibus stations serving Mid-Levels – Old Peak, Bowen, Macdonnel and Conduit Roads, and Queen Mary's Hospital – are located at Star Ferry car park and round the corner from City Hall. From Causeway Bay, buses run to Happy Valley (No. 30 from Pak Sha Road), Stanley (No. 40 from Tang Lung Street) and Kennedy Town (from Jardine's Bazaar, opposite Sogo).

You should pay with the exact change or your Octopus card when you board. If there is no Octopus card reader or slot box when you get on, then pay the driver directly when you get off. Note that some routes have sectional fares and concessions for children under 1.2 metres tall.

You have to shout when you want to get off the bus. Commonly, one of the following phrases is used:

- 'jyun waan yauh lohk' (meaning 'round the corner');
- 'kyuu dai yauh lohk' ('at the steps');
- 'dang wai yauh lohk' ('at the traffic lights');
- just the name of the street; or
- 'yauh lohk' if you want to get off right away.

Bus timetables and routes are given in the pamphlet enclosed in the *Hong Kong Guidebook* (see above).

FERRIES

There are more than ten different ferry operators in Hong Kong. The **Star Ferry Company** runs services between Hung Hom and Central, Central and TST (Star Ferry Pier, Central), Wanchai and Hung Hom and Wanchai and TST (Wanchai Ferry Pier). Services run from 6:30 am to 11:30 pm (Central) and 7:30 am to 11:00 pm (Wanchai). They are every five to eight minutes at peak hour and every ten to twenty minutes at off-peak times, and cost $1.70–2.20 per trip.

Major daily services
- Central Pier No. 3 – Discovery Bay, Lantau. Journey time: 25–30 minutes. Intervals vary between 10–30 minutes. Service runs through the night. Adult fare: $27.
- Central Pier No. 6 – Mui Wo (Silvermine May), Lantau. Journey time: 35–50 minutes. Intervals vary between 15–40 minutes. Service runs through the night. Adult fare: varies (Monday–Sunday).

- Central Pier No. 6 – Peng Chau. Journey time: 25–40 minutes. Service runs every 45 minutes through most of the day and night. Adult fare: varies (Monday–Sunday).
- Central Pier No. 5 – Cheng Chau. Journey time: 32–48 minutes. Service runs at half-hourly intervals through most of the day and night. Adult fare: varies (Monday–Saturday). The slow ferry 'Deluxe Class' allows you to sit out on deck.
- Central Pier No. 4 – Yung Shue Wan, Lamma. Journey time: 27 minutes. Service runs between 6:30 am and 12:30 am. Time intervals vary between 15–60 minutes. Adult: $14.5–20 (Monday–Sunday).
- Sok Ku Wan, Lamma. Journey time: 30–40 minutes. Infrequent service.
- Aberdeen-Pak Kok Tsuen-Yung Shue Wan (Lamma). Journey time: 25 minutes. Intervals vary.

The location of the Central piers is shown on the Central City Map (see Figure 4.2). Other ferry services include Central–Ma Wan, Central–Hung Hom, Wanchai–Hung Hom, North Point–Hung Hom and Central–TST East.

For more information on ferry services and Kaito ferry services, timetables and fares, visit **www.td.gov.hk/en/transport_in_hong_kong/public_transport/ferries/service_details/index.htm**.

TRAMS

The Peak Tram runs from the terminus station on Garden Road (see Figure 4.2) up to the Peak between 7:00 am and midnight. There are four stops along the route and the journey takes about 15 minutes. Adult fares are $22 single.

Hong Kong Tramways runs trams along the north of Hong Kong Island from Kennedy Town in the west to Shau Kei Wan in the east and also to Happy Valley from 6:00 am to midnight. The flat fare is $2 for adults and $1 for children and senior citizens.

TAXIS

There are over 18,000 taxis in Hong Kong and they provide an excellent, ubiquitous and comparatively cheap service throughout the day and night. Red taxis serve Hong Kong and Kowloon, green taxis serve the New Territories and blue taxis serve Lantau. Urban taxis charge slightly more than their

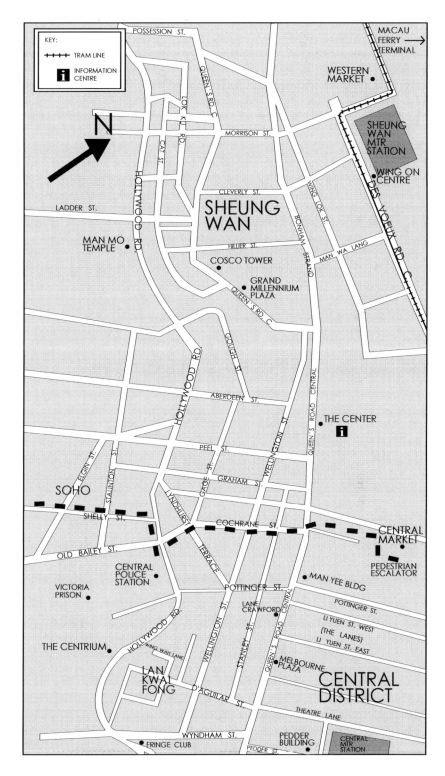

Figure 4.1 City map: Sheung Wan to Central

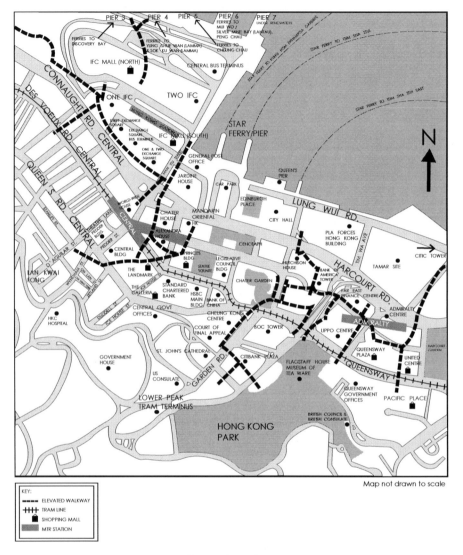

Figure 4.2 City map: Central to Admiralty

rural equivalents. A flagfall urban taxi fare of $18 applies for the first two kilometres; thereafter the fare is charged at $1.5 per 0.2 kilometre.

Some taxis on Hong Kong Island only travel to Kowloon. These taxis have their own taxi ranks and frequently display a sign covering the taxi lamp that says 'Not For Hire' – in fact they are, but only for passengers going over to Kowloon.

Taxis are only allowed to pick up and drop off at designated zones and will not stop for you if you're standing on a double yellow line. They are not allowed to refuse to take a fare, although some try to if the distance is not sufficient to be attractive. If they do, you can report them on the **Complaints Hotline** (tel. 2889 9999). Drivers in Hong Kong are not permitted to use handheld mobile phones but frequently do use ear-piece mobile phones while driving.

Front- and back-seat passengers are required by law to wear seat belts and an extra charge of $5 is applied to taxis booked by phone, if animals are taken or if luggage is put in the boot. Passengers are also liable to pay the return tolls for cross-harbour tunnels, but Shing Mun, Lion Rock, Aberdeen, Tseung Kwan O, Tai Lam and Tate's Cairn tunnel fares should be paid by the driver. Avoid handing the driver a $500 note – he probably won't have change. Taxi drivers don't expect tips, although it's usual to round up to the nearest dollar when paying them.

Most drivers can speak some English, although the level of English varies considerably. Drivers may connect you via walkie-talkie to their headquarters so you can repeat the place name to them, or just ask you to direct them. It pays to learn the name of your own road in Cantonese. Major tourist land-marks such as MTR stations, Times Square, Central, Peak Tram, Ocean Park and so on won't be a problem, but keep a bilingual map handy if you want to avoid trouble.

'Every taxi ride is a true Hong Kong experience, be it a swervy ride through the Cross-Harbour Tunnel in the early hours while the driver is trying to continue his phone call, or the brave but crazy manoeuvres through back streets to avoid a traffic jam. Once, the driver purposefully took off as soon as I put my bags on the back seat without yet having climbed in, and I had to chase the taxi to the next set of traffic lights, which thankfully turned red. When I retrieved my bags and foiled the attempted robbery, he just shrugged his shoulders. Expect the unexpected!' (Dr Trevor Lane.)

ELEVATED WALKWAYS

The elevated covered walkways in the city make walking around more pleas-ant and less crowded. Major elevated walkways include those in Central and Wanchai – see Figures 4.1 to 4.6 for details.

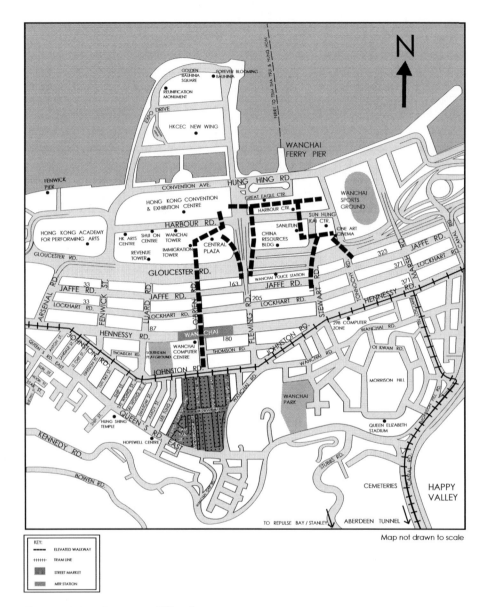

Figure 4.3 City map: Wanchai

DRIVING

Because running a car is comparatively expensive in Hong Kong – estimates vary between $8,000 and $15,000 per month – and because the public transport network is efficient and good value, many expats opt not to have a car. Second-hand cars can, however, be acquired inexpensively.

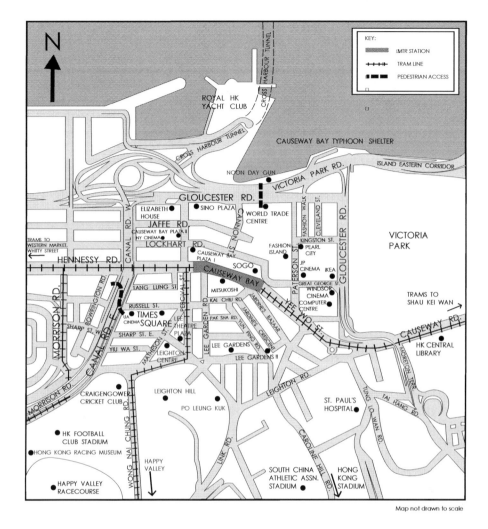

Figure 4.4 City map: Causeway Bay

The main direct costs associated with running a car in Hong Kong are the insurance, vehicle licence and petrol:

- Insurance is dependent on not only the type of car, but also the age of the person buying it. Sample costs can be obtained from www.thecarlocator.com.hk.
- The annual vehicle licence fee varies according to engine capacity: $3,929 for less than 1.5 litre engines, ranging up to $11,329 for 4.5 litres and above.
- Petrol is not cheap, at approximately $12 a litre.

As in the UK, cars drive on the left-hand side of the road. Driving is reasonably safe in Hong Kong, although there are frequent complaints about the recklessness of some drivers. *Automotive* magazine has commented:

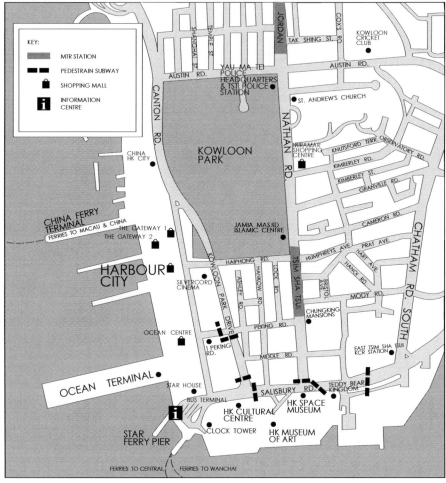

Map not drawn to scale

Figure 4.5   City map: TST

The most common mistakes by Hong Kong drivers are related to signal-ling. The main one is turning with no signal. Next up is signalling without turning. Third is signalling half-way around the turn.

Importing a car for personal use

If you are importing a car for personal use, you will need to prove that your car complies with vehicle exhaust and noise requirements. Some exemptions apply to petrol-driven private cars if vehicles have been used for less than six months, or used by the owner for six months or more in the country of normal residence prior to the application.

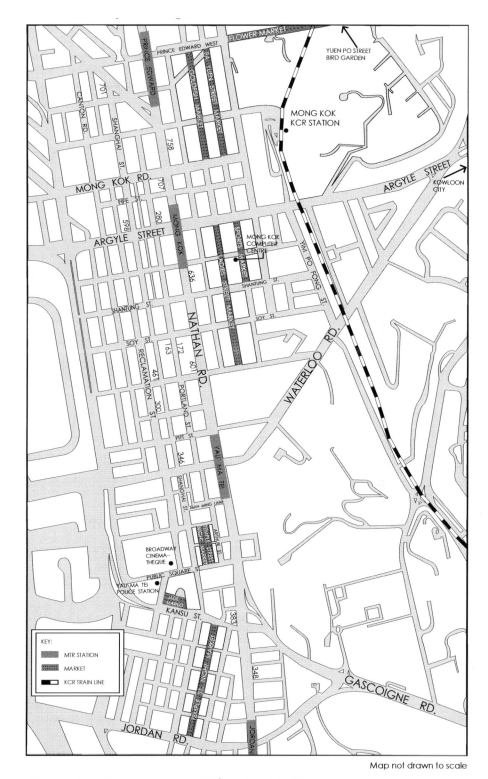

Map not drawn to scale

Figure 4.6 City map: Mong Kok to Yau Ma Tei

There is no customs tax to pay, but you will need to pay a 'first registration tax' administered by the Transport Department on the basis of the car's retail price; or, if that is unavailable, tax will be calculated on the purchase price plus insurance and freight fees, brokerage fees and so on. Rates of tax are posted at **www.info.gov.hk/customs/eng/major/import/motor_e.html**. Depreciation allowances can be given if the imported vehicle has previously been registered in the name of the importer in a foreign country. Left-hand drive vehicles are not usually permitted to be imported.

You will also need to file an 'Import Return' (form CED 336) and a 'Declaration on Particulars of Motor Vehicles Imported for Personal Use' (form CED 336A) with the Customs and Excise Department. Forms can be completed electronically at **www.info.gov.hk/customs/eng/forms/forms_e.html**, or call 2231 4390. More information is available from the **Customs and Excise Department** (11/F, North Point Government Offices, 333 Java Road, North Point; tel. 2231 4391).

A vehicle inspection should then be carried out at a specified Vehicle Examination Centre (tel. 2333 3112). After the taxable value of the vehicle has been ascertained and the vehicle has passed its inspection, you can apply for registration and licensing of your vehicle at one of the **Licensing Offices** of the **Transport Department** (e.g. 3/F, United Centre, 95 Queensway, Admiralty; tel. 2804 2637).

Licence renewal and change of registration details

A vehicle licence may be renewed four months before its expiry by submitting Form TD 23112 (for one year) or TD 2314 (for four months). The owner is required to inform the Transport Department within 72 hours of any changes with regard to registration particulars (TD150). All forms can be downloaded from **www.td.gov.hk**.

Transfer of ownership

The fee for transfer of vehicle ownership is $1,000 for vehicles except motorcycles and tricycles, where the fee is $250. The new owner is legally required to deliver a Transfer Notice (TD25) to the Transport Department and give the duplicate to the former owner. Third party insurance is necessary when registering or transferring ownership.

Applying for a driving licence

You can drive here with a foreign licence as long as you have visitor status – that is, you are expecting to reside in Hong Kong for less than 12 months. Once you are issued with a Hong Kong ID Card, you are required to apply for a Hong Kong licence. No test is necessary if you:

* hold a valid overseas driving licence issued by an approved country;
* have a licence that expired less than three years ago;
* have resided in the place of issue for at least six months during which time the licence was issued;
* held the licence for five years or more prior to application and hold a passport of the country where the licence was issued.

TD63A application forms are available at the Transport Department Licensing Office or can be downloaded from the website address above, or from any post office. A driver's licence costs $900 and is valid for ten years.

Learning to drive in Hong Kong

If you are 18 years of age or above, you can apply for a learner's driving permit at the Transport Department Licensing Office. You will need a Hong Kong ID card and you will have to pay an application fee of $548. The learner's permit is valid for 12 months. A test on Hong Kong Island can also be arranged via the same office: fees are $510 for the written test and $800 for the driving test. Details of government and private driving instruction centres are provided on the Transport Department's website.

Parking

The cost of parking varies depending where the car is parked, and even within which building. You can purchase monthly tickets for most car parks, Star Ferry car park being particularly popular. These are sold on a first-come, first-served basis and cost $4,100 a month without a reserved spot or $23 per hour. A list of multi-storey car parks and motorcycle spaces, with details of monthly pass and hourly rates, is provided at **www.td.gov.hk/transport_in_hong_kong/parking/carparks/index.htm**. All street parking meters are operated by Octopus card.

Toll roads and tunnels

There are ten toll roads and tunnels in Hong Kong, including the cross-harbour tunnels (Eastern Harbour Tunnel, Western Harbour Tunnel and Cross-Harbour Tunnel). If you want to avoid hold-ups while paying the toll, you can join the Autotoll prepaid system (see **www.autotoll.com.hk**).

Traffic situation

The **Traffic Department** posts camera images and videos of busy areas for drivers to view online at http://traffic.td.gov.hk/selection_e.htm. If you are involved in or witness an accident, call emergency services on **999**. Take down the vehicle registration number and driver's details, including their ID card number.

Hong Kong Automobile Association

The Hong Kong Automobile Association (tel. 2739 5273) offers 24-hour emergency vehicle rescue, car care services, insurance and motorsports. Membership is $200 plus an annual subscription of $660. For more details, see their website **www.hkaa.com.hk**.

Maintenance

Car maintenance services are offered by dealers' garages or street garages all over Hong Kong, including Happy Valley, Tin Hau, Wanchai, Sai Kung, Kowloon City and Mid-Levels. Garages offer a range of services, including repair, car wash, shine, interior steaming, vehicle safety inspection and oil changing.

11. Happy Valley Panorama
Photograph taken by Mimi Mori

Chapter Five

Looking for Accommodation

As a husband of a friend once succinctly put it, 'if you don't want to live in an apartment, don't come to Hong Kong.' Another fact impossible to ignore is that housing in Hong Kong is *very* expensive – a problem if you are paying for it yourself. Employees being relocated to Hong Kong by their companies may be offered a company flat or, more commonly these days, given a budget with which to find their own accommodation. Most high-end apartment blocks have their own estate management office equipped with English-speaking staff to whom you can report problems with the property.

At the other end of the scale, you may be paying for your flat yourself and renting from a landlord who cannot speak English. In this case, make full use of the property agent who introduced the apartment to you and get them to act as a middleman, relaying information from you to the landlord and vice versa. It's worth bearing in mind how helpful the property agent is likely to be in the future, after you've already signed on the dotted line.

FINDING A HOME

Depending on your budget, the size of your family and the area you wish to live in, Hong Kong can offer a variety of accommodation options. Expect to spend a few weeks looking at apartments before you find the one appropriate for your needs. Apartments are measured in square feet: one square metre equals 10.762 square feet. Any space less than 450 square feet is going to be very small, even for one person; that said, the longer you spend in Hong Kong, the more comfortable small spaces become.

Price is affected by many factors including size, location and age of the building. Generally, the higher you are in an apartment block, the better the view, so high-floor apartments command a premium. Apartments with a sea view (listed as 'S/V') command higher prices than those with a mountain view ('M/V'), which in turn is preferable to rooms without a view. Distance from the centre of town is also a factor. Many locals shun residential areas more than an hour from downtown. Most also prefer the security of living in

12. High Street 'Ghost House'
Photograph taken by Stanley Ng

populous areas and are reluctant to live in quiet rural neighbourhoods. Anything over fifteen years old is considered 'old' in Hong Kong and therefore less desirable, so the landlord may be more amenable to negotiation.

It's quite common to move apartments during your stay in Hong Kong, either because of a change of workplace, change in economic situation or to take advantage of fluctuations in property market prices. It is acceptable to renegotiate the rent when your tenancy agreement comes up for renewal, especially if the market has dropped. In my five and a half years in Hong Kong, I moved five times, shared flats three times and lived in four completely different neighbourhoods. I have always experienced harmonious relationships with my landlords, all of whom were local, individual owners. However, some friends have experienced problems trying to recover their deposit at the end of their lease or getting their landlord to make repairs, and have even received threatening letters directed at their landlord from Triads. These are the vagaries of renting outside the corporate landlord zone. Recent changes to the Landlord and Tenant Ordinance may also leave tenants less secure when seeking renewal.

The most important factors affecting choice of accommodation are:

- proximity to work and schools;
- access to transport;
- neighbourhood amenities, such as doctors, hospitals, supermarkets and fitness centres; and
- nightlife (if important) – clubs and bars.

POPULAR NEIGHBOURHOODS

Below are the main neighbourhoods favoured by expats who are renting, although the connectedness of Hong Kong means that you can live in virtually any area of the city without too much difficulty. To view images of each area, examples of property available and tables indicating price ranges ('How far your money will go'), browse Compass Real Estate's website at **www. hongkongpropertyman.com**. The website **www.hongkonghomes.com** lists buildings by areas, sorted into high- and low-rise, and displays images of specific buildings.

Hong Kong Island – north side
The Peak
The Peak is the most expensive location on Hong Kong Island, with rents often over $100,000 per month. Apartments occupied by expats are inevitably corporate-sponsored.

Soho
Soho is a lively, mixed area and is home to antique shops, art galleries, designer offices, street markets, clothes shops and flower shops. It's popular with expats and locals who are part of the club or gay scene and is sprinkled with bars, clubs and restaurants of all kinds. The downside is all the steps and steep hills, and the lack of supermarkets in the neighbourhood: ParknShop branches are located at Caine Road, Queen's Road, Gage Street and on the Mid-Levels escalator just below Robinson Road.

Sheung Wan
Sheung Wan, at the Western end of Hollywood Road, has several blocks with lower-priced units (typically $4,000–9,000) owned by the Tung Wah group (www.tungwah.org.hk).

Mid-Levels
Mid-Levels is more grown-up and upper-middle class. It encompasses the upper reaches of the mid-level escalator, an 800 metre long escalator that runs downhill before 10:30 in the morning and uphill for the rest of the day, including Caine Road, Robinson Road, Seymour Road down to the University of Hong Kong and Pokfulam. Apartments in this area tend to be expensive and tightly packed, and a good view is worth its weight in gold. A steady procession of minibuses and double-deckers wind their way along the roads to Central and the rest of Hong Kong, and the area is often congested, making walking and jogging unpleasant. Despite this, the area remains popular and desirable with expats and affluent locals who send their children to prestigious local schools in the area. May Road and Old Peak Road appeal to the higher end of the market who want to be close to Central.

Running eastwards above Hong Kong Park, Admiralty and Wanchai, Macdonnell Road and Kennedy Road are also desirable locations and very pleasant. Macdonnell Road is well situated for sports activities: it is close to Seasons Sports Club in Citibank Tower and the YWCA, both of which have pools, and not far from squash courts and a ParknShop on Garden Road.

Pokfulam

Pokfulam is situated high up in west Mid-Levels and is generally regarded as a place where you can get more for your money. Well served by minibuses, it's particularly popular with British expats prepared to do without club facilities and unperturbed by the graveyards in the area. In return, older properties can provide spacious accommodation, green surroundings and great sea views. Schools in the neighbourhood include Kennedy (primary), Kellet and West Island schools.

Happy Valley

Set back from Causeway Bay and much quieter, Happy Valley is leafy and affluent, with girls' schools, churches and the excellent private Sanitorium Hospital nearby. The race course can cause delays getting in and out of the neighbourhood on Wednesday nights and Saturdays, but the course also provides a pleasant green space for walking, jogging and watching the various amateur and schools sports activities going on. There's a Wellcome, Parkn-Shop and Pacific Coffee, a few upscale restaurants, and plenty of moderately priced Cantonese restaurants, beauty shops, flower shops and boutiques. The Hong Kong Football Club and Craigengower Cricket Club are nearby.

A range of older and newer properties are available, but apartments tend to be expensive, cramped and viewless. Those that are better value (more space for your buck) are in 'Chinese buildings' not served by lifts and have little security. Expect to pay around $7,500 for about 450 square feet. In many buildings in Hong Kong, especially older Chinese buildings, what would be called the ground floor in the UK is counted as the first floor.

Jardine's Lookout

Jardine's Lookout, above Happy Valley, is green and quiet, and home to some older, larger ex-civil service apartments. These can be good value as they are leased below market rates. These apartments are leased through selected agents, usually for one or two years. The French International School is nearby.

Taikoo Shing

Taikoo Shing and Braemar Hill are popular with Japanese and Korean families – international schools for both nationalities are close by – and expats working in Quarry Bay's Taikoo Place. Shopping centre Cityplaza hosts a cinema complex, ice rink, restaurants, supermarkets and department stores, including Japanese stores Jusco and Uny. Fitness centres are located nearby and hiking opportunities include the Quarry Bay to Violet Hill route.

Hong Kong Island – south side

Shouson Hill

Shouson Hill Road is located above Deep Water Bay and is, with Repulse Bay and the Peak, one of the most prestigious areas to live in Hong Kong. Properties are low-rise and older style. Minibuses run along Shouson Hill Road into town.

Repulse Bay to Stanley

This stretch of the Hong Kong coastline is idyllic and preferred by expats who enjoy accommodation paid for as part of their employment packages or who have families. Residents can enjoy upscale apartment complexes equipped with leisure facilities, supermarkets, car parks and free shuttle buses into Central. Getting into town usually takes about 40 minutes by car on a good run, but traffic in the Aberdeen Tunnel can cause delays. Buses and minibuses run regularly into town.

Repulse Bay is popular with Americans because the Hong Kong International School is close by. Luxury high-rise developments **Parkview** and **Red Hills** are located at the edge of Tai Tam Country Park, so there are opportunities for hiking and barbecues right on your doorstep.

Stanley is a bit cheaper and provides a greater range of apartment styles. The town is equipped with a large shopping centre, waterfront Western-style restaurants and cafes, the eponymous market – which gets packed with tourists and locals at the weekends – beaches, schools and St Stephen's, a church popular with expats. Near to Stanley are **Tai Tam** and **Chung Hom Kok**, luxury low-rise properties.

South Horizons, Ap Lei Chau

South Horizons is a middle-class development that offers features such as:

- 24-hour security;
- residents' club facilities such as swimming pools, nurseries and children's classes;
- a shopping complex housing a ParknShop superstore; and
- convenient bus links into town.

Apartments are a reasonable size for the money and many have an ocean view. The nearby **Horizons Plaza** offers mixed shopping including discounted fashion outlet Joyce Warehouse, furniture and interior design shops, wine merchants, toy shops, etc.

Kowloon
TST

TST is in the touristy, commercial heart of Kowloon, and is like a wilder version of Causeway Bay. Merchants touting copy watches, street-side tailors and leather merchants add to the hustling atmosphere, while the unsavoury and decrepit Chungking Mansions and Mirador Mansions act as hostelries to people from all walks of life and all corners of the globe. TST is handy for those who work there or in Central and there are numerous serviced apartments in the area.

Kowloon Tong

Kowloon Tong is close to City University and Hong Kong Baptist University and is an upscale area of Hong Kong served by Festival Walk, a plush shopping centre. It's rather mixed, with health clubs, international schools and kindergartens, wedding photos studios, old people's homes and love hotels side by side. It's also the linking station between the MTR and KCR – the East Rail link to China. It's about half an hour from Kowloon Tong into Central by MTR and 20 minutes to TST by bus.

MTR travel times to Central

Tai Koo – 15 minutes.
Prince Edward – 12 minutes.
Tseung Kwan O – 24 minutes.
Tung Chung – 34 minutes.
Kowloon Tong – 17 minutes.

New Territories
Clearwater Bay

Clearwater Bay is an area of outstanding natural beauty, with dramatic mountain scenery and clean beaches (by Hong Kong standards). The University of Science and Technology, Clearwater Bay School (primary), King George V (secondary) and the exclusive Clearwater Bay Golf and Country Club are located here. The area is secluded and quiet (except for the dogs – the most common form of security in the rural areas of Hong Kong), with very few restaurants or shops. Houses are mainly low-rise, and vary in price from very affordable ($5,500) to expensive.

All 'village houses' conform to strict specifications in terms of size and layout. Usually, there are three floors plus a roof area and the space per floor is around 700 square feet, including a kitchen, bathroom, living room and two bedrooms. If you rent the ground floor flat, you will have use of the garden; if you rent the top floor flat, you will usually enjoy the use of the roof terrace. Ideally, the roof area will be at least partly covered to offer protection during the hot summer months.

An efficient minibus service operates between Clearwater Bay and Tseung Kwan O MTR station until about 1:00 am. Another bus runs to Kwun Tong MTR and ferry.

Sai Kung

Prices are slightly lower in nearby Sai Kung, which is popular with expat families who want to be part of a community and like the green, island feel. Sai Kung is a medium-sized fishing town, equipped with kindergartens, ParknShop and Wellcome supermarkets, Western and Chinese restaurants, bakeries, pet product shops, second-hand bookshops, and so on. Buses run from Sai Kung to Hang Hau and Choi Hung MTR stations, as well as other parts of Kowloon. The town gets busy at weekends and on public holidays when people from all over Hong Kong descend on the famous waterfront seafood restaurants.

Taipo and Shatin

Both new towns are well placed for access to the Chinese mainland via the KCR East Rail link. The Chinese University and Lingnan College are also in this area. Luxury developments such as Shatin Heights enjoy more space than their equivalents downtown and rents can be up to 40% less. Village house accommodation, often preferred by expats, is another reasonably inexpensive option.

Outlying Islands

Lantau

Car-free **Discovery Bay** is well set up for residents, with a club house, swept beach, shopping centre and expat-oriented nurseries and schools. Properties vary in price, starting at about $6,000–7,000. The place has the feel of a holiday town and you can forget you're in Hong Kong. A very efficient ferry service links Discovery Bay with Central – a journey that takes 20 minutes – and runs throughout the night. Buses link Discovery Bay to Tung Chung and from there by MTR or bus to the rest of Hong Kong. More details about Discovery Bay can be found at www.discoverybay.com.hk.

Long-term expats Shelagh and Ethan Heath have lived in several different parts of the city, but relocated to car-less Discovery Bay (population 16,000) after they had children. 'There are very few negatives about living in DB. Our three blocks is like a little village. There are lots of other expats with kids and lots of Chinese with kids who speak English. There's more fresh air and lower population density. And for lower end rentals, it's cheaper than elsewhere. Friends of ours moved here just so they could get a garden.'

The couple looked at property in the New Territories and Lantau but found their choice often limited to either a three-storey village house, a standard 700 square feet and about $2 million to buy, or an apartment in a luxury development, $10–20 million for 1,000–2,000 square feet. There was little in between. They comment, 'In DB, we found 900 square feet we could actually afford.'

Mui Wo (Silvermine Bay) is also popular with expats, although government plans to build a super-jail on Hei Ling Chau Island, to be connected by bridge to Mui Wo, are being fiercely resisted by residents.

Lamma

Lamma is a smaller car-free island, but has a loyal expat following. Traditionally residents have a reputation for being alternative, artistic, eco-friendly, child-friendly and dog-keeping. Yung Shue Wan is the main town centre; other residential areas include Pak Kok, Hung Shing Ye and Sok Ku Wan. English teacher Kate Allert, a resident on the island, comments:

> The social scene in Lamma is fabulous. It's almost like living in a gigantic shared house but with more privacy. You can go out for a quiet drink and never be sure how the evening will turn out. Everyone has to come up the Main Street to get home, so you see everybody all the time.

Ferries to Central run between 6:20 am and 12:30 am, which is when the last ferry returns to Yung Shue Wan. And if you get stranded on the mainland late at night, you can always get back from Aberdeen Fish Market by hiring a sampan. Village houses cost $6,000–8,000 per month for a top-floor flat with roof, less for a middle floor. There are also 350 square feet units that are $2,000–3,000 per month.

Short-term holiday or weekend lets are also possible on the island – details of vacant apartments are posted in the property agents on the Main Street. The island gets busy at weekends with day-trippers. Visit the Lamma resident forums at **www.lamma.com.hk** to find out more about the community.

SEARCHING FOR A PROPERTY

Once you get to Hong Kong and have decided where you want to live, the best resource for properties are the agents in the immediate neighbourhood of where you're looking. They'll know specific buildings in the area that other expats have liked and may be able to offer appropriate advice. Register your details with them and spell out exactly what you are looking for so they don't waste your time by showing you properties way over your budget or something that doesn't meet your criteria. Most residential apartments are measured in square feet and represent the gross floor area. This means that the area quoted will include external walls, the lift lobby, fire escapes and other common areas.

Details of properties available, market trends and statistics are published every Wednesday in the *South China Morning Post*; shared flats are also advertised in *HK Magazine*.

Relocation services

These days, many property agents and removals companies also offer relocation services. Relocation takes into account the whole spectrum of your family's needs when moving abroad, such as:

- packing and shipping your goods;
- arranging viewing of potential properties at your destination;
- negotiating the lease;
- fixing up school viewing appointments; and
- offering face-to-face support once you get to Hong Kong.

Other benefits may include spouse support through complimentary memberships to international (women's) clubs.

International relocation companies serving Hong Kong include **Crown Relocations** (www.crownrelo.com; tel. 2636 8388). A more personalized service is offered by Rehana Sheikh of **Personalized Relocation Assistance** (tel. 2891 8664/9105 0593).

Property agents and property websites

One of the most comprehensive websites for searching properties with different agents is **www.gohome.com.hk**, which lists rental properties of $4,000–50,000+. They also list properties for sale. Also visit **hongkonghomes.com**, **hongkongpropertyman.com** and **http://hongkong.craigslist.org**. For market trends, information on new property developments and lists of properties to buy and rent, visit the website of the **Centaline Property Agency (www. centanet.com.hk/ehome.htm)**.

Medium and high-end property agents dealing with properties with a rental from $30,000 per month include **Savills** (www.savills.com.hk), **Colliers** (www.colliers.com), **Jones Lang LaSalle** (www.joneslanglasalle.com.hk) and **Habitat Property** (www.habitat-property.com).

RENTING A PROPERTY

Signing a tenancy agreement

After selecting a suitable property you will be asked to sign a tenancy agreement, which commits you to leasing the property usually for a minimum of one year. One agent points out that when you commit to a new lease, you are generally committing to 14 months, not 12, because after 12 months you have to give two months' notice. You will usually be asked to pay a deposit of two months' rental plus one month's rent in advance. Most agents will also take a fee from the tenant of a half-month's rent. Both parties sign two copies of the agreement: one is held by the landlord, the other by the tenant. The documents should be sent to the Inland Revenue for official registration and stamping before being returned to landlord and tenant.

Usable Space

'Check the flat's "usable space", as opposed to its "official size",' warns a veteran expat. 'The usable space can be as low as 60 per cent or as high as about 90 per cent of the official size.'

Illegal structures

If you have been promised the use of a roof or balcony and any store rooms there as part of the useable space of the apartment, check that this fact is specified in your tenancy agreement. If it isn't, then the chances are high that the balcony or roof may be an 'illegal structure': you risk losing this space if it is identified as such by a government inspector during a routine check. Usually owners are required by law to remove an illegal structure within a month.

Swimming pools

If your apartment includes the use of an outdoor pool and you don't plan to stay in Hong Kong long, double-check which months the pool is open because it is usually a comparatively short section of the year.

Stamp duty

This is a fee charged by the Inland Revenue for stamping the tenancy agreement and is usually shared between the landlord and tenant. Some landlords and tenants ignore it.

Break clause

A break clause gives either or both parties the option to terminate the agreement prior to the lease expiry date. The most typical lease in Hong Kong is for a two-year term with a tenant's option to break the lease after one year. Written notice is required when the tenant intends to break the lease.

Renewing the tenancy agreement

This can be done formally for a new fixed period, but commonly in cheaper properties after the tenancy agreement has expired, the tenant can just continue to pay month by month, with either side giving one month's notice.

Management fees and government rates

A **management fee** is paid to the building's management company to cover the cost of electricity and lighting in common areas, security staff, upkeep of facilities such as elevators, cleaning, and so on. All apartments are also liable for **government rates**, which are roughly 5% of the annual rental, paid quarterly. When negotiating rental costs, try and ensure that the agreed figure includes government rates and management fees.

Household insurance

Although your landlord will insure your apartment, it is wise to take out contents insurance, covering your furniture and belongings against fire, theft, typhoons and burst pipes. The major banks offer insurance quotes online, or try **www1.speedinsure.com** (tel. 8209 0020). Other insurers include **Zurich Insurance Group** (tel. 2968 2222) and **AIA** (tel. 2232 8888).

Pets

Some apartment blocks do not allow pets, so check before you agree to move in. In many cases, although the tenancy agreement specifies no pets, you may be able to negotiate special permission from the landlord. For more information on pet keeping, see below.

OTHER OPTIONS

Buying a property

Buying a property in Hong Kong can be difficult if you are not a permanent resident. Banks are unwilling to lend against older properties and there may be restrictions on the term of a loan, which is typically 15 years. The property market in Hong Kong is considered volatile, so unless expats plan to stay long term, most don't choose to buy. According to Berthold Chik of ANZ Banking Group, many expats aren't aware of foreign currency loans they can take out against a property back home, should they decide to buy a property. ANZ clients, for example, can borrow up to 75% in Hong Kong dollars (HK$) against the property value in Australia or New Zealand. Clients then use these funds to contribute to the equity portion of their Hong Kong property. Barclays and Lloyds TSB also have branches in Hong Kong that can lend HK$ against property held in the UK. (Address details are given in Chapter Ten, 'Money'.)

According to Chik, if expats are on a local package and are being paid a salary in HK$, a HK$ loan can act as a 'natural hedge' when buying property back home, rather than risking depreciation of the HK$ against the home currency during mortgage repayments. This means they do not need to repatriate an ever-increasing amount of HK$s to service their loans back home. The other major attraction is the fact that HK$ interest rates are lower than those in the home country and interest savings in the past have been as much as 5% per annum. However, borrowing in HK$ does involve risk, and it is best to speak to a bank consultant.

Flat share

One way for singles to save money is to share a flat, especially if you're new to Hong Kong and want an immediate circle of acquaintances. Commonly flatshares are advertised in the *South China Morning Post* Property section, *HK Magazine* or – best of all – by word of mouth. Some flatshares include maid service and club facilities. Paying your way in a flat in Mid-Levels, Soho, Sheung Wan or Happy Valley will work out at between $3,500 and $15,000. Anything below $3,500 is most likely going to be a bedsit and/or in an old, unkempt building.

Serviced apartments

Serviced apartments are increasingly popular with expats on short contracts or with those who often travel outside Hong Kong. Breakfast, a daily newspaper, maid service, sheet change, fitness club membership, clubhouse facilities or night club memberships and dining discounts are common add-ons. For a variety of serviced apartments in different areas of town, browse **www.gohome.com.hk**.

Serviced apartments usually cost from $10,000 per month upwards depending on space, location and design. Developments include:

- Kush (www.kushliving.com) – includes 750 square feet apartments less than ten minutes from Central.
- Soho Habitats (Lan Kwai Fong) – 500 square feet for $12,000 per month;
- Bijou Apartment at Prince Edward MTR – 390 square feet for $8,000 per month;
- Gateway and Waterfront Apartments in TST – $24,000+ per month; and
- Harbour Plaza Metropolis Hung Hom – 860–1,120 square feet for $25,880 to $70,000 per month.

Serviced apartments near the Chinese border are cheaper; for example, the Harbour Plaza Resort City in Tin Shui Wai has 400–1,200 square feet for $6,000 to $11,000 per month.

Prices given here are rough guides only. **Century 21**'s website (www.century21-hk.com) has the latest quotes.

SHORT-TERM HOTEL ACCOMMODATION

If you are staying in a hotel and money is not a consideration, two of the most popular and luxurious are the Shangri-la and Conrad hotels, which are conveniently built above Pacific Place – a large shopping plaza which includes a UA cinema complex showing mainstream English-language films and a quality 'fast food court' in the basement of supermarket Great. For a luxury suite of rooms try the wireless-connected Upper House, near the Conrad. Just across the elevated walkway from Pacific Place in United Centre is the Metropole Chinese restaurant, which serves excellent dim sum. The shopping/arts area of TST and Hong Kong's Central business district are one stop away (in different directions) on the Mass Transit Railway. The Four Seasons Hotel is located in the IFC building above the Airport Express Station in Central.

Hotels offering less expensive deals to short-termers (especially out of season) include **The Wesley, Charterhouse** and **Bishop Lei International House** (details below). The **YMCA Salisbury** (www.ymcahk.org.hk) has rooms with stunning views overlooking the TST harbour front (from around $760/day weekly; monthly packages for $3,675/week), whilst the **Helena May** ladies club (www.helenamay.com; tel. 2522 6766) has standard 'studios' for men and women from around $12,000/month, or 'rooms' for single women only from $200/day (or $6,500/month). There are, of course, always cheaper rooms ($200/night) available at Chinese hotels and guesthouses around Causeway Bay and TST or from **Rent-a-Room** in TST (http://rentaroomhk. com; tel. 2366 3011). Licensed holiday flats, guesthouses and hotels can be found at www.hadla.gov.hk.

Major hotels
Central and Admiralty hotels
The following hotels are shown in Figure 5.1:
1 **Mandarin Oriental**, ★★★★★, 5 Connaught Road Central; tel. 2522 0111.
2 **Ritz-Carlton**, ★★★★★, 3 Connaught Road, Central; tel. 2877 6666.
3 **JW Marriott**, ★★★★★, 88 Queensway, Pacific Place, Admiralty; tel. 2810 8366.

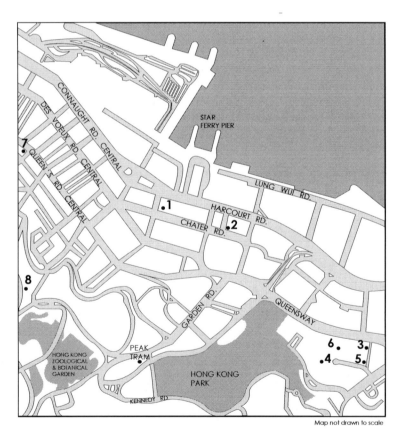

Map not drawn to scale

Figure 5.1   Central and Admiralty hotels

4 **Island Shangri-La**, ★★★★★, Pacific Place, Supreme Court Road, Admiralty; tel. 2877 3838.

5 **Conrad**, ★★★★★, 88 Queensway, Pacific Place, Admiralty; tel. 2521 3838.

6 **The Upper House**, 88 Queensway, Pacific Place, Admiralty; tel. 2918 1838.

7 **Novotel Century Harbourview**, ★★★, 508 Queen's Road West, Sheung Wan; tel. 2794 1234.

8 **Bishop Lei International House**, ★★★, 4 Robinson Road, Mid-levels; tel. 2868 0828.

(Not shown) **Four Seasons Hotel**, ★★★★★, 8 Finance Street, Central, tel. 3196 8888.

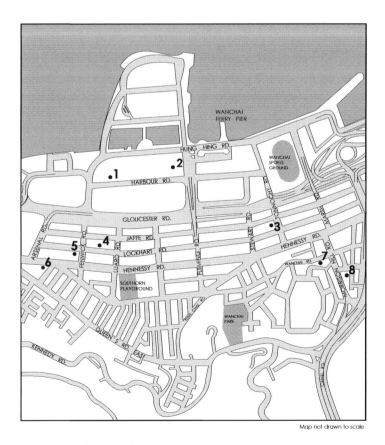

Map not drawn to scale

Figure 5.2   Wanchai hotels

Wanchai hotels

The following hotels are shown in Figure 5.2:

1 **Grand Hyatt, ★★★★★**, 1 Harbour Road; tel. 2588 1234.
2 **Renaissance Harbour View, ★★★★**, 1 Harbour Road; tel. 2802 8888.
3 **Novotel Century, ★★★★**, 238 Jaffe Road; tel. 2598 8888.
4 **Wharney, ★★★**, 57–73 Lockhart Road; tel. 2861 1000.
5 **Empire, ★★★**, 33 Hennessy Road; tel. 2866 9111.
6 **Wesley, ★★★**, 22 Hennessy Road; tel. 2866 6688.
7 **Charterhouse, ★★★**, 209–219 Wanchai Road; tel. 2833 5566.
8 **South Pacific, ★★★**, 23 Morrison Hill Road; tel. 2572 3838.

Causeway Bay hotels

The following hotels are shown in Figure 5.3:

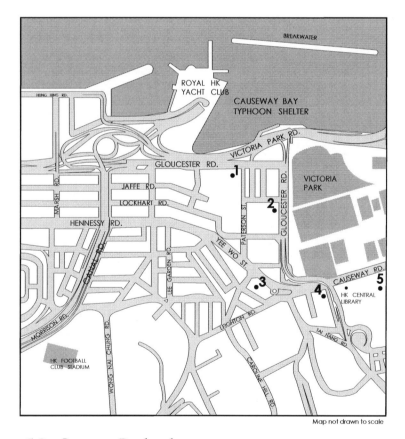

Figure 5.3   Causeway Bay hotels

1 **Excelsior**, ★★★★, 281 Gloucester Road; tel. 2894 8888.
2 **Park Lane**, ★★★★, 310 Gloucester Road; tel. 2293 8888.
3 **Regal Hong Kong**, ★★★★★, 88 Yee Wo Street; tel. 2890 6633.
4 **Rosedale on the Park**, ★★★★, 8 Shelter Street; tel. 2127 8888.
5 **Metropark**, ★★★★, 148 Tung Lo Wan Road; tel. 2600 1000.

TST hotels

The following hotels are shown in Figure 5.4:

1 **BP International House**, ★★★, 8 Austin Road, tel. 2376 1111.
2 **Stanford Hillview**, ★★★, 13 Observatory Road (enter via Knutsford Terrace); tel. 2722 7822.
3 **Empire Kowloon**, ★★★★, 62 Kimberley Road; tel. 2685 3000.
4 **Kimberley**, ★★★, 28 Kimberley Road; tel. 2723 3888.

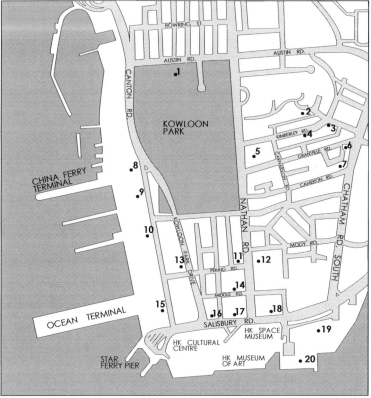

Figure 5.4 Tsim Sha Tsui (TST) hotels

5 **Miramar,** ★★★★, 118–130 Nathan Road; tel. 2368 1111.
6 **Ramada,** ★★★, 73 Chatham Road South, TST East; tel. 2311 1100.
7 **Park,** ★★★, 61 Chatham Road South; tel. 2366 1371.
8 **Royal Pacific,** ★★★★, 33 Canton Road, China HK City; tel. 2736 1188.
9 **Marco Polo Prince,** ★★★★, 23 Canton Road; tel. 2113 1888.
10 **Marco Polo Gateway,** ★★★★, 13 Canton Road; tel. 2113 0888.
11 **Hyatt Regency,** ★★★★, 67 Nathan Road; tel. 2311 1234.
12 **Holiday Inn Golden Mile,** ★★★★, 50 Nathan Road; tel. 2369 3111.
13 **Langham,** ★★★★★, 8 Peking Road; tel. 2375 1133.
14 **Kowloon,** ★★★★, 19–21 Nathan Road; tel. 2929 2888.
15 **Marco Polo Hongkong,** ★★★★, Harbour City, 3 Canton Road; tel. 2113 0088.
16 **YMCA Salisbury,** ★★★, 41 Salisbury Road; tel. 2268 7000.
17 **Peninsula,** ★★★★★, Salisbury Road; tel. 2920 2888.
18 **Sheraton,** ★★★★★, 20 Nathan Road; tel. 2369 1111.
19 **New World Renaissance,** ★★★★, 22 Salisbury Road; tel. 2369 4111.
20 **InterContinental,** ★★★★★, 18 Salisbury Road, Tsimshatsui; tel. 2721 1211.
21 Hyatt Regency Hong Kong, ★★★★★,18 Hanoi Road; tel. 2311 1234

Hullet House, 2 Canton Road, Tsim Sha Tsui, opened in January 2010 and is located in the former Marine Police Headquarters (now called 1881 Heritage).

UTILITIES

Electricity

The current in Hong Kong is 200–220 volts. Plugs can be either square or round pin, with many apartments having a mixture of both, so you may have to buy plug adapters (which are available from hardware shops and Parkn-Shop) for your appliances.

To arrange for electricity connection, you should call the appropriate supplier at least **two days** before it is required:

▪ For Hong Kong Island and Lamma Island, call the **Hongkong Electric Co.** (tel. 2887 3411).

▓ For Kowloon, the New Territories, Lantau and Cheung Chau, call the **China Light and Power Co.** (tel. 2678 2678).

A deposit of an estimated two months' electricity charges is usually required, although in some cases this has already been paid for by the landlord and the tenant may just take over paying the monthly bills.

If you forget to pay your bills you will receive several demands before being disconnected. After payment, electricity will be restored immediately. Emergency 24-hour electricity work can be provided by **Hoo Kee Water Electrical Pumping Works** (tel. 2572 3706), amongst others.

Electronics
Video players in Hong Kong use the PAL and NTSC systems. DVDs for playing in Hong Kong are labelled 'Zone 3'.

Gas
Most areas of Hong Kong are linked to the **Towngas** network. Accounts can be opened by making an application and paying a deposit of $600 (www.towngas.com; tel. 2880 6988).

Older apartments, especially those in parts of the New Territories and apartments in the Outlying Islands, have no mains gas supply. You will therefore need to use bottled LPG gas, which can be delivered to you, or make do with electricity.

Water
Water bills are minimal in Hong Kong and are paid quarterly. For the **Water Supplies Department Customer Service**, call 2824 5000. For 24-hour plumbing services, call Hoo Kee Water Electrical Pumping Works on 2572 3706.

Telecommunications services
Local calls are free in Hong Kong. Activation of a telephone landline in most buildings is managed by the phone company **PCCW** (www.pccw.com; tel. 1000), who charge a few hundred dollars every quarter for the privilege of using the line. If you fail to pay, your connection will be terminated and you will need to pay the bill in full plus a reactivation charge.

Most telecommunications companies offer residential and business telephone services, international direct dialling (IDD) and broadband or dial-up Internet services. Well-established phone service companies in Hong Kong include **New World Telecom** (www.newworldtel.com; tel. 1239), **Wharf**

T & T (www.wharftt.com; tel. 121 000) and **Hutchison Global Communi-cations** (www.hgc.com.hk; tel. 1220).

Companies specializing in IDD and Internet services are springing up all the time, so shop around to get the best deals. PCCW's Netvigator service is the most widely used in Hong Kong. Others include:

- HKNET (www.hknet.com; tel. 3793 0388); and
- HongKong Broadband (www.ctinets.com).

Zone 1511 (www.zone1511.com) offers members a one-stop shop for call management, allowing you to compare the cheapest IDD service providers for different destinations and buy IDD roaming services, and so on.

Calling cards with stored value are another option and may work out much cheaper when calling destinations that don't generally enjoy special rates from phone companies, such as South Africa. Buy them from **Worldwide House** in Central or from the many booths advertising them around town.

Mobile Phone service operators

- Mobile Hong Kong Company Limited (tel. 2945 8888)
- Hutchison Telephone Company Limited ('3') (tel. 2121 1228 for '2G' service; 3162 3333 for '3G' service)
- SmarTone Mobile Communications Limited & SmarTone 3G Limited (tel. 2880 2688)
- CSL Limited (tel. 2888 1010 for '1010' customers; 2512 3123 for 'One-2Free' customers and 178 178 for 'New World Mobility' customers)
- Hong Kong Telecommunications (HKT) Limited, tel.1833 800.

Television
Free television
Hong Kong has two Chinese language channels and two English language channels – Pearl and ATV World. No TV licence is required.

Pay television
Broadband is widely available in Hong Kong. Star TV can be obtained via pay TV operators **Hong Kong Cable Ltd** (www.i-cable.com) and PCCW's **now Broadband TV** (www.nowtv.com; tel. 1000). PCCW is also in the vanguard of IPTV (Internet Protocol Television), installed in 40 per cent of Hong Kong homes.

Radio

Dedicated English language radio channels include RTHK Radio 3 (567 kHz) and the BBC World Service (675 kHz).

Home help

It's common in Hong Kong to hire home help, which is very reasonably priced. Cleaning companies offering hourly services include **Merry Maids** (www.merrymaids.com.hk; tel. 2857 4038). A local worker charges roughly $50 to $70 per hour.

Alternatively, you can undertake the cost of hiring a full-time Foreign Domestic Helper or FDH (see Chapter Eight, 'Having and Raising Children'). FDHs are prohibited from working for anyone other than their contractual employer, even with that employer's consent, although in practice many helpers do work part-time. Punishment for the employer is a maximum fine of $150,000 and one year's imprisonment. The FDH may be imprisoned and deported. Visit **www.amahnet.com** and **www.proxy-maid.com.hk** for more information.

PETS

Bringing your pet to Hong Kong

You will need to obtain a special permit in advance to import dogs and cats into Hong Kong or for transit purposes. The fee for one animal is $432; every additional animal costs $102. Apply at least five days in advance of the pet's arrival at the **Agricultural, Fisheries and Conservation Department** (AFCD). This form, as well as other information regarding the eligibility of your pet, is available at **www.afcd.gov.hk**.

All dogs and cats imported must be implanted with an ID chip. Dogs and cats imported directly from the UK, Ireland, Australia and New Zealand are normally exempted from quarantine subject to certain conditions. These include possession of a recent veterinary health certificate, continuous residence in the country of origin for six months or more, vaccinations and airline certification. Detailed procedures on how to collect your pets from the airport are given on the AFCD website.

Export-a-Pet can assist with pet relocation into and out of Hong Kong (www.export-a-pet.com; tel. 2358 1774).

Buying a pet in Hong Kong

The **SPCA** (Harcourt Road and Fenwick Pier St, Wanchai; www.spca.org.hk; tel. 2802 0501) is often looking for adoptive parents for their cats, dogs and rabbits. The branch at 5 Wan Shing Street in Wanchai is open every day till 5:00 pm for walk-in adoption. Dog behaviour training classes and details of veterinary clinics are also available.

The SPCA does not recommend that you buy pets from unregistered pet shops or illegal hawkers on the street. Some of these animals are imported from China illegally without the requisite medical certificates and vaccinations, although microchipping of animals is being introduced. They may also have been clipped and dyed to resemble another more expensive breed – stories abound of Dalmatians whose spots come off in the wash and schnauzers revealed to be shih-tzus in disguise. Before buying, ask a vet to come with you to the pet shop to check the state of health of the animal. All dogs over five months must be licensed and inoculated against rabies every third year. Rabies is not a problem in Hong Kong.

Keeping pets in Hong Kong

Most cat owners keep their cats indoors, either because there is nowhere for them to roam or to protect them from marauding wild dogs – a problem all over Hong Kong but especially on the Outlying Islands. Dogs should be kept on a lead when taken out in public and dog faeces scooped up on a newspaper and deposited in a rubbish bin – the fine for non-compliance is $1,500.

Veterinary centres include:

- **Valley Veterinary Centre** (Happy Valley; tel. 2575 2389);
- **Stanley Veterinary Centre** (tel. 2813 2030);
- **Veterinary Housecall Practice** (tel. 2892 1567);
- **Sai Kung Animal Hospital** (tel. 2792 2206/emergencies 747410572); and
- **The Ark Veterinary Hospital** (Sai Ying Pun, tel. 2549 2330 – 24 hrs).

Grooming is available through a home visit from **Dogfather's Treatment** (www.dogfathers.com.hk; tel. 9460 0389) and **Pet Shop Girls** (G/F 40B, Blue Pool Road, Happy Valley; tel. 2891 9972), amongst others.

Pet-minding in your own home and day-time walking is available from **Wish You Were Here** (www.wishyouwereherehk.com; tel. 2899 0817). Kennels include **Ferndale Kennels and Cattery** (tel. 2792 4642) and **Kennel Van Dego** (cats and dogs; http://kennelvandego.com) in Sai Kung; **Pokfulam Kennels** (tel. 2551 6661) and **Hong Kong Kennels** (tel. 2551 8586/2550 9211) on Hong Kong Island.

Details of pet product shops are provided in Chapter Seven, 'Shopping'.

Pests

Most apartments are visited by small geckos and cockroaches from time to time. Whilst the former don't usually present much of a problem, apart from leaving faecal deposits indiscriminately round the place, getting trapped in door hinges and occasionally tripping electric circuits, cockroaches are roundly despised by everyone.

To avoid attracting cockroaches:

* keep rubbish wrapped up;
* don't leave food hanging around;
* make sure plug holes and drainage holes are kept covered; and
* buy roach baits from the supermarket to put around the apartment.

If you still have problems with roaches or termites, you could consider fumigation. Pest control companies include:

* **Biocycle Ecological Pest Control Services** (tel. 2799 6206);
* **Truly Care Environmental Pest Control Services** (tel. 2458 8378); and
* **Rentokil** (tel. 2954 6888).

LIFE IN YOUR NEW HOME

Humidity and air conditioning

Air conditioners are a prerequisite for comfortable living during the summer months and many rental apartments are ready-fitted. Most people also find it worthwhile to invest in at least one dehumidifier, which can be kept running throughout the humid months from March to September. Their main function is to prevent clothes, books and leather, etc. from rotting, but they can also be used to dry out damp clothes.

Furniture leasing

An alternative to shipping your furniture out to Hong Kong or buying lots of new furniture when you get here is to lease, particularly if you plan to stay in Hong Kong for only a short time. Companies leasing furniture include **Tree** (www.tree.com.hk), touted as the city's first eco-chic furniture business, **Home Essentials** (22/F, Horizon Plaza, Ap Lei Chau, tel. 2870 1400; www.

homeessentials.net) and **Indigo Expressive Living** (6/F, Horizon Plaza; tel. 2555 0540; www.indigo-living.com). Indigo ensures that long-term rental furniture (two years) is brand new and offers an option to purchase after lease expiry.

For details of where to buy furniture, refer to Chapter Seven ('Shopping').

Painting and decorating

Your apartment will probably have been newly painted in advance of the start of your rental, but if it hasn't, feel free to ask the landlord to give it a lick of paint. If you need anything else installing, for example shelves or light fittings, ask your landlord to help you arrange for a workman to do this for you. This will usually be a lot cheaper than finding an expatriate workman, but agree the price before the work starts. If your landlord doesn't speak English, then ask the property agent to help you find a local workman. Expat-oriented companies providing maintenance and home services include **Winkle Design & Decoration** (tel. 2554 1269) and **Alan Engineering Co.** (tel. 2887 6638). Other companies advertise in Dollarsaver (www.dollarsaver.com.hk).

Locking yourself out

Emergency locksmiths serving Hong Kong Island and Kowloon include the **24-Hour Open Lock Service Centre**. The **Fair & Good Security Locks Centre** (tel. 2498 1777) serves the New Territories. Expect to pay a few hundred dollars. **Mr Locksmith** (tel. 2887 6638) can also open doors, make keys and increase security.

Maintenance of your apartment

Over the course of time, you may discover patches of mould spreading over the wall, the roof may start to leak during the typhoon season, the toilet flush may break down, the shower fixture may spring a leak or the air conditioner may play up. More serious problems may also occur, such as the hot water tank exploding. Generally speaking, when equipment such as the hot water tank breaks down, it will be your responsibility to fix it; but for structural problems, your landlord should take responsibility. Some landlords, of course, are sweeties and will help to fix anything for you for minimal or no cost. You should always report leaks and rotting to the landlord (or property agent, if you use them as a middleman in communication) as soon as possible. Depending on the landlord, your problem could be fixed within a few days or may never be fixed. Make sure you have the approval of your landlord before you pay for someone to fix structures or fittings – including putting extra locks on doors.

Service is usually polite and efficient, and workmen can often come out during the evening and on Sundays.

Leaving your apartment

It is usual to give your landlord at least one month's notice, according to the terms of your tenancy agreement. You will need to pay all outstanding bills before quitting the property and leave it in the same state as it was when you arrived, unless you have agreed with the landlord to leave equipment or furniture in place.

You can get rid of unwanted furniture and equipment by having a moving sale, which you can advertise in the *South China Morning Post*, or by calling up a recycling company. Waste collectors and recyclers are listed on the **Environmental Protection Department**'s website (www.epd.gov.hk). Removals companies (see below) will also remove unwanted items for a minimum charge. Charities such as **Crossroads International** (tel. 2984 9309) receive used furniture and equipment in good condition. Clothing can be deposited in recycling bins or given to one of the many charities that take second-hand clothes, for example the **Salvation Army** (tel. 2332 4433). Books can be given to the YWCA for its borrowing library or a second-hand bookshop.

REMOVALS COMPANIES

Removals companies who can pack and ship your household internationally include:

- **AGS Four Winds** (www.agsfourwinds.com; tel. 2885 9666);
- **Crown Relocations** (www.crownworldwide.com; tel. 2636 8388);
- **Links Relocations** (www.linksrelo.com; tel. 2366 6700); and
- **Santa Fe** (www.santafe.com.hk; tel. 2574 6204).

Contact them three to four months before your intended move date and they will give you a free survey and quotation.

Chapter Six

Eating and Drinking

Food is such a central part of Chinese culture that it merits a whole book on the subject – certainly more than I can cover briefly here. Hong Kong is definitely a place where people live to eat – a few years ago, there were over 10,400 restaurants counted – and the enjoyment taken in food, as well as the widespread sophisticated, discriminating appreciation for it, is palpable. The attention paid to the presentation of food, however, can sometimes be quite cursory, so don't be put off by appearances.

Food is what brings people together – family, colleagues, friends – and for most people who live in small apartments in the city, a restaurant is the preferred place for meeting socially. It's less common than in the West for friends and colleagues to invite you over to their place to eat. There isn't really much etiquette involved with eating Chinese food, but there is a lot of symbolism: chopsticks stuck vertically into rice should be avoided, as it reminds people of incense sticks and death; chopsticks held very high up are thought to signify travelling far from home – again, not good.

Food is often eaten because it sounds good. Pig's tongue (*lei*) sounds like a word meaning 'profit', so it's supposed to be lucky for those starting up a business. *Fat choi*, a black, stringy, now endangered moss that often serves as a garnish to green vegetables or is cooked in soup, sounds the same as a word meaning 'make wealth'. It is gobbled up by everyone during the Lunar New Year, when eating auspicious-sounding food starts the year on a positive note. There used to be a tradition practised by bosses who had to lay off staff at this time of the year – considered very unfortunate, when everyone else is celebrating – that involved a cooked chicken. At the office dinner, the boss would point the head of the bird towards the employee who was going to lose his job. It delicately dispensed with the need for words.

At times, English translations of food names on menus can be maddeningly unspecific. 'Dumpling' seems to cover over a hundred varieties of food, all having very different flavours, textures and appearances. A certain amount of experimentation will be necessary. 'Rice cake fried with pork and cabbage' is altogether savoury; 'barbecue pork bun' will appear on the table as a white,

13. Eating dim sum
Photograph taken by the author

sweetened pork donut, steamed. Dishes are often christened with fabulous or preposterous names, impossible to decipher. 'Dragon, tiger, phoenix', available just over the border in Shenzhen, is one such example. This is dressed up snake, cat and chicken.

Precious little goes to waste in Chinese restaurants. The extremities, innards, tendons and gelatinous parts of fish, fowl or beast are often prized because of their texture and their ability to soak up piquant sauces. Fish eyes, pig's ears, nose and tail, goose web and head, chicken's heart and feet are all dished up. Many foods are believed to be good for the health, such as snake bile and ox blood (served in chunks and cooked in a hotpot).

LOCAL DELICACIES

Below is a sampler of some common Hong Kong delicacies.

Dim sum

Dim sum (or 'little bits of heart') are a cherished feature of Hong Kong cuisine and rightly so. Standard meals in the lunch-time institution of *yum cha* ('drink tea') that are served at Cantonese restaurants all over Hong Kong include:

- *siu mai* – steamed mince and prawn dumplings decorated with bright orange crab eggs;
- *har gau* – steamed prawn dumplings;
- *cheung fen* – soft white rice flour rolls sloshed with soy;
- *luo buo gau* – fried squares of turnip, pork and mushroom mash; and
- *char siu bao* – sweet pork stuffed in the centre of a white steamed bun.

Eaten briskly with colleagues on weekday lunch-times or lingered over with family at the weekend, several hundred types of dim sum fry and steam their way onto tables from 11:00 in the morning till past three in the afternoon. The noise generated by customers in a big restaurant can be deafening.

In some places, the serving ladies still push around trolleys from which you make your selection, whilst in other restaurants the waitress brings food to your table. Trolley ladies can be found at **Maxim's Palace** (2/F, Low Block, City Hall) and **The Metropole** (4/F, United Centre, Admiralty – but watch your bag, as thieves are known to operate there). You select a dish from the trolley and the serving lady stamps your order card. When there are no trolleys, you first mark up your order sheet, which also shows the price of each item – low, medium, high or special price. Then give the order sheet to the waitress, who brings the dishes, often in bamboo steamers, to your table. The only problem with this is that most Chinese restaurants do not have an English translation of dim sum menus. A nice pictorial guide to many of the most famous dim sum is *Dim Sum: A Pocket Guide* by Kit Shan Li (Chronicle Books).

Sauces and dips served with dim sum include soy sauce, vinegar (garnished with thin strips of ginger), chilli oil, XO sauce (oil flavoured with chilli and seafood), chilli sauce, sweet sauce and mustard sauce (especially good with roast pork). Tea is usually drunk as an accompaniment – *sao mei, bo lei* and *tik guan yum* being among the most popular with local Hong Kongers. Lift the tea-pot lid to the side when you want a hot water refill.

Beside the dim sum, which usually come in three or four strips or items per helping, it's common to order other side dishes such as a roast meat plate – pork, goose, duck and eel are common – and one of the many fried rice, congee or fried noodle dishes. (Fried rice with dried scallop and egg white is tasty.) Chinese also commonly order a plate of blanched *choi sum*, green stalky vegetables served with oyster sauce.

There is usually a small selection of desserts served after dim sum. Amongst the most popular are:

- mango pudding in a lagoon of evaporated milk;
- sweet red bean soup flavoured with sun-dried tangerine peel;
- mini-egg tarts with the centres almost runny; and
- sesame or peanut balls in sweet soup (*tong yun*).

Expect to pay about $130–160 per head for a meal of dim sum, depending on what is ordered. An excellent restaurant for dim sum is **Victoria City** (5/F, Citic Tower, Admiralty), which has a splendid view of the harbour.

One last note – you may or may not be able to book a table for dim sum, depending on the rules of the establishment concerned. Having booked a table, you may well have to wait ten minutes or more for it to be cleared for you, even though you have arrived on time. If time is tight, it's better to get there before midday to avoid the stampede and before the egg tarts start to run out. Alternatively, go later – usually after 3:00 pm – to enjoy half-price dim sum at many of the restaurants.

Roast meats

One of the most common and distressing sights around Hong Kong – until you get used to it – is the display of carcasses on hooks in restaurant windows. These roasted meats include:

- *siu yok* roast pork – with crispy crackling;
- *char siu* pork – sweet honey roast pork that is red at the edges;
- chicken – yellow-skinned;
- duck – dark brown, very rich and fatty; and
- goose – light brown.

A standard lunch box for office workers consists of rice plus one or more roast meat, topped with a splash of soy sauce, a dab of crushed garlic and spring onion in oil and a slip of green stemmed vegetable. They usually cost around $25 and are extremely good value and tasty.

Roast pigeon is the house speciality at **Han Lok Yuen** on Lamma Island (on the steps above Hung Shing Ye Beach; tel. 2982 0608/0680).

Chinese dessert houses

These are a very popular hang-out for locals, although some desserts are an acquired taste for expats. Common desserts include:

- *dau fu fa* – soft, semi-solid beancurd, sweetened with brown sugar or syrup;
- walnut and sesame soups;
- tapioca and tarot egg pudding;
- mango and durian pancakes – fresh fruit and false cream wrapped in a yellow skin; and
- a large range of clear soups supposed to be good for your skin and health that include exotic ingredients such as papaya, gingko nuts, Job's tears and white fungus.

An excellent selection of desserts can be found at **Honeymoon Dessert** (9–11 Po Tung Road, Sai Kung), **Moon House Dessert** at the bottom of Sing Woo Road in Happy Valley and 50–56 Paterson Street, Causeway Bay, and **Heung Fa Lau** (D'Aguilar Street).

Delicious milk desserts of semi-solid milk mixed with egg or other ingredients served hot and cold – try the ginger one – are found on the menus of many small restaurants and in dedicated Formica-tabled diners such as **Yee Shun**

Milk Co. (85 Percival Street, Causeway Bay; 519 Nathan Road and elsewhere).

Cakes, Chinese-style

To be brutally honest, cakes are a bit of a disappointment in Hong Kong. You can find a small selection of French patisserie-style cakes at **Great** and **Olivers**, but mouth-watering Chinese cakes without false cream are harder to find, despite the profusion of local bakeries selling all manner of sweet and savoury combo buns and flaky pastries. However, maybe this is all an elaborate ploy to enhance the impact of the virtuoso **mooncake**, which makes its appearance around the time of the full moon at Mid-Autumn Festival. A meal-in-a-cake, it's built like a fortress. Once you breach the heavy brown pastry walls and wade through the viscous melon paste, you are rewarded with the golden treasure – a hard-boiled, salty egg yolk. Irresistible.

Cha chantengs

I guess the closest equivalent in English to the *cha chanteng* is a builder's caff or greasy spoon. It's a place where people drop in for breakfast, lunch or dinner to get a filling meal cheaply and quickly. Breakfast 'sets' include *nai cha* ('milk tea' made with very strong black tea and evaporated milk), egg tarts or toast, eggy bread sandwiched with peanut butter, a plate of macaroni and spam in cooking water, and scrambled egg with a sweet bun on the side. Lunch sets are typically noodle or rice sets – choose from beef tendon on top of noodles in soup, roast duck pieces on top of noodles in soup, rice smothered with a curry beef sauce, etc. It's very Hong Kong, so there's bound to be one close to your home or office.

AFTERNOON TEAS, TEA BUFFETS AND TEA SETS

Most small Chinese restaurants and cafes do a 'tea set', usually from 3:00 to 6:00 pm. Tea sets generally comprise a hot meal, such as spaghetti and pork chop, a drink (for example, ice lemon tea) and coffee or dessert, which could be ice cream, waffle or pancake. The meal may cost as little as $30.

Hong Kongers expect a lot of 'bang' for their bucks and afternoon tea buffets can often be the equivalent of a hearty meal. Spreads laid on by the big hotels are extravagant affairs and built to withstand extensive grazing. There is usually a selection of Western and Asian food, including sandwiches, dim sum, rice, fried noodles, soup, cooked dishes, cooked meats, sushi, salads, oysters and French cheeses, as well as an assortment of cakes, fruit, desserts, mousses, chocolate puddings, petit fours, tarts, brownies, fresh pancakes and ice cream. Popular buffets include the excellent value **Marriott** hotel afternoon tea buffet.

For more demure dining, you can enjoy a very English afternoon tea in the opulent surroundings of the **Peninsula Hotel Lobby**. Here, your afternoon tea is brought to your table on tiered plates while you are serenaded from the minstrels' gallery.

Other popular afternoon tea venues include the **Mandarin Oriental's Clipper Lounge** and the well-positioned **China Tee Club** (101 Pedder Building, 12 Pedder Street, Central). Strictly speaking a members-only club, they allow first-time visits and you get the membership fee back in dining coupons.

Dessert buffets and late night buffets from 9:00 pm onwards are also available in some hotels – check *HK Magazine* for details.

STREET SNACKS

Street snacks in Hong Kong are not as varied as in other parts of China, but the hawkers who vigorously ply their wares add to the vibrant atmosphere of this 24/7 city. The same old favourites seem to grace the corner of **Temple Street Night Market** in Jordan, the bus stops in Wanchai and the Sai Kung seaside. Take-away snacks include fish balls on sticks dunked in curry sauce, 'stinky' tofu (rare these days), octopus tentacles, curly pig intestines (coloured orange to make them more appetizing), fish balls (deep fried or broiled), beef balls, red and green pepper halves stuffed with fish paste and imitation shark's fin soup. Snack stalls are usually right on the main road, metres away from roaring traffic and bus exhaust fumes.

Sweet snacks sold on hawker's stalls include *tong chong beng*, a crisp rice flour wafer folded or rolled and sprinkled with peanut powder or dessicated coconut, and *dan zai* ('little eggs'), a kind of almond-flavoured waffle ball cooked in pitted iron moulds.

SANDWICHES

Oliver's Supersandwiches and **Delifrance** are two sandwich chains serving expats who refuse to trade in their daily bread for a rice box. **Pret a Manger** (in Central MTR station, Lippo Centre Admiralty and other locations) does brisk business.

DRINKS STALLS

Drinks stalls supply take-away drinks for people on the move. Common drinks found at stalls around Hong Kong include herbal/health teas, soya milk and 'pearl' drinks that contain fruit juice and pulp, sago, coconut milk, grass jelly, red beans, ice and jellied candy.

One of the things that always gets my brother's mouth watering when he comes to visit is the fresh fruit juice stalls dotted around the city; imagine being able to watch your favourite fruit being juiced and handed over in a large cup for immediate consumption at a cost of $5–10. Fresh juice menus feature orange, grapefruit, apple, strawberry, kiwi, pear, watermelon, mango, pineapple, star fruit, dragon fruit, as well as special combos such as celery, aloe vera and carrot, or honeydew melon, bittersquash and papaya – or you can select your own mix. Fruit is seasonal and depends heavily on imports from Thailand and China. Juice bars also often sell boxes of mixed fresh fruit or sandwich and fruit box sets as take-away. The prices, needless to say, are half the price for an equivalent bought from a supermarket. You can also often order flower arrangements or fruit baskets – mixed whole fruits in a wicker basket, cellophane-wrapped with a bow – as presents. Try **Funny Shop** (corner of Lockhart Road and Luard Road).

COFFEE SHOPS

The main coffee shop chains operating in Hong Kong are the home-grown **Pacific Coffee**, notable for its plush red velveteen sofas, and the world-dominating **Starbucks**, which entered Hong Kong in 2000. Most coffee shops are along the north of Hong Kong Island in the area between Causeway Bay and Central, with outlets also in the upmarket shopping malls in Kowloon (Harbour City, TST; Festival Walk in Kowloon Tong – be warned, though: most of Kowloon and the New Territories is a frappuccino-free zone.). All Pacific Coffee shops are equipped with Internet access.

Caffe Habitu has branches in Pacific Place, Three, Kowloon Station and Hutchinson House and is a luxurious though very enjoyable place to meet for a gossip.

You can pick up a nice, cheap coffee and snack at **Ali-Oli Bakery** and **The Colour Brown** in Sai Kung, and the town is well-equipped with coffee shops generally due to the presence of a significant number of expats in the neighbourhood. **Café Lavande** off the Mid-Levels escalator and **Café Corridor** opposite Times Square (26A Russell Street) have also earned good reviews from coffee-lovers and are well-positioned for shopping and sight-seeing pit-stops.

yin-yang (yuen-yeung)

No, it's not a dodgy haircut, it's a Hong Kong mixed drink concoction: half milk tea, half coffee. You can find it in the Chinese cafes near Hollywood Road.

TEA SHOPS

Traditional Chinese tea shops specialize in serving and selling different varieties of Chinese tea to discerning customers. Service is very attentive and staff are knowledgeable, sometimes offering classes on tea preparation. Shops include the well-known **Ying Kee** (152 Queen's Road, Central and 170 Johnson Road, Wanchai), **Lok Cha Teashop** (290B Queen's Road, Sheung Wan; tel. 2805 1360), and **Kai Fat** (G/F, 132 Wing Lok Street, Sheung Wan; tel. 2666 9328).

More recently, Hong Kongers obsessed with health have turned to tea to help with weight loss, coughs, colds, stress and digestion. These tea shops are commonly found in MTR stations. Brews cooked up by **Chinese Urban Healing Tea Shops** include Heat Cough Tea, Mulberry & Self-Heal Spike Drink and Perilla Herbal Soup for Enhancing Immunity.

FAST FOOD

McDonald's faces stiff competition from local food and this is reflected in the price of its burger meals – at about $22, reputedly one of the cheapest in the world. Other burger restaurants include **Monster Burger** and **Atomic**

Patty (near Lan Kwai Fong), **Burger King** at the Airport and Peak Tower and **Fatburger** (196–206 Queen's Road East, Wanchai). Twenty-four hour restaurants operate at China Chem Johnston Plaza, 178–186 Johnston Road, Wanchai and in TST (Peking Road branch). McDonald's' younger sibling, **McCafe**, offers salads, pastries, muffins and so on. Other American-style fast food chains include **Jollibee, Hardee's, KFC** and **Spaghetti House**. Chinese fast food outlets include **Café de Coral, Fairwood** and **Maxim Fast Food**, serving up East-meets-West combos such as pig knuckle and rice, ham and cheese toast, and American baked potato and egg salad. They also do party-size take-aways.

Popular and cheap Japanese fast food chains include **Genki Sushi** and **sen-ryo** for Japanese conveyor-belt sushi and **Yoshinoya** for stringy beef and rice bowl sets.

Besides sandwiches, **Delifrance** does soup and sandwich sets, quiche and salad, baked potatoes, and tempting basketfuls of French-style sweet breads (chocolate croissants, raisin rolls, muffins, etc.).

A tasty fish and chips or pie and chips is served up at **Chips**, Pottinger Street, Central. In the same neighbourhood is the delectable but more expensive **Archie B's** (7–9 Staunton Street, on the Mid-Levels escalator), which features speciality sandwiches such as hot pastrami and Swiss cheese melts. Both provide for eat-in and take-away diners.

Kebab vendors and take-away Thai food sellers can be found around the Lockhart Road area in Wanchai.

Food courts, which generally serve food till about 9:30 pm, are usefully located in shopping malls all round Hong Kong. **Great's Food Hall** (Basement, Pacific Place) features speedy dining from a range of vendors selling oysters and sashimi, roasts, pasta, Korean and Chinese food, burgers from Canadian Triple O's White Spot and pizza by Pizza Express. Another food court on the Lower Floor of Pacific Place includes standard fast food from round the world. Branches of **City'super Food Court/Pit-Stop** (Times Square Basement, Harbour City and Basement of Silvercord building, Haiphong Road) include Indian, Taiwanese, Japanese, Korean, Chinese and Thai food counters.

If you're shopping in Whampoa, the **Gourmet Plaza** in 'Screen World' is well worth a visit. Featuring a range of famous Chinese restaurants, some of which were former *daipaidong* – restaurants catering to the masses with rows of tables laid out in the street – this is the place to pick up a steaming bowl of hand-made noodles, dim sum or dumplings at a very reasonable price. Another tasty daipaidong-style restaurant that is now indoors is the **Wong Nai Chung Cooked Food Centre** at the top of the Urban Council Building in Sing Woo Road, Happy Valley.

Although you don't often see locals eating snacks as they walk along the street, ice cream is the exception. **Häagen-Dazs** has over ten branches, including Lan Kwai Fong, Pier No. 3, Central, Festival Walk and Times Square; there are also several **Ben & Jerry's** outlets, including those in D'Aguilar Street, Festival Walk, Two IFC and Level 2, World Trade Centre. Alternatively, try the delicious local lick **XTC on Ice** (Central, Threesixty, Happy Valley, TST).

Hong Kong dishes

Fish maw: The bladder of a fish, often served in a soup or stew, reputed to be good for the lungs and skin.

Turtle jelly: Reputed to have cooling properties, this black, bitter-tasting semi-solid food is made from Chinese herbs and turtle shell (or meat in the more expensive version), and can be eaten with brown sugar or syrup to make it more palatable.

Bird's nest soup: Soup made from a swallow's nest that has been first dried, then stewed. Reputed to be good for the skin, it can be served as a savoury or sweet dish.

Abalone: An edible mollusc that is extremely popular in Hong Kong and prized because it is rare – and therefore expensive.

1,000-year-old eggs: Duck eggs preserved in salt and ash for 100 days. The yolks have a dense texture and strong flavour; the whites are black.

RESTAURANTS

Hong Kong diners are extremely discriminating and because food is taken seriously, restaurants have to compete on quality and price. There is a considerable range of prices when it comes to Chinese and non-Chinese restaurants, so you are well-catered for no matter what your budget. Lower down the price chain, Chinese restaurants are usually better value, and the price comes down even further the more people you have around the table.

Even for solitary diners, Chinese food often works out cheaper. For example, tea and a bowl of freshly made and cooked noodles (usually served with a meat sauce and a green vegetable), or a plate of dumplings and soup, at a downtown air-conditioned Shanghainese restaurant with proper seats, space between each table, a good level of cleanliness, an English/Chinese menu and English-speaking serving staff costs about $28 with no added service charge. A plate of Asian food from cafeteria-style **Canteen** (IFC Mall, Prince's Building, etc.) would cost roughly $100, no service charge necessary. Any Western-style establishment in Lan Kwai Fong is going to work out more expensive than that.

Gourmands can choose from a vast array of local and international cuisine, including French, Spanish, Indian, Indonesian, Russian, Cambodian, Mongolian, Egyptian, Lebanese and Nepalese. Chinese restaurants often specialize in specific provincial cuisines that all have their distinct flavours and signature dishes: Cantonese (local), Hunanese, Szechuanese, Shanghainese, Yunnanese and Chiuchow are some of the better known. For detailed information on restaurants, prices and ratings, check out the weekly **HK Magazine** or the *'Tatler' Guide to HK's Best Restaurants*, updated annually. Foodies can also join the local online gourmet community at **www.openrice.com** to keep track of new restaurants opening all the time and enjoy member discounts at restaurants. Another food appreciation society is **Slow Food (Hong Kong)** – call 2836 3938 to find out about meetings. Look out also for the free Japanese magazine *Concierge* (available in Great supermarkets), which usually has a few pages of restaurant discount coupons in English.

Restaurants waiting to get liquor licences and those not licensed to serve alcohol usually allow you to bring your own. Some waive the corkage charge; others can charge up to $100 per bottle.

Below, I've tried to provide an overview of the dining options in Hong Kong to get you started. If accumulating **Asia Miles** (www.asiamiles.com) is important to you, make sure you take advantage of the many restaurants and service providers in Hong Kong which are partners in the scheme.

Famous Chinese restaurants

These are some of the longest-established, most famous Chinese restaurants in Hong Kong, imbued with history and ambience (and often octogenarian waiters):

- **Tai Ping Koon** (40 Granville Road, TST; 6 Pak Sha Road, Causeway Bay, etc.). An early experimenter in East–West fusion; very Hong Kong.
- **Luk Yu Teahouse** (24–26 Wellington Street, Central). Claims to fame include the retro interior décor, the favouritism of the elderly waiters and an assassination carried out over dim sum in 2002.
- **Yung Kee** (32–40 Wellington Street). Famous for its roast goose.
- **Fook Lam Moon** (35–45 Johnston Road, Wanchai). Famous for the black Mercedes parked outside and the excellent food.

Good value restaurants serving regional cuisine

These include:

- Cantonese: **Che's** (4/F, The Broadway, Lockhart Road, Wanchai).
- Hakka: **Hak Ka** (21/F, Lee Theatre, Percival Sreet, Causeway Bay).
- Chiu Chow: **Chiu Lau** (No.1 Peking Road, Tsimshatsui).
- Shanghainese: **Siu Nam Kwok** (Sugar Street, Causeway Bay).

Hotel restaurants

Some of the best restaurants in Hong Kong are located inside hotels such as the Mandarin Oriental, Peninsula, Conrad, Shangri-La, Hyatt Regency and Regent. They often enjoy stunning views of the harbour and have excellent service, as well as plenty of space – lacking in some other expensive venues. Prices are high, but you can buy discount cards that allow two to dine for the price of one for a fixed number of visits or period of time.

DINING LOCALES

International

Many of Hong Kong's 'international' restaurants and bars cluster together in pockets. The most famous of these is probably **Lan Kwai Fong** in Central, closely followed by the **Soho/Mid-Levels** escalator area. The restaurants in these two locales are generally pricey, although there are cheaper options. Restaurants open and close all the time in this neighbourhood, so it's well worth checking these areas on a regular basis to keep abreast of new arrivals.

Knutsford Terrace (TST) and **Cleveland Street** (Fashion Walk) in Causeway Bay are two smaller pedestrianized areas that play host to a variety of bars and restaurants.

The **Lockhart Road/Luard Road** area in Wanchai is cheaper, on average, and includes Thai, Mexican, Balinese, pub grub and kebabs.

The restaurant with arguably the best view of Hong Kong's breathtaking skyline is **Café Deco** on the Peak. Other stunning views can be had at **Felix** (38/F, The Peninsula), **Aqua** (29–30/F, 1 Peking Road) and **Tott's Bar and Grill** (34/F, The Excelsior).

Al fresco restaurants that allow diners to enjoy views and/or a sea breeze include the restaurants on the **Stanley** waterfront, **Harbour Plaza Resort City** (18 Tin Yan Road, Tin Shui Wai), **Spices** at The Repulse Bay, **The Viceroy** in the Sun Hung Kai Centre and **The Peak Café** on the Peak.

Many restaurants, including **Bombay Dreams** (Wyndham Street), the **Fringe Club** and **Bamboo** (4/F, The Plaza, 21 D'Aguilar Street), have private rooms/roof terraces that can be booked for larger groups.

Cheaper eats
There are many mini-dining zones where you can pick up a tasty Western/ Asian fusion meal for less than you'd pay at equivalent restaurants in TST or Causeway Bay. **Wing Lok Street**, outside Sheung Wan MTR, and **Sanlitun**, on the elevated walkway between the Sun Hung Kai Centre and the Harbour Centre in Wanchai, represent good value for money.

'Korea Street'
Kimberley Street and **Kimberley Road** in TST are pleasant backwaters just off the main drag and home to a string of Korean food supermarkets, cooked food shops and restaurants serving up genuine Korean food at an affordable price.

Little Japan
Causeway Bay is sometimes dubbed 'Little Japan' for its mix of teppanyaki and sashimi restaurants, Japanese curry houses and snack bars. Other places to get good Japanese food include the Hung Hom area – try **Katiga** (37 Shung Kit Street; tel. 2764 6436) – and 'Ramen Alley', six ramen stalls serving their own style noodles, at 517 Jaffe Road, Wanchai.

Lei King Wan/Island East
Further along the north Hong Kong Island shoreline to the east, a cluster of al fresco restaurants line **Tai Hong Street** in Lei King Wan serving a mix of reasonably priced seafood, Japanese, Thai and Brazilian style cuisine. It's very popular with those living in the Sai Wan Ho/Taikoo Shing neighbourhoods.

Seafood heaven
Lei Yue Mun is reputed to be *the* place for seafood in Hong Kong, but it is expensive and awkward to get to. Take a taxi from Kowloon side, or a ferry from Sai Wan Ho.

Lamma Island's **Sok Ku Wan** is noted for its strip of seafood restaurants, the most famous being the **Rainbow Seafood Restaurant**, which provides a free ferry shuttling customers between the restaurant and Queen's Pier (opposite City Hall).

The **Sai Kung** waterfront, not far from the minibus terminal, is also home to a number of excellent seafood restaurants, including the popular **Chuen Yee Seafood Restaurant**. You can pick out your own fish or prawns and take them home to cook, or give them to the kitchen to cook. Relaxed al fresco dining with friends on chilli salt prawns, bamboo clams, steamed garoupa and Qingdao beer is one of the most pleasurable ways to spend an evening in Hong Kong. Buses to Sai Kung connect with Kwun Tong, Hang Hau and Choi Hung MTR stations, amongst others. At the end of Clearwater Bay Road, near the Clearwater Bay Golf and Country Club, **Po Toi O** village has a few seafood restaurants – but it's quite a way to go for your prawns.

Prices are significantly lower on **Cheung Chau** – try **Hong Kee**, where my aunt and uncle go regularly for their boiled prawns, lobsters, crab and scallops with broccoli.

Oyster restaurants are also popular in Hong Kong – **The Oyster and Wine Bar** at the Sheraton Hotel, Kowloon, is one of the best and most romantic. Another popular venue is **Oyster Talks Seafood & Wine Bar** (13 King Kwong Street, Happy Valley).

Kids' favourites
The most popular restaurants with children and teens include Fat Angelo's (1/F, Elizabeth House, 250 Gloucester Road; 49A–C Elgin Street; G/F Wu Chung House, 213 Queen's Road East, Wanchai; Panda Hotel, Tsuen Wan, etc.) and Amaroni's Little Italy (LG132 Festival Walk, Kowloon Tong),

which are Italian-American style family restaurants serving up big portions. Other child-friendly restaurants include:

- Dan Ryan's Chicago Grill (Pacific Place, Ocean Terminal and Festival Walk);
- TGI Friday's (26 Nathan Road);
- Shooters 52 (G–1 The Peak Galleria and Times Square);
- California Pizza Kitchen (Level 3, Ocean Terminal; 13/F Food Forum, Times Square, 56 Dundas Street, Mongkok);
- Ruby Tuesday (Cityplaza 1; Ocean Terminal; New Town Plaza Shatin, etc.);
- Jaspa's (Sai Kung and Staunton Street, Central); and
- Pepperoni's (Sai Kung and Stanley).

Younger kids like Trendy Toon Town (Shop B101, Basement 1, 1 Peking Rd, TST), a scaled down version of Disneyland complete with popular Disney characters. Turkish restaurant **Bahce** in Mui Wo (Unit 19, Mui Wo Centre, tel. 2984 0221) does *mezze* platters that please kids and adults alike. Even more important, the owners and staff are great with toddlers.

Private dining restaurants

Private dining restaurants are small-scale, privately run restaurants located unobtrusively in residential or commercial blocks. They usually have one or two sittings each evening and places need to be booked in advance. There's no a la carte menu; either you get what the owners have prepared or you're offered a choice before you come. The selling points are that they provide a more private experience and authentic, home-cooking cuisine. You can probably get recommendations from Cantonese colleagues in the know (a Chinese language book listing these restaurants is also available at bookshops). Better-known ones include **Yellow Door Kitchen** (www.yellowdoorkitchen. com.hk; 5 and 6/F, 37 Cochrane Street, Central, tel. 2858 6555), **Mum Chau's Sichuan Kitchen** (5B, 37 D'Aguilar Street, Central, tel. 8108 8550) and **Helen Chiang's Kitchen** (1/F, 26 Leighton Rd, Causeway Bay, tel. 2805 7533). Expect to pay about $200–400 per person without wine.

TAKE-AWAY/HOME DELIVERY

Many restaurants around Hong Kong now belong to a delivery co-operative. Large delivery companies include:

- www.foodbyweb.com.hk, which has a very comprehensive listing of restaurants;
- **Food by Fone** (www.foodbyfone.net; 2868 6969), which delivers food from restaurants in the Lan Kwai Fong, Sai Ying Pun, Wanchai Happy Valley areas; and
- **Dial A Dinner** (www.dialadinner.com.hk; 2598 1718), which also covers the south of Hong Kong Island and Kowloon;
- **Soho Delivery** (www.sohodelivery.com.hk; 2526 2029).

Order food from one or several restaurants by phone or via the Internet and your meal will be whisked to you within an hour. Companies will also cater for large parties.

Other take-away/delivery services are offered by **Wildfire** pizza (2/F, Murray House, Stanley and 13 Bonham Road, Mid-Levels; www.igors.com) and **Pepperoni's** (www.pepperonis.com; tel. 2869 1766).

HALAL/KOSHER RESTAURANTS

Habibi's (116 Wellington Street, Central; tel. 2544 9298) is an Egyptian Halal restaurant; **Islam Food** (1 Lung Kong Road, Kowloon City) serves Chinese Muslim and Shanghai food. Kosher restaurants include **Shalom Grill** (2/F, Fortune House, 61 Connaught Road; tel. 2851 6300).

VEGETARIAN AND VEGAN RESTAURANTS

There is a good selection of Chinese vegetarian restaurants and a few Western ones if you know where to look. Many of the Chinese vegetarian restaurants have Buddhist connections – traditionally, Hong Kong Chinese eat vegetarian food on the first and the fifteenth of the Lunar calendar months, especially the first meal of the first month of the Lunar New Year.

Chinese vegetarian restaurants that come recommended include **Bo Kong Vegetarian** (12/F, Times Square Food Forum; tel. 2506 3377) and **Kung Tak Lam** (G/F, Block B, Lok Sing Centre, 31 Yee Wo Street, Causeway Bay; tel. 2890 3127 and 7/F, 1 Peking Road, TST; tel. 2312 7800).

Good non-Chinese vegetarian restaurants include **The Bookworm Café** on Main Street, Lamma Island, the owner of which is also behind **Life** on Shelley Street, Central, and **Woodlands** Indian restaurant at 61 Mody Road,

TST; tel. 2369 3718. The **Fringe Club** in Central offers a vegetarian buffet Monday to Friday. A list of vegan and vegetarian restaurants can be found on the website of the **HK Vegan Society** (www.ivu.org/hkvegan).

Vegans do not seem to find it particularly difficult to find suitable food in Hong Kong. As the Chinese traditionally are not heavy consumers of dairy products, there are plenty of tofu-based foods available in supermarkets as well as vegetarian restaurants.

For information on food and wine shops and supermarkets, please refer to Chapter Seven, 'Shopping'.

Chapter Seven

Shopping

As you become more familiar with Hong Kong, you'll develop your own personal stamping ground for shopping – no two people I have spoken to have exactly the same preferences. I've included here a selection of shops, malls and streets devoted to particular merchandise that will hopefully act as a useful starting point. The general consensus is that you can get pretty much anything you want, but you may have to hunt for it. To locate a phone number, call directory enquiries free on 1081, or visit www.timway.com.hk or www.yp.com.hk. The *Yellow Pages* website also has a handy 'location search' facility. Reductions are best found during Shopping Festival (end of June through August) and Winterfest (late November to January 1).

QTS SHOPS

It's worth looking out for shops that display the **Quality Tourism Services (QTS) Scheme** logo. If you do encounter problems, give the **Consumer Council** a call on 2929 2222. The idea that the 'customer is king' has not caught on here and generally speaking it is difficult to return goods that have been opened or worn, or if the delay between buying the item and bringing it back is too long. Always check what 'right of return' you have before you buy. Large department stores offer goods at a fixed price, but in smaller shops, as with markets, bargaining is allowed.

MALLS

Hong Kong has several large shopping malls, many of which are plush marble-floored buildings decorated with orchids and water features. They are popular with expatriates and locals because they provide a mix of entertainment, dining and shopping options close together, and are air-conditioned havens from the hot and humid summer weather. The major malls include:

- **Harbour City** (www.harbourcity.com.hk) is accessed from Ocean Terminal next to the Star Ferry Pier or from the upper reaches of Canton Road – an eight-minute walk from TST MTR. The mall includes City'super and Wellcome supermarkets.

14. Wanchai street market
Photograph taken by Stanley Ng

- **Elements** (www.elementshk.com, 1 Austin Road West, TST) includes organic supermarket Threesixty, a roof-top garden, playground and kindergarten.
- **Festival Walk** (www.festivalwalk.com.hk), above Kowloon Tong MTR station, includes a ParknShop superstore.
- **Times Square** (www.timessquare.com.hk), above Causeway Bay MTR, should be avoided on Saturdays and Sundays if you dislike large crowds. It includes ParknShop and City'super supermarkets.
- **IFC Mall** (www.ifc.com.hk) above Central's Airport Express Station is the newest mall and includes a City'super supermarket.
- **Pacific Place** (www.pacificplace.com.hk) includes Great supermarket. Access is from Admiralty MTR station and via the elevated walkway from Central's Harcourt Road.
- **Wonderful Worlds of Whampoa** in Hunghom (www.whampoaworld. com). Not strictly speaking a mall, this huge shopping hub is divided into Fashion World, Treasure World, Screen World and Home World. A free air-conditioned shuttle service can ferry you between worlds.
- **Cityplaza** (www.cityplaza.com.hk) and the interconnected Kornhill Plaza are located near Taikoo MTR station. They include the Japanese department stores Uny and Jusco.
- **Langham Place** (www.langhamplace.com.hk), 8 Argyle Street, Mongkok.

All the malls have, or are very close to, a cinema. Festival Walk and Cityplaza have ice rinks. Other amenities such as parking, clean public toilets, banks and ATM machines are also conveniently available. The malls are enlivened by occasional performances of live music, model shows, art displays and advertising stands.

SHOPS

Below is an A–Z listing of the main types of shopping available in Hong Kong. Services are mentioned under the relevant chapter. New website www.aiiyah. com allows users to find, share and compare information about shops.

Antiques
Hong Kong has a thriving antiques business, mostly centred around the **Hollywood Road** neighbourhood. For late nineteenth and twentieth century European and Scandinavian art and antiques, go to **Manks** in Wong Chuk Hang (www. manks.com; tel. 2522 2115). At the bottom of Hollywood Road, past the Man Mo Temple and down the steps, is **Cat Street**, an interesting place to browse for fortune sticks, curios, posters and second-hand household bric-a-brac. Antique

furniture can also be found at warehouse-style shops such as **Shamabala** (2/F, Horizon Plaza, Ap Lei Chau; www.shambala.com.hk). **Wah Tung China Ltd** (G/F and 1/F, Lee Roy Commercial Building, 57–59 Hollywood Road; www. wahtungchina.com) is well known for its reproduction ceramics and porcelain.

The shops offer a wide selection of genuine antiques and reproductions, including furniture, silk fragments, ceramics, fossils and sculpture, for the connoisseur and the casual browser. Serious acquisitions can be made at Sotheby's and Christie's auction houses, both in Central.

Genuine antiques are accompanied by Oxford Test certificates that establish the age of the piece; several tests should be performed at different sites on a large object. Perhaps most importantly, find a dealer who you trust – there is no professional body you can contact, so it's very much a case of caveat emptor. Reproduction antiques are advertised as such by reputable stores and are good value for money, but make sure that they have been properly made: reproduction lacquerware, for example, is very popular, but hastily prepared lacquer can crack in Hong Kong's humidity.

Consider how you will care for your antique once it is installed in your home. Hong Kong's humidity can damage silks, leather and wood, so take professional advice.

Art
Many art galleries reside in the neighbourhood of Hollywood Road, a stone's throw from the Mid-Levels escalator. Online links to many of the galleries are provided at **www.hongkongartwalk.com/galleries.html.** Modern and traditional Chinese art and other Asian art is exhibited for sale at galleries such as **Schoeni Art Gallery** (21–31 Old Bailey Street; www.schoeni.com.hk), **10 Chancery Lane Gallery** (Soho) and **Karin Weber Gallery** (20 Aberdeen Street; www.karinwebergallery.com). John Batten (batten@netvigator.com) advises clients collecting contemporary art to take basic precautions, such as tracing the ownership back to the artist to prove the originality of the art, doing research in magazines such as *Asian Art News* and *Art Asia Pacific*, which can be informative, and taking the time to network with other art collectors and find art dealers who are honest. He says:

> *Expats are driven by sentiment, so when they're in Hong Kong they want something to remind them of their stay here.*

This usually means that expats buy Chinese or Vietnamese art – the latter is usually a lot more expensive to buy here than in Hanoi – and for a lot of

Asian art, there's no secondary market. Well-established overseas artists occasionally mount exhibitions and because they're not well-known here, prices may be lower.

The main benefit of buying art in Hong Kong is that there's no VAT, meaning that prices are 17.5% less than what they would be in the UK, for example. Also, there are no import duties or taxes applied to art brought into Hong Kong. It's perfectly acceptable to bargain with an art dealer, and depending on situations sometimes as basic as the current financial status of the artist, you may be able to pick up a good deal. Most small art galleries take a 40% commission, with the rest going to the artist.

Down the road, **Picture This** (603B, 6/F, 9 Queen's Road; www.picturethiscollection.com; tel. 2525 2820) stocks a large range of antique maps, vintage film and travel posters and early photographs. Other art dealers can be found in Prince's Building (including **Alisan Fine Arts**) and Pacific Place **(Galerie du Monde)**. Local ceramics studios include **Pottery Workshop** (2 Lower Albert Road, Central); glass studios include **Gaffer Studio Glass** (17/F, Hing Wai Centre, Aberdeen; www.gafferstudioglass.com; tel. 2521 1770).

Stanley Market is another popular place for picking up art and Asian kitsch. Besides selling prints and original watercolours, oil paintings and pen-and-ink drawings by well-known local artists, shops such as **Wong's Art** display oil reproductions of European and Chinese art. At the far end of the market, two or three home-grown artist-entrepreneurs accept commissions to copy any picture in oils. They have catalogues of Chinese, Vietnamese and Burmese art for you to select from. Prices vary from about $500 for a smaller work to a few thousand dollars, depending on size, and may take several weeks to complete.

If you require a picture or small object to be framed, **Queen's Road East** in Wanchai is studded with framers that can put together a shadow box in less than a week. Shadow boxes are similar to a frame, but have depth and are often used to display objects such as 'lotus slippers'. They are a beautiful way to display any personal items. On one occasion when I was collecting a Pyrex dome made for a Japanese doll that my parents have, a customer was picking up a finished shadow box that proudly displayed memorabilia from her time as a press correspondent in Sarajevo. The framers also sell posters and, occasionally, black and white photographs.

Traditional Chinese crafts (for example, gold ornaments, jade sculptures, cloisonné, ceramics and silks) can also be bought at **Yue Hwa Chinese Products Emporium** (301–309 Nathan Rd and Peking Road in TST), and

Chinese Arts and Crafts (Star House, TST; 26 Harbour Road, Wanchai; Queen's Road, Central and Pacific Place, etc.).

Art materials

Artland (3/F, 301–7 Lockhart Road, Wanchai; www.artland.com.hk; tel. 2511 4845) stocks a large range of acrylic and oil paints, pastels, colouring pencils, paper, card and artist's tools. **Sam & Company** (38 Stanley Street, Central; tel. 2523 0338) has a reasonable selection of paints, paper and pencils, and staff are very helpful. The basement of the **Shenzhen Book Centre** (Shenzhen) also reputedly has good-quality cheap materials for Chinese art.

Baby products

There is very little standards-checking of products available in Hong Kong, so exercise caution when buying cots and other baby products. **Eugene Group** has shops stocking bottles, nappies, pushers and so on around Hong Kong (Shop S8-S12, 2/F, North Tower, Kornhill Plaza, Quarry Bay and Shop B215–217, Basement 2, New World Centre, TST, etc.). **Mothercare** (3/F Prince's Building) and **Bumps to Babes** (5/F Pedder Building and Ap Lei Chau) are popular with mums.

Boats

Fragrant Harbour is a magazine widely available at bookshops and magazine stores, and is probably your best first port of call if you plan to buy a boat in Hong Kong. It also has advertisements from parts suppliers, boat fumigators, clothing merchants and hiring companies. The *South China Morning Post* lists boats for sale in the classified ads on a Sunday, or try **www.asiaxpat.com**. You can also contact yacht clubs and marinas (see Chapter Nineteen, 'Sports') to get leads on boats for sale. Discovery Bay residents can find second-hand boats for sale listed at **www.lantauboatclub.com**.

Books

A large selection of general English and Chinese books and magazines can be found at **Page One** (Basement One, Times Square, D'Aguilar Street in Central, Festival Walk and Harbour City Level 3). **Bookazine** and **Dymocks** stock a smaller selection of general books and imported newspapers. Local bookshops worth browsing include:

- **Commercial Press** (Yee Wo Street, Causeway Bay and 3/F, Star House, TST, etc.);
- **Cosmos Books** (30 Johnson Road, Wanchai, etc.);
- **Swindon Bookstore** (13–15 Lock Road, TST, etc.);
- **Hong Kong Book Centre** (25 Des Voeux Road, Central, etc.); and
- **Joint Publishing** (D'Aguilar Street, etc.).

Most of the universities have campus bookstores stocking textbooks. Art books can be purchased at **Tai Yip** bookstores (branches include 1/F, Central Library, Causeway Bay and Hong Kong Museum of Art, TST) and **Kelly & Walsh** (Pacific Place, One Exchange Square, etc.).

Bloomsbury Books (1/F, Hutchison House, 10 Harcourt Road, Central) stocks new and second-hand law and business titles, as well as general books. Online booksellers include **Paddyfield** (www.paddyfield.com) and **www.shopinhk. com**. **Waterstones** in Ocean Terminal sells many imported books.

Christian books are sold in the **St John's Cathedral Bookshop**, which also specializes in children's books, and the **Catholic Centre Bookshop** (2/F, Grand Building, 15–18 Connaught Road, Central; www.catholiccentre.org. hk).

Parentheses stocks French-language books, novels and videos (4/F Duke of Wellington House, 14 Wellington Street, Central; tel. 2526 9215).

For second-hand books, check out **http://hk.auctions.yahoo.com** – this site is in Chinese – or visit book and CD shop **Flow** (40 Lyndhurst Terrace, Central; tel. 2964 9483 and 14 Wan King Path, Sai Kung; tel. 8104 0822). Other second-hand stores include **Collectables** (11 Queen Victoria Street, Central; tel. 2559 9562).

Detailed maps of the Hong Kong countryside and trails as well as official government publications are available from the government bookstore (via www.gov.hk). Self-designed photo books can be ordered via **www.mud.hk** or **memoMiiO** (www.memomiio.com.hk).

Cars
Brand new cars are prohibitively expensive in Hong Kong due to the hefty import duties, so most expats choose to buy a second-hand car. One of the largest showrooms is **Automall** (B1, 1 Harbour Road, Wanchai, beneath the Hyatt Hotel; www.auto22.com), which has over 800 new and second-hand cars, and provides information and service on all cars. The website also has information on new car launches, test drive reports and car-related events. Besides buying direct from the showrooms, second-hand cars are advertised on Sundays in the *South China Morning Post* and via a host of websites, including **www.geoexpat.com/classifieds/**.

Children's parties
In Prince's Building, **Hobby Horse** (Shop 209; www.allinafamily.com/hh/ index.htm) and **Toy Museum** (Shop 320) stock a selection of gifts, toys and

party paraphernalia or visit **Matteo Party** (3/F, 530–532 Jaffe Road, Causeway Bay). Online party planners **Party Caramba** (1101 Tung Chai Building, 86–90 Wellington Street, Central; www.partycaramba.com; tel. 2851 8320) sell cards and cakes, offer bouncy castle hire, costume hire, partyware and piñatas, and provide advice on planning your party.

Children's toys

Imported children's toys are generally expensive in Hong Kong and so the selection is smaller than you'd get back home. **ToysRUs** is popular and has seven stores – check their website, www.toysrus.com.hk, for store locations. **Toys Club** is also popular (Unit 901, Horizon Plaza, Apleichau; 15/F, 8 Queen's Road Central; www.itoysclub.com). In Causeway Bay, **Sogo's** Childrens' Floor has a large selection of games and gifts for children, **The Disney Store** (Shop 501, Times Square) and **A Barrel of Monkeys** (Sinoplaza, Causeway Bay) also have a good selection.

Learning toy shops include:

- **Early Learning Centre** (Shop 315–316, 3/F Prince's Building);
- **Kiss my Kids Educational Toys**, all over the city;
- **Wise Kids Educational Toys** (Shop 134, Pacific Place; G/F Hennessy Centre, 500 Hennessy Rd, Causeway Bay; Shop B233, New World Centre, 20–24 Salisbury Rd, TST, Shop 301, Prince's Building etc.);
- **Stepping Stones** (Rm 1002 Century Square, 1–13 D'Aguilar St, Central etc.); and
- **Children's Corner** (Rm 601, 6/F, 1 Hysan Ave, Causeway Bay).

Also selling children's toys and clothes in Hong Kong is **www.shopinhk.com**.

Clothes

There is a wide choice of clothing of all styles in Hong Kong, but women who are taller than 5'7 or larger than a UK size 12 may find it difficult to source fashionable, dressy clothes, especially blouses and trousers, and may need to opt for having things tailor-made – as will men who are taller than six foot. **Marks & Spencer** (28 Queen's Road, Central; Times Square; Harbour City) stocks larger sizes, as do the small shops in Grand Progress Building (58–62 D'Aguilar Street, Lan Kwai Fong) run by American expat women for expat women. Other shops stocking women's smart casual wear up to size 16 include **Episode** (30 Queen's Road, Shop 320–321 Times Square; Gateway 11 Harbour City and 4–6 Hankow Road, TST) and **French Connection** (Shop 501 Times Square; Shop 119 Pacific Place; Shop 325 New Town Plaza, Shatin, etc.).

The same goes for shoe size. For women who are larger than a UK size 6, the range of fashionable shoes is limited. **Nine West** (Pacific Place; Harbour City) is one of the few high street stores that stock some styles up to size 42. For men, sports and leather shoes up to a UK size 12 are readily available. Although it is possible to have shoes made here, in practice it's cheaper and easier to stock up when you're home for a holiday.

Casual wear

Local Hong Kong stores **U2**, **Baleno**, **Bossini** and **Giordano** produce simple, well-made casual wear in great fabrics and are excellent value. **Mango** (Harbour City, Pacific Place, etc.), **Zara** (IFC Mall), **Uniqlo**, **H&M** and **Esprit** are also good options for expat women. They are comparatively cheap and likely to have up to size 12/14.

Children's wear

Upmarket children's clothes can be found at department stores such as **Seibu** (Pacific Place; 311 Gloucester Road, Causeway Bay, and Langham Place, Mongkok) **Sogo** (555 Hennessy Road, Causeway Bay) and seven or eight stores in Prince's Building. French label **Jacadi** sells clothing for children up to 12 years old (Prince's Building, Lee Gardens 2, Sogo Causeway Bay; Shop G05, Ocean Terminal, TST). Other good quality local stores stocking kids' clothes include **Giordano**, **La Compagnie des Petits** (2/F, Windsor House, Causeway Bay; Shop 251, Cityplaza, etc.) and **Chickeeduck** (Shop 103–104, Vicwood Plaza, 199 Des Voeux Rd; Shop 248, City Plaza; Shop 909, 9/F, Times Square, etc.). **Eco-Mama** sells second-hand baby goods and clothes (A2, 7/F, Tung Chong Factory Building, 653–5 King's Road, North Point).

Clothes markets and sample/export stores

For inexpensive clothing, check out the export shops in **Wanchai Road**, which also do sample bras and lingerie. **Fa Yuen Street** market (Prince Edward MTR) has over 60 small shops selling assorted men's, women's and children's wear – you can often find clothes by French Connection, Gap, Debenhams and other UK/US high street brands, as well as outsize clothes. Always ask to try on before you buy, although some shops won't allow this. Just a bit further south is **Ladies Street Market**, which gets going in the late afternoon and runs till late in the evening. Here you can find men's shirts, T-shirts, bags, belts, toys and other accessories. A smaller version of Ladies Street can be found in **The Lanes** (Li Yuen Streets East and West, opposite H&M in Central). Market locations are shown on city maps. You can also try Cheung Sha Wan Road Fashion Street (Sham Shui Po MTR, Exit C1).

Casual wear, linen clothing, hats, bags, jewellery, sports shoes and much more can also be found on the south of the island at **Stanley Market**.

Designer wear and designer outlets

All of the famous labels are here – Gucci, Prada, Boss, Armani, Hermes, Mui Mui, Chanel, Vivienne Tam, Kate Spade, La Perla, Pal Zileri, Hilditch & Key, Gieves & Hawkes, etc., as well as mid-priced designers such as Max Mara, Max & Co, Sportsmax, iBlues, Agnes B, Ralph Lauren, Polo Ralph Lauren, and CK. Department stores such as **Seibu** (Pacific Place; 311 Gloucester Road, Causeway Bay and Langham Place, Mongkok), **Harvey Nicholls** (Landmark), **Lane Crawford** (Pacific Place; Times Square; Canton Road; IFC Mall) and **Joyce** (23 Nathan Rd, TST and New World Tower, 16 Queen's Road Central) play host to high-end fashion concessions. **Lee Gardens 1 and 2**, in Causeway Bay, and **Style House** (Park Lane Hotel) are also where you'll find a concentration of topflight designer brands.

It's worth waiting for the summer and Christmas sales, when clothes are often discounted by 40% or more, but there are other ways to pick up a bargain. These include designer outlet stores in:

- the **Pedder Building** (discounted Anne Klein, second-hand Chanel, Gucci, etc.);
- **Kaiser Estate** (Hung Hom – for detailed information and maps click on the *Hong Kong Yellow Pages* website, http://yp.ypdomain.com/mv_templates/ SHP/mv_ypshopping_e.html); and
- **Dickson Warehouse**, which deals in fashion and sportswear (Kowloon MTR station, etc.).

Other outlet stores include:

- **Nike Outlet** (Shop 1, 1/F, Enterpise Square, 9 Sheung Yuet Road, Kowloon Bay);
- **IT Sale Shop** (3/F, Silvercord Shopping Centre, TST); and
- **Esprit Outlet** (www.esprit.com.hk).

Second-hand designer shoes and handbags can be found at **Milan Station** in Causeway Bay (and other 'stations' around Hong Kong).

Evening and bridal wear

For evening and bridal wear, there is a cluster of upmarket shops around the Soho and Lan Kwai Fong areas, including:

- **Brides and Gowns** (www.bridesandgowns.com; 8/F Asia Pacific Centre, 8 Wyndham Street), which stocks Australian and Hong Kong-made designs;

- **The Wedding Shop** (4/F On Lan Street, 11–15 On Lan Street), which stocks Italian labels;
- **Anaiss** (301 Tak Woo House, 17–19 D'Aguilar Street), which stocks London and Parisian labels; and
- **Chimes** (7/F, 1 Lan Kwai Fong).

On Kowloon side, **Kimberly Plaza** in Kimberly Road, TST, is devoted to wedding dress shops or try the wedding shops close to **Prince Edward** MTR station.

Eye wear

Eye wear is a key fashion statement in Hong Kong. Designer opticians include **Alain Mikli** (D'Aguilar Street, Central), **Senses Optik** (28 Wellington Street) or the more reasonably priced **Optical 88**, which has stores around the city. A free eye test is provided with any purchase of glasses or contact lenses. All types of contact lenses are available in the city, including coloured and disposable.

Fancy dress

There are several fancy dress shops that sell or hire costumes. **Festival and Party** (Shop 30, Basement, Queen's Theatre, 31 Queen's Road, Central; tel. 2529 5921) is open from midday. Costumes in **House of Sirens** (23 Staunton Street; tel. 2526 2877) are flamboyant and sexy. The **Hong Kong Academy for Performing Arts** also hires out costumes to the public (call Wardrobe on 2584 8574).

Maternity wear

Pregnant mums can find stylish maternity wear at:

- **Formes** (8 On Lan Street, Central; G/F, 19 Yun Ping Road, Causeway Bay and Shop 230B, Ocean Centre);
- **Bumps to Babes** (5/F, Pedder Building); and
- **Mothercare** (3/F, Prince's Building; Shop 137, Ocean Terminal, TST; 2/F, Windsor House, 311 Gloucester Rd, Causeway Bay).

Other maternity wear shops can be found in **Melbourne Plaza** (33 Queen's Road, Central), including **Mother's Work**, **Mother Court** and **Wendy's Maternity Wear**.

Second-hand and vintage clothes

For second-hand clothes, check out www.asiaxpat.com.hk or www.red-dots. com – note that some of the latter site is in Chinese. **Castaways Charity Shop**, run by St John's Cathedral, also sells quality second-hand clothing.

There hasn't traditionally been much of a market in Hong Kong for vintage clothes because of negative associations with the dead, although one place that sells 1960s and 1970s clothes is **Beatniks** (221 Gloucester Road, Causeway Bay and Shop 1, Rise Commercial Building, Granville Circuit, TST).

Sportswear

Cold weather clothes or outdoor wear can be found cheaply at Stanley Market or at a dedicated outdoor sports shop such as **Camping Protrek** (46 Hennessy Road, Wanchai; www.protrek.com.hk). There is a good selection of sportswear (including swimwear) in **Mitsukoshi** and **Sogo** (both in Causeway Bay), and the sports shops in Times Square (6/F, Leisure & Pleasure) or **Dickson Warehouse** outlets (details above).

A collection of small sports shoes and sportswear shops can also be found at the **Sports Market** in Sai Yee Street, Mongkok (see city maps).

Tailors

Tailoring in Hong Kong does not come cheap, in spite of the many tailors operating in and around the Humphrey's Avenue area. Many people head over the border clutching Ellen McNally's *Shop in Shenzhen*, which gives useful hints on finding tailors and has floor plans of the whole of Lowu Shopping Plaza – chock-full with the latest Grade A and B imitation Tod's bags, Gucci belts, Cartier watches, Oakley sunglasses, jewellery, cloth and Chinese crafts.

For local tailors, get recommendations from a friend. I've been happy using Theresa at **Tailor & Alteration** (1/F, Teda Building, 87 Wing Lok Street; tel. 2543 6328). She charges around $700 for a summer dress before material – you should buy material from a wholesaler. There are also plenty of alteration tailors in **Melbourne Plaza** (33 Queen's Road, Central).

To buy linen cloth, silk, beads, ribbon, feathers and buttons and other materials in Hong Kong, head to the Cheung Sha Wan Road area in **Sham Shui Po**, which is lined with wholesale merchants. Expat shoppers have used:

- **Ming Sang Button Manufactury** (G/F, 114 Nam Cheong Street;
- **Luen Fung Bead & Gems Company** (G/F, Yu Chau Street); and
- **Lung Moon Elastic Weaving** (G/F, 126 Nam Cheong Street).

Closer to downtown, you can obtain cloth by the yard from one of the many sellers upstairs in the **Western Market** in Sheung Wan, which closes at 7:00 pm; try **Yau Fat Textile Company** (Shop 105–6, Western Market, 323 Des Voeux Road, Central; tel. 2850 5169). A large selection of traditional Chinese designs on silk is available from **CRC Department Store** (Whampoa

Garden, Hunghom), and you can buy ribbons, feathers and beads from the stalls on the steps of **Pottinger Street**. Nearby **Wing Kut Street** and **Gilman's Bazaar** are lined with haberdashery shops, scarf-sellers and so on.

Shanghai Tang (Pedder Street) is famous as much for the beautifully fragrant scent, which spills out onto surrounding pavements, as for its bold patterned silks. It's all the rage with wealthy tourists, but I've yet to find something off-the-peg that comes close to fitting me properly. When I've saved up, I'll use their tailors. **Siriporn** (47A Caine Road) has Thai silks and tailoring.

Caring for clothes and shoes

Hong Kong's humidity can seriously affect clothing and shoes, even when they've been packed away. Dehumidifiers left running day and night can reduce the risk of clothes going mouldy, and expensive clothes such as leather jackets can be put in cold storage at the dry cleaners (**Clean Living**, which has branches all over Hong Kong, is one of many dry cleaners offering this service).

Trendy

For teens and trendies, the best shopping area is undoubtedly **Causeway Bay**, with its many independent boutiques and trashy-glam cubby-holes. A mini-Causeway Bay can be found on the Kowloon side in the **Granville Road/Carnarvon Road** area of TST. Local Japanese-influenced stores **IT** and **LCX** (Ocean Terminal) are the preferred shopping haunt of local teens; **D-Mop, H&M, Cotton On, Diesel** and **Kitterick** (Central and Causeway) are also popular brands.

Computers

The main shopping malls for hardware and software are:

- **Wanchai Computer Centre** (Wanchai MTR Exit A1);
- **298 Computer Zone** (298 Hennessey Road, Wanchai);
- **Mongkok Computer Centre** (8 Nelson Street);
- **Star Computer City** (Star House, 3 Salisbury Road, TST);
- **Golden Building Shopping Centre** (146–156 Fuk Wa Street, Sham Shui Po); and
- **Windsor House** (10/F–13/F).

Cosmetics and skincare

Your favourite brand of face cream will probably be here, but it might take some time to locate. If it's high end, start with **Joyce** (16 Queen's Road Central; 38 Russell Street, Causeway Bay and Pacific Place), which stocks a number of international skin care brands and is constantly updating its beauty lists. Individual concept stores include:

- **Bobbi Brown** (Festival Walk);
- **Lancôme** (Festival Walk);
- **Shu Uemura** (Pacific Place);
- **Jurlique** (68 Des Voeux Road); and
- **Clarins, Clinique** and **Estée Lauder** (all in the IFC Mall, as well as elsewhere).

Large department stores such as **Lane Crawford** stock most internationally famous cosmetic brands, but you can get many of these discounted at local cosmetics stores. Chief among these are **Sasa** (www.sasa.com), with its trademark white, black and shocking pink logo, and **Strawberry**, which also has a large virtual shopping operation at www.strawberrynet.com. It's unusual in Hong Kong to obtain free take-away samples of creams and perfume in any store unless you're buying, but Sasa sells sample-size perfumes and creams.

Other cosmetics and fragrance stores in Hong Kong include:

- **The Body Shop**;
- **H_2O**;
- **Red Earth**;
- **Watsons**, which stocks Boots No 7, Simple, Ulay and Neutrogena products;
- **Lush** (Festival Walk, Admirality MTR Station, UNY Basement, City Plaza 2, etc.);
- **Crabtree & Evelyn** (Pacific Place, Landmark, etc.);
- **L'Occitane En Provence** (Pacific Place, etc.); and
- **Aveda** (Harbour City and concessions in Lane Crawford).

Mannings has low-priced shower gel, soaps, creams and hair colour products. ParknShop and Wellcome run to Badedas and Pears.

Herbal Bliss (Unit 11A, 128 Wellington Street, Central; www.herbalbliss. com.hk; tel. 2676 2885, and Unit 1808, Workingport Commercial Building, 3 Hau Fook Street, TST) sells holistic and organic skincare products and cosmetics.

Spas such as Elemis Day Spa (9/F, Century Square, 1 D'Aguilar Street, Central) and Ellespa (10/F The Centrium, 60 Wyndham Street, Central and

Shop G106A, The Repulse Bay) sell a range of spa products. For more information on spas, see Chapter Nine, 'Health'.

Food

Cake shops

Chinese brands such as **Saint Honore** and **Maxim's** offer a range of Western-style and Chinese baked goods. For authentic French-style patisseries, visit **Mandarin Oriental Cake Shop**, **Sift Patisserie** (22/F Horizon Plaza, Unit 17–19, Ap Lei Chau and 51 Queen's Road East, Central), or **Sift Dessert Bar** (G/F, 46 Graham Street, Central). For fancy cupcakes, try **Complete Deelite** (6/F California Entertainment Building, 34–36 D'Aguilar Street, Lan Kwai Fong), **Babycakes**, (Shop 1114, 11/F Horizon Plaza, 2 Lee Wing Street, Ap Lei Chau) and **Coco** (G/F, The Mira, 118–130 Nathan Road, TST, 2315 5566), amongst others.

Chocolates

Godiva have branches across the city. City'super in the IFC building stocks one of Japan's premier brands, **Royce** (try the Nama chocolates). **Vero Chocolate Lounge**, (1/F Fenwick Pier), **La Maison du Chocolat** (Prince's Building, Elements, IFC, Pacific Place), **Monde Chocolatier** (online at http://development.sunnyvision.com/mc_b/eng/aboutus.php), **Jean Paul Hevin** (IFC Mall, Harbour City, Times Square), and **Chocolux** (57 Peel Street, Soho) have all garnered good reviews.

Chinese

You may feel you get enough Chinese food and the last thing you want to do is start cooking it at home, but in case you do, here are a few ideas. Fresh noodles can be bought at many shops around Hong Kong; it's just a case of finding your nearest. Two that I visit from time to time are in Wanchai: **Kang Kee Noodles** (4 Tai Wo Street) and **Wanchai Ferry Peiking** [*sic*] **Dumpling** (51 Wanchai Road). Condiments such as soy sauce, sesame oil and chilli oil can be easily obtained from supermarkets.

Wing Wah Cake Shop is an institution and has branches in Mongkok, Whampoa, Airport and so on. **Kee Wah**, which has a number of branches, including one in the IFC Mall, sells a similar range of egg rolls, mooncakes, butter cookies, etc.

Almost every small town has its string of shops selling dried seafood, but the **Queen's Road West/Des Voeux Road West** area in Sheung Wan is noted for its dried fish, bird's nest and shark's fin.

Indian

The **Indian Provisions Store** at the end of Bowrington Road in Causeway Bay furthest away from the wet market stocks a large range of spices, rice and condiments.

Italian

In addition to City'super, Great and Olivers, the Italian wine shop and delicatessen **Castello del Vino** (12 Anton Street, Wanchai), stocks a large selection of Italian wines, biscuits, oils, food and hand-painted porcelain. Other Italian food shops include:

- **Il Bel Paese** (Shop B, G/F, 95 Caine Road, Mid-Levels, 10/F Coda Plaza, 51 Garden Road and 25 Queen's Road East, Wanchai); and
- **Viva Italia Supermarket** (Shop 12, G/F, Palatial Crest, 3 Seymour Road, Mid-Levels and 10/F Horizon Plaza, Ap Lei Chau).

Japanese

Although ParknShop superstores have a Japanese food section that stocks the basic, vital ingredients of Japanese cuisine – rice, rice vinegar, dipping sauces, wasabi, fresh ginger and instant miso soup – you may find it more rewarding to venture into the basement supermarkets of the Japanese department stores **Uny** and **Jusco** (Cityplaza and Kornhill Plaza respectively, both near Taikoo Shing MTR). Other branches of Jusco are located at Whampoa (Hung Hom), Tseung Kwan O, Tsuen Wan, Tuen Mun, Lok Fu and Tai Po. **City'super** supermarkets also stock an extensive range of Japanese food and condiments.

Organic

The fair number of organic shops in Hong Kong include:

- **Health Gate** (8/F, Hung Tak Building, 106 Des Voeux Road, Central; tel. 2545 2286);
- **Simply Organic** (1/F, 21 Canal Road West, Causeway Bay; tel. 2488 0138), which supplies locally grown organic vegetables and will deliver to subscribers;
- **Green Concepts** (2/F, Prosperous Commercial Building, Causeway Bay);
- **All Things Healthy** (Unit 1503, The Centrium, 60 Wyndham Street; www.allthingshealthy.com.hk); and
- **Organic Farmers' Market** @ Central (Sundays at Star Ferry Pier No. 7).

Alternatively, you can order direct from **The Organic Farm** in Yuen Long (www.organic-farm.com; tel. 2483 9966). Most of the supermarket superstores also stock organic produce.

Thai

If you are lucky, you'll have a Thai speciality shop near where you live; if you can't find any, there are three shops on **Stone Nullah Street** in Wanchai that stock a range of fresh Thai vegetables and cooking ingredients. Large supermarkets such as Great and ParknShop also do packs of fresh and dried Thai herbs, spices and sauces.

Supermarkets

The past five years have really seen a boom in the number of Western products available on the shelves of major supermarkets in Hong Kong. Old-timers recall how you could never get hold of things like Oxo cubes and goat's cheese. These days, you can find Godiva chocolates, Covent Garden soups, Waitrose lemon curd and free-range sausages, gluten-free bread, Kettle Chips and Kellogg's Fruit 'n' Fibre. Needless to say, imported products are generally more expensive than they would be back home.

If you're planning an impressive dinner party or a romantic candle-lit dinner and want to splurge on expensive food, including nice cakes and bread, most people's taste for extravagance are catered for by:

- **Olivers The Delicatessen** (2/F, Prince's Building, Central);
- **Great Food Hall** (LG/1, Pacific Place, Admiralty); and
- **City'super** (Basement 1, Times Square, Causeway Bay, Harbour City, TST and IFC Mall, Central; www.citysuper.com.hk).

These shops source fresh and packaged food from all over the world. Sushi is discounted after 8:00 pm in both places; **Great** also has discounted fresh fish near the Rotisserie counter.

Supermarkets in the basement of Japanese stores **Sogo**, **Uny** and **Jusco** are also worth a browse. More than one friend rates the bread at the bakery in the basement of **Sogo** to be the best crusty French stick in town.

For food that doesn't have to be agonized over, **Wellcome** (www.wellcomehk.com) and **ParknShop** (www.parknshop.com), Hong Kong's two mainstream supermarkets, stock most of what you'll need to prepare Western or Asian food – go to the superstores to find the largest range of products. They also sell pre-packaged, ready-to-eat hot and cold food. **Gateway** (Basement, 188 Des Voeux Road, Central) stocks American food.

You may have to shop around to see what you can buy from where – for example, Covent Garden soups are only available at Great, Kettle Chips at Parkn-Shop – but you can find many familiar brands in Hong Kong. Service in all supermarkets is generally of a very high standard: staff are friendly and will pack your bag for you. You can shop in person or go online and have your shopping delivered the same day, free of charge for a minimum amount spent. Price wars and incentives such as free kitchenware have kept costs competitive.

Wet markets

'Wet market' is a catch-all term used in Hong Kong for fresh vegetables, fruit, meat and fish sold on individual stalls in designated areas – usually along a street or inside an urban council market building. Most residential areas of Hong Kong have their own wet market. Ideal for singles who want to buy small quantities of food, prices are generally a little lower than supermarkets and products are very fresh. They are also places you can try out your 'market Cantonese' and establish good relations with a flower seller – good-quality market flowers can be a *lot* cheaper than a standard florist.

Large street markets on Hong Kong Island include **Graham Street** in Central (Mon–Sat), **Cross Street** in Wanchai (Mon–Fri), **Bowrington Road**, Causeway Bay (Mon–Sun) and the intersection of **Centre Street** and **Second Street** in Sai Ying Pun. On Kowloon side, large wet markets include **Yamati Market** in Reclamation Street and **Nelson Street Market**, Mongkok.

Wine merchants

Since import duty on wine was abolished, there has been an explosion in the number of wine merchants in the city. Visit www.jancisrobinson.com/articles/directorymerchantshongkong to find a thorough list of reputable wine importers and sellers. The only large-scale wine merchants with stores all over Hong Kong is **Watson's Wine Cellar** (www.watsonswine.com), which has shops in Stanley Plaza, Sai Kung, Discovery Bay Plaza and downtown. **Boutique Wines** (Room 1603, 16/F, Horizon Plaza; www.boutiquewines.com.hk; tel. 2525 3899) specializes in wines from Western Australia, New Zealand and Tasmania. **Soho Wines and Spirits** (37 Staunton Street, 49 Shelley Street and 18–32 Chan Man St, Sai Kung; www.sohowines.com.hk) will deliver for a minimum charge and offer free loan of glasses.

Appellation Limited (1102B, 11/F, The Centrium, 60 Wyndham Street, Central; tel. 2866 6335) specializes in New World wines and offers membership of the Appellation Club for $120 per year, entitling members to discounts of 5–15% on wines and accessories.

Other recommended wine shops include **Berry Bros** (3/F, The Lee Gardens, 33 Hysan Avenue, Causeway Bay; tel. 2907 2112), which has a fine selection of wines and spirits, wine accessories and dedicated tasting rooms.

Houseware

Designware

Top-notch designer sanitary ware is carried by **Colour Living** (333 Lockhart Road) and **The Professional Depot** (371 Lockhart Road) in Wanchai. Fine tubs and kitchenware can also be found at Italian brand **Boffi** (81 Wong Nai Chung Road, Happy Valley). Also good for a browse are:

* **Alessi** (Shop 247, Prince's Building, Central etc.);
* **Dentro** (Shop 4, Tai Sang Commercial Building, 24 Hennessy Road, Wanchai; Shop A, G/F, Winway Building, 50 Wellington Street, Central); and
* **Design Gallery** (Hong Kong Convention and Exhibition Centre, Wanchai).

DIY/hardware

Christmas lights, Black & Decker drills, screws, inexpensive self-assembly barbecue sets and a thousand and one other things are sold all over Hong Kong in 'houseware' shops. The big ones are the best – packed like treasure troves and likely to eat up hours of your time. It's useful to locate your local houseware shop early, because they also stock light bulbs, plugs, adapters, mugs, kitchen knives, ironing boards, pet products, plant fertilizer and lots of other stuff that'll come in handy.

Electrical appliances/electronics

For new appliances, **Fortress** (www.fortress.com.hk) is the first place most people turn to. They stock a range of everything electric, from washing machines to TVs, DVD players, MP3 players, digital cameras, vacuum cleaners and food processors, and are competitively priced. They also offer free delivery, a ten-day money-back guarantee policy and a trade-in service for certain goods. Check their website to locate the store nearest you.

Other stores stocking audio-visual equipment include:

* **Broadway** (Electronics World, 7/F, Times Square);
* **Universal Audio Video** (Shop 135, Pacific Place);
* **Bang & Olufsen** (Shop 228A, Level 2, Pacific Place, etc.);
* **Bose** (Shop 322, Ocean Centre); and
* **Sony Shop** (Shop 209, Man Yee Building, 60–68 Des Voeux Road) and **Sony Style HK** (16/F, East Point Centre, Causeway Bay).

There are plenty of small shops specializing in cameras on **Stanley Street** and **Queen Victoria Street** in Central and **Nathan Road** in TST, but be wary of buying at non-accredited shops, especially those on Nathan Road, where tourists are regularly fleeced. Another electronics shopping centre is **Sai Yeung Choi Street** in Mongkok (MTR Exit E2).

Second-hand electrical appliances, telephones and radios can be found at the flea market in Ap Liu Street, **Sham Shui Po** or via **www.hkclassifieds.com**, **www.asiaxpat.com.hk**, or the *Sunday Post* magazine.

Department stores stocking a range of kitchen appliances include **Wing On** (211 Des Voeux Road, Sheung Wan MTR Exit B), **Uny, Jusco, Sogo** and **Mitsukoshi.** The prices are pretty similar, but it's worth looking out for promotions.

Fixtures and fittings

There are a few well-known streets devoted to house hardware. The most convenient for Hong Kong Island is probably **Lockhart Road**, Wanchai; on the Kowloon side, the **Shanghai Street/Fife Street/Portland Street** area in Mongkok (near MTR Exit C2) have a quantity of shops stocking these things. Upscale stores in Wanchai include **Fired Earth** (2404 Dominion Centre, 43–59 Queens Road East). Sisal and parquet flooring are available from some of the interior design stores along **Queen's Road East**, Wanchai.

Furniture and furnishings

The *South China Morning Post*'s *Sunday Post* magazine is a useful source of information on local interior design and provides leads on shopping and recommended designers.

GOD (Goods Of Desire) is a local designer brand that's witty, modern and stylish. They stock living room, bedroom and office furniture; kitchenware and bathroom accessories; and printed handbags, amongst other things (48 Hollywood Road, Central, and Leighton Centre, Causeway Bay, etc.; **www.god.com.hk**). The Causeway Bay store also has a pretty flower and plant design section, as well as Home Cooking, a restaurant that is famed for its mango Napoleon.

Moving down in the design stakes, **IKEA** has five stores in Hong Kong (www.ikea.com.hk) that stock a whole range of furniture and fittings, along with comprehensive information that allows you to work out the cost of equipping a furnished apartment from scratch. You can also pay to have the parts assembled for you, so you don't have to get frustrated figuring out the self-assembly plans.

A more cost-cutting option is provided by **Pricerite**, which has 30 stores in Hong Kong, some of which stock kitchenware as well as bedroom, living room and office furniture. Check the website, www.pricerite.com.hk, for store locations, weekly specials and stock.

Muji (Lee Theatre Plaza, Causeway Bay, etc.) has a range of household goods in rustic colours, such as duvet covers, toothbrush holders, magazine racks and storage boxes. **Ito Futon Japanese Furniture** (G/F, 64–66 Wellington Street, Central) stocks just what it says.

A fascinating place to browse is **Jusco $10 Plaza** (9 Kingston Street, Causeway Bay, as well as branches in other parts of Hong Kong Island, Kowloon and the New Territories). The huge floor space is dedicated to cheap Japanese house-hold utensils and tools from plastic toilet seat covers to house decorations, lint remover and shoe brushes. In the same mould is **Japan Home Centre** – a cheap chain stocking stationery, houseware and kitchenware for $10 an item.

Horizon Plaza in Ap Lei Chau (Aberdeen) contains a mix of furniture, outdoor furniture and antique shops. Amongst the most popular – if you have room for their spacious designs – are **Tequila Kola** and **Banyan Tree**, which are also in United Centre and Prince's Building respectively. For upmarket Italian furniture, browse **Prince's Building** or **Wong Nai Chung Road**, Happy Valley. You will find a glut of lighting shops not far away in **Morrison Hill Road**.

Queen's Road East, Wanchai, is the place to go to check out mid-priced products, whether they be Italian-style sofas, Chinese rosewood or rattan furniture, and soft furnishings – custom-made curtains, sofa covers, sisal rugs and carpeting. **Avant Garde**, a small shop in Pacific Place, sells Designer's Guild fabrics and functional designware for the home.

Reproduction antique furniture can be found in Hollywood Road (see above under the 'Antiques' heading), but locals often go to Macau or Zhuhai for cheaper custom-made reproduction antique Chinese chests, screens, ward-robes, cabinets, bookshelves, tables and chairs. Modern Chinese furniture and mainland knick-knacks as well as general household goods, clothes and food can be found at **CRC Department Store** (Whampoa Garden, Hunghom).

Shops stocking trendy furniture by international designers include **Aluminium** (G/F, Shop 1B, Capitol Plaza, 2–10 Lyndhurst Terrace and 2 Kingston Street, Causeway Bay etc.).

Retro furniture can be found at **flea + cents** (1/F, 34–38 Queen's Road East, Wanchai). The Hong Kong Trade Development Council Design Gallery (www.hkdesigngallery.com) in Wanchou showcases innovative local products.

Kitchenware

Japanese department stores **Sogo, Uny** and **Jusco** combine high-quality bone china with a good range of Japanese-style bowls, cutlery, cups and serving utensils. **GOD, IKEA** (details above) and **Wing On** (Des Voeux Road, near Sheung Wan MTR) stock tableware and cutlery, whilst at **The Panhandler** (Shop 318–319, 3/F, Prince's Building) there is a distinctly professional feel to the implements and crockery.

At the cheaper end, local houseware shops all over Hong Kong sell everything from tea strainers, bamboo steamers and woks to cookie cutters and chopping boards. **Shanghai Street** (the section nearest Yaumatei MTR) has three or four professional kitchenware shops that stock a large selection of good quality metalware – pans, knives and utensils.

Papers such as the *Sunday Morning Post*'s *Trading Post* section and free magazines such as *Inside DB* (a magazine for Discovery Bay residents) list house sales and can be a good place to pick up cheap second-hand furniture. Websites such as **www.asiaxpat.com.hk** also have advertisements and e-bay style bartering for second-hand furniture. Discovery Bay residents can check out **www.dbay. com.hk**.

If you're not planning to be in Hong Kong long, you may be better off leasing furniture rather than buying. More information on this can be found in Chapter Five, 'Accommodation'.

Linens

Besides the department stores, cotton and lace tablecloths and napkin sets can be bought at embroidery specialist **Chun Sang Trading Co.** (3–4 Glenealy, Central) and **Stanley Market**. **Bed & Bath** (Prince's Building) and **Inside** (Prince's Building, Horizon Plaza and The Repulse Bay www.inside.com.hk) also stock a nice selection of soft furnishings and linens. **White Contemporary Homeware** (Harbour City; Prince's Building; 60 Wellington Street) stocks a range of interior furnishings.

Office furniture

Office furniture specialists include **Kam Luen Office Furniture** (G/F, 135 Connaught Road Central) and **Mister Furniture** (APEX) (G/F, 125 Connaught Road, Central; tel. 2581 0323).

Steelcase Worklife Hong Kong (1/F Tai Yip Building, 141 Thomson Road, Wanchai; tel. 2828 6083) offers consulting services and ergonomic furniture designed to make the most of a small space.

Rugs and carpets

You can buy silk and wool Persian rugs from shops along **Hollywood Road** and **Wyndham Street**; other shops are located in **United Centre**, Admiralty. **Tai Ping Carpets and Rugs** (213 Prince's Building, Central; www.taipingcarpets. com; tel. 2522 7138) sells excellent-quality carpets, and silk hand-woven carpets are available from **Fort Street Studio** (www.fortstreetstudio.com; tel. 2889 5150).

Jewellery and precious stones

Hong Kong is famous for its '999' pure gold shops. You can visit one of the many gold shop factories in Kowloon and see how it's fashioned, but to see if Chinese gold is really your style, wander down the Mongkok-to-Jordan stretch of Nathan Road – that's where you'll find **King Fook**, one of the largest gold retailers in the city.

Tiffany, one of the most sought-after brands in Asia, is located in the **Landmark Building** and **Pacific Place**. **Van Cleef & Arpels** and **Cartier** are close by in **Prince's Building**, whilst **Bulgari** sits proudly across the road.

For slightly more affordable jewellery, try a recommended individual jeweller, many of whom are located in TST. One often used by corporate clients is **Mariane** (G/F Shop 21F, Hankow Road, TST; tel. 2376 1527), which is run by the very affable lady herself. I'm partial – she made me my engagement ring. Another reputable jeweller is the family-run **Premier Jewellery** (G14–15 Holiday Inn Golden Mile Shopping Mall, 50 Nathan Road; tel. 2368 0003). Founded over forty years ago, the company specializes in ideal cut diamonds and pearls; gemmologist Henry Cheng, who gives jade and pearl appreciation classes, is a keen proponent of educating consumers.

For something sparkly that looks like the real thing but won't cause such a dent in your wallet, check out the designs at **Carat** (23 D'Aguilar Street, Central). Mid-price international brands with stores in Hong Kong include **Links of London** (Shop 141, Pacific Place; Prince's Building, etc.) and Spanish chain **Folli Follie**. Local chains include **Ma Belle**, **Just Diamond** and **Chow Sang Sang** (74 Queen's Road, Central, etc.).

The **Jade Market** in Kowloon has knick-knacks in jade, coral and semi-precious stones. It is located at the junction of Kansu Street and Battery Street, at the Yau Ma Tei MTR Exit C. Not far away, **Nam King Jade Hong** (29 Austin Road, Jordan) has a large selection of jade craftwork.

Hong Kong is an important centre for the trading of **Tahitian black pearls** and **Australian pearls**, which are auctioned several times a year by Robert Wan of Tahiti Perles and the Australian Paspaley Pearling Company respectively. At the other end of the spectrum, Chinese freshwater pearls can be obtained cheaply at many jewellery shops round the city. Wholesale pearl merchants include **Om-International** (1/F, 6 Canarvon Road, TST; tel. 2366 3421).

Watch collectors can visit Queen's Road Central, especially **Chow Tai Fook Jewellery** (44–46 Queen's Road) and **Vacheron Constantin** (Shop A, G/F, Melbourne Plaza, 33 Queen's Road).

Mobile phones

A mobile phone is a must in Hong Kong, and rates and call plans are extremely competitive. Networks include **One2Free**, **3**, **Sunday** and **Trident Telecom**, and they have stores all over Hong Kong. Handsets can be bought at many of the electronic shops mentioned above, or at mobile phone specialist shops, particularly around the Times Square area.

Motorbikes

Man Lee Tak Car Company is a Yamaha motorcycles agent (G/F, 9 Caroline Hill Road, Causeway Bay; tel. 2576 3079); **Motorbikes Ducati Hong Kong** has a showroom in Jaffe Road and **Kelly Motors** (G/F, 19 Caroline Hill Road, Causeway Bay; tel. 2890 9668) sells a range of bikes. **Kustom Culture Cycles** (Unit 3, G/F, Lai Sun Yuen Long Centre, 27 Wang Yip Street East, Yuen Long; www.kcchk.com; tel. 2540 6596) specializes in custom-built American twin-V motorcycles.

Other shops stocking bike accessories include **Sanwa Motorcycle Company** (9 Junction Road, Kowloon City).

Music and film

The largest selection of CDs, VCDs and DVDs can be found in **HMV** (28 Hankow Road, TST; 1/F, Central Building, near The Landmark; 1/F, Queensway Plaza; 1/F Style House, Causeway Bay; Telford Plaza, Kowloon Bay). Other chains include **Hong Kong Records**, which has a branch in Festival Walk with a large classical collection, **CD Warehouse** and **Shun Cheong Records**, the largest local distributor of independent labels (www.shuncheongrec.com).

Local online sellers include **www.cd-wow.com.hk**. Visit the website **www.hkclubbing.com** for information on DJs and the music scene. Second-hand CDs, VCDs and DVDs can be obtained at **Flow** (Central and Sai Kung).

You used to be able to buy or rent videos at Blockbuster Video, but they pulled out of Hong Kong a while back because pirate software companies were undercutting their business. A VCD costs about $10 in China and you can pick them up for about $20 at the small cupboard shops around Causeway Bay – try Lockhart Road behind Sogo.

Musical instruments

Tom Lee (www.tomleemusic.com) is the largest music chain in Hong Kong, with branches all over the territory selling instruments, music and music lessons. The largest showroom is at 1–9 Cameron Lane, TST. Another popular chain is **Parsons Music** (www.parsonsmusic.com).

Strings shops include:

* **Hong Kong Strings** (4/F, Parker House, 72 Queen's Road Central; tel. 2529 2616);
* **Orfeo Strings** (Flat 2D, Southorn Mansion, 1 Luard Road; tel. 2866 4328);
* **Ngai Violins** (26 Po Tung Road, Sai Kung; tel. 2792 9199); and
* **Violmaster Studio** (G/F, 14 Wood Road, Wanchai, tel. 2870 2177).

An excellent selection of sheet music is available at **Rhythm Music House** (3/F, 2 Queen Victoria Street, Central; tel: 2801 4939). A list of further instrument shops around Hong Kong can be found at **www.hkpo.com**. Click through 'Member's Corner' to 'Club Bravo' and then on 'Discounts around Town'.

Pets

You may have brought a pet with you from home, or you may like to acquire a pet while you're here. The **SPCA** (www.spca.org.hk) can provide advice about keeping pets in Hong Kong and seeks animal sponsors, dog walkers and foster homes for animals on a regular basis. They can also offer veterinary, grooming and boarding services to members' pets.

Pet product shops include **Honey Pet Shop** (Shop 1A–B, Wood Road, Wanchai), **Central Pets Supply** (270–276 Queen's Road) and **www. creaturecomforts.com.hk** (tel. 9773 0372).

Pharmacy

Pharmacy counters can be found at larger branches of **Watsons** and **Mannings**, or you may prefer to visit independent pharmacies such as **Victoria Dispensary** (Theatre Lane, Central). **Eu Yan Sang** (G/F, 152–156 Queen's Road, Central, etc.) is one of the leading dispensers of traditional Chinese medicine (TCM), herbal infusions, tonics and health-protecting soups.

Plants

There are several nurseries along Hiram's Highway on the way into Sai Kung, including **Green House Nursery** and **KK Horticulture** (Tau Chung Hau Road – a left turn just past Pak Sha Wan), Sai Kung; tel. 2792 7440). Most will deliver, for a fee; expect to pay more to get plants carried up flights of stairs.

Downtown, you will find **Chun Hing Gardening & Landscape** inside the Parsi cemetery on Wong Nai Chung Road, Happy Valley. **Flower Market Road** in Prince Edward is famous for its flower shops, but it can be a bit far to travel home with your blooms unless you've got transport or live over Kowloon side. Gardening supplies can be bought at hardware shops. **Agnès B Fleuriste** (Festival Walk) offers beautiful arrangements.

Printed materials and pens

The neighbourhood around **Lee Tung Street** in Wanchai is full of small printing operations that can print anything from name cards to wedding invitations and pamphlets. There are also lots of copy shops in this neighbourhood.

For elegant stationery and beautiful greetings cards, try **Papyrus** (U/L Pacific Place, Prince's Building and IFC Mall, etc.). Greeting cards can also be found at **Kalms** (www.kalms.com.hk), selected branches of **Watsons, Mannings** and **Loft** (inside Seibu). For Cross, Parker and other brandname pens, visit **Pens Museum** (1/F, Convention Plaza, 1 Harbour Road, Wanchai, TST; K3 Citylink Plaza, Shatin; and 318 Telford Plaza Phase II, Kowloon Bay, etc.).

Public toilets

Whilst out shopping you'll most likely need to use the public washroom facilities, although you can always use those at one of the hotels inconspicuously. Most large shopping malls are equipped with clean, well-maintained ladies' and men's washrooms, including Pacific Place (1/F, near HSBC), and at various locations in the basement and on upper floors in IFC Mall, Peak Tower and Times Square. In the Pedder Building, toilets are locked, so ask to borrow a key from the shop owner. Lane Crawford in Central has a very nice ladies' cloakroom on the first floor behind an unobtrusive mirrored door.

Sports equipment

For information on sports clubs, see Chapter Nineteen, 'Sports'.

Cycling
* **Bicycle World** (15 Wood Road, Wanchai; tel. 2892 2299).
* **Shun Lee Bicycle Company** (G/F, 2A Lucky Plaza Commercial Complex, Shatin; tel. 2695 7195).

- **Flying Ball Bicycle Shop** (478 Castle Peak Road, Cheung Sha Wan; tel. 2381 3661).

Diving
- **Bunns Diving Equipment** (tel. 2558 9345).
- **Pro-Dive** (127 Lockhart Road, Wanchai; tel. 2890 4889).
- **The Dive Shop HK** (375 Portland Street, Mongkok; tel. 2397 6222).

Fishing
- **Po Kee Fishing Tackle Company** (6 Hillier Street, Sheung Wan; tel. 2543 7541).

General
- **World Top Sports Goods** (49 Hankow Road, TST; tel. 2376 2937; 6/F, Times Square; Sai Yee Street, Mongkok).

Golf
- **Super Golf** (26 Nathan Road; tel. 2368 7654).
- **Metro Golf** (47 Connaught Road, Central; tel. 2537 6709).
- **AbcustomGolf** (1795 C, Po Tung Road, Sai Kung; tel. 2194 4977) offers club repair, custom club building and components.

Horse-riding
- **Bits & Boots Saddlery (HK)** (1721B, 17/F, Star House Arcade, 3 Salisbury Road, TST; tel. 2735 0123).

Mountaineering
- **Chamonix Alpine Equipment** (G/F, On Yip Building, 395 Shanghai Street, Yau Ma Tei; tel. 2388 3626).

Ski-ing and snowboarding
- **Fun N Snow** (tel. 2866 7847) sells ski equipment and has seasonal opening hours.
- **Island Wake** (20 Pak Sha Road, Causeway Bay; tel. 2895 0022) sells snowboards.

Wakeboarding
- **Island Wake** (20 Pak Sha Road, Causeway Bay; tel. 2815 0027).

15. D'Aguilar Street
Photograph taken by the author

Chapter Eight

Having and Raising Children in Hong Kong

Expatriate children living abroad – or 'third culture kids' as they are sometimes known – are often worldly, well-travelled and confident when compared to their peers back home. They have the advantage of being able to mix with many nationalities, are taught by teachers recruited from around the world and experience a very different culture.

This also brings challenges: children who grow up in Hong Kong are at home neither in their parents' culture nor their foster culture, and may find it difficult to make the transition and feel comfortable in their new multinational peer group. Frequent partings with friends can reinforce this insecurity. International schools have started to take this issue more seriously and have implemented schemes to provide counselling and buddies for new students: **English Schools Foundation** (ESF) schools have an hour a week for personal and social education built into the curriculum. (More details about ESF schools are below.) Lesley Lewis is a psychologist involved with these programmes and also offers counselling services (lewis@culture3counsel. com; tel. 9055 2211). The **Kely Suppport Group** (www.kely.org; tel. 2521 6890) provides free counselling and workshops for schoolchildren facing peer pressure, emotional problems, eating disorders and drug- and alcohol-related problems.

Hong Kong is very safe when compared with big Western cities, a particular advantage for teens wanting to stay out late with friends. Being able to jump in a taxi and call home on a mobile phone, both of which are very affordable in Hong Kong, can allay parents' fears.

A major difference here is that 'free' play – just being able to just go outside and play in the garden or have a casual game of football in a park – is virtually impossible in Hong Kong due to pressure on space. You need to join a team, club or class. Concerned parents may find themselves overcompensating for a lack of play space by organizing activity after activity to keep youngsters amused.

16. Foreign Domestic Helpers are common in Hong Kong
Photograph taken by Stanley Ng

PREGNANCY AND CHILDBIRTH

Public versus private

Quite a few women I know have given birth successfully in Hong Kong and received their full pregnancy care, including IVF treatment, through both private and public hospitals here. Where you give birth will be determined to a large extent by where you live, how much money you are prepared to spend and how much privacy you require for your birth. The standard of healthcare in private and good public hospitals is pretty similar. In public hospitals, episiotomy is standard, so you should advise the midwife or doctor during your antenatal visits if you would prefer not to have one. If your antenatal care is with a private doctor, prepare a birth plan and hand it to the midwife when you're admitted to the hospital. Newborns in Hong Kong are routinely given BCG, polio and hepatitis B vaccinations.

Partners are generally allowed into the labour ward for routine deliveries and newborns are allowed to stay in the room with their mothers. In private hospitals, you can expect more perks, such as having a 'lodger' stay for free, a complimentary baby care product set and web-baby photo service.

A full list of public hospitals, grouped by location, is available on the **Hospital Authority**'s website (www.ha.org.hk). A list of registered private hospitals is available at www.dh.gov.hk/english/main/main_orhi/list_ph.htm.

Fees

Private hospitals such as the **Matilda** (www.matilda.org), **Canossa Hospital** (www.canossahospital.org) and **Hong Kong Adventist Hospital** (www.hkah.org.hk) have a range of maternity packages that cost between $20,000 and $100,000+. By contrast, public hospitals such as the university teaching hospital **Queen Mary** (www3.ha.org.hk/qmh/index.htm) charge $68 per visit for Hong Kong residents, which includes all procedures. Queen Mary and some other public hospitals also offer a private service (single and double bedrooms, rather than a shared ward), which costs $2,000–3,500 per day. A normal delivery costs around $4,880 and a Caesarean Section is between $20,000 and $41,000 plus anaesthesia charges.

If you decide to move from the general ward to a private room after the birth, all medical procedures (including the delivery) and doctor's fees are recalculated based on your new accommodation.

Birthing experiences

An Australian friend in her late thirties chose to go public to have her baby daughter. She had her antenatal care at Tsan Yuk and delivery at Queen Mary, and said that 'you couldn't have paid for better care than we had'. The only thing she would advise new mothers to do is to hire the services of a qualified midwife to help with lactation from the day of the birth: hospital staff were too busy to spend the time required to assist and she had problems breastfeeding. She then went to her (private) GP for post-natal baby clinic check-ups, a service that is often free for patients' babies.

A Scottish expat had this to say about going the public route: 'Some people complain about the food. It's pretty basic, like chicken and rice. It's no frills, but it's cheap. I was in for six days and it cost me $650 ($100 per day + $50 admission fee). Benjamin (her baby, who had to spend some time in the ICU) was charged for nine days at $50 per day, although he was there for 12 days altogether. I think that the first three days must have been free. So our total bill was $1,100!' (The market rate, provided by the hospital, was $65,000).

Neither the semi-private or ward beds offer overnight accommodation for partners and husbands are only admitted during visiting hours. 'You have to be very firm that your husband is present at the time of delivery, especially for C-sections. You have to be "pushy".'

If anything goes wrong, not only do teaching and research hospitals like Queen Mary's and Prince of Wales have the best technology and best-trained doctors, but private hospital bills can quickly balloon to astronomical proportions if there are problems. 'Mathilda is like a glorified hotel. If there's a problem, they have to send people down to Queen Mary's, which might take 45 minutes in a taxi.'

For information about women's health, sexual health, pregnancy, smear tests and so on, log onto the **Family Planning Association of Hong Kong**'s website (www.famplan.org.hk), which offers a free e-counselling service. Low cost ante-natal and post-natal care is provided at local mother-child centres.

Breastfeeding

Hong Kong society is not particularly comfortable with women breastfeeding in public. **La Leche League** (www.lllhk.org) offers information, support and encouragement to women who want to breastfeed, and holds regular meetings that are advertised in *HK Magazine* or via its website.

Baby products

Details of where to find baby clothes and baby products are provided in Chapter Seven, 'Shopping'.

Mother and Father and baby groups

Stay-at-home dads can hook up with others at **www.hkdads.org**. Associations such as the **American Women's Association** (AWA – www.awa.org. hk) and the **Australian Association** (www.ozhongkong.com/) are good places to network with other young mums and share information. The AWA has several Moms and Toddlers groups that meet for coffee and tea and conversation at child-friendly venues. The Australian Association has a monthly 'Mother and Toddlers' meeting in Happy Valley. Geobaby.com also organises informal playdates around the city and mums seeking playmates for their children can post messages on the website. As there is no official regulation or accreditation of private companies offering babysitting services or running playgroups, word-of-mouth plays an important part in helping mums to decide the best pre-school activities and care for their children. Most playgroups for under-threes require a parent/helper's participation due to licensing requirements. Daycare is not widely available.

The **YMCA** in TST (www.ymcahk.org.hk; tel. 2268 7756) hosts an English language 'Parents and Toddlers' group every Monday and Thursday morning for children from newborns to three years old. Attending a meeting costs $55 and it is run on a first come, first served basis. One of the longest-running pre-school organizations offering help and advice to parents is the **Hong Kong Pre-School Playgroups Association** (HKPPA – 2/F, East Wing, 12 Borrett Road, Mid-Levels; tel. 2523 2599), which:

- runs 'open play' sessions for members on alternate weekdays; HKPPA membership is $320 and no pre-registration required;
- holds a 'Mother and Baby Group' on weekday mornings; and
- has health visitors that provide weekly check-ups for three months, costing $650.

Other HKPPA-linked playgroups for babies and young toddlers can be found in Heng Fa Chuen (tel. 2898 2308), Tai Hang Road (tel. 2576 5859) and Tai Po (tel. 2640 2014).

Other expat-oriented mother and baby groups include the 'Matilda Mum and Baby Group' (details on the Matilda Hospital website) and those connected with family-oriented churches, such as **St Stephen's Chapel, Stanley**, which has a Sunday service crèche facility and daily 'Mother and Toddler' group meetings, the English-speaking **Methodist Church Alice Playgroup** (271 Queen's Road East, Wanchai, tel. 2575 3105) and **St John's Cathedral** (Tuesday and Thursday – $30/child; tel. 2523 4157).

Classes and workshops
Antenatal, post-natal classes and midwives
Most public hospitals provide antenatal classes for a modest fee. There are also workshops held by various private companies, such as **Annerley Midwives** (Room 1801, Car Po Commercial Building, 18–20 Lyndhurst Terrace, Central; www.annerly.com.hk). The staff is made up of Western-trained midwives and nurses. Classes offered include antenatal classes, infant/toddler CPR workshops, yoga sessions and baby massage. They also offer sale and rental of breast pumps, babysitting and nanny services. The **Everdawn Midwives Counseling Service** (Room 1502, Star Commercial Building, 366 Lockhart Road, Wanchai; tel. 2705 9322) offers bilingual Chinese/English services, including home delivery, antenatal classes, post-natal visits and lactation consultation. They also sell nursing and baby products.

Parenting skills
The **Matilda Hospital** offers courses in parentcraft, as well as antenatal sessions and holistic care. The YWCA (see below) runs classes on Parent Effectiveness.

Babies and toddlers
The **YWCA English-Speaking Members Department** (3/F, 1 MacDonnell Road, Central; http://esmd.ywca.org.hk) has a range of courses for mothers and young children under the 'Parents and Parents-to-Be' section of their programme, including baby care and healthy cooking for toddlers.

Play and movement classes for babies include:

- body-stimulating **PEKip** (www.pekip.com.hk; tel. 2573 6623) for mothers and babies from six weeks to ten months old;
- **Kindermusik by Catherine** (www.kateskids.com.hk; tel. 2518 4840) for children up to seven years old; and
- **Gymboree Play & Music** (www.gymboree.com.hk; tel. 2899 2210), for children up to four years old.

BABYSITTERS/NANNIES/FULL-TIME HELP

Finding a domestic helper

Word-of-mouth is often the way expat women find helpers to look after their babies, as tried-and-tested helpers who come highly recommended by their employers are in demand. Advertisements are sometimes placed by employers on behalf of their helpers or by the domestic helpers themselves on noticeboards in supermarkets or websites (such as **www.asiaxpat.com.hk/domestichelp/**). You can also use an online domestic helper search service, such as **www.amahnet.com**, which lists regulatory information and provides links to the Labour Department. Domestic helpers preferred by expats are often from the Philippines or Sri Lanka, as their English language skills are generally better than their Indonesian counterparts.

Helpful advice for managing your helper is contained in Julie Jacobson's *Helper's Helper*. The **YWCA** also runs classes on subjects such as cooking, first aid and kitchen hygiene for helpers. Communication issues can sometimes arise, complicating the relationship between a helper and her employer. Employers recommend that the person who will be dealing with the helper should be the one to hire her, rather than the husband deciding who to hire and leaving his wife to manage the helper.

Mother of two, Kavita Jindal, comments:

> *One of the things I didn't realize is that Filipino helpers who were qualified midwives in the Philippines and have experience of looking after children or working with other expat families expect to be offered more than the minimum wage. I couldn't understand why, after shortlisting helpers, interviewing them and then finding a suitable one and offering them work, they never called back. It's definitely worth offering more money to get a good helper.*

Full-time help

There's very little free help available to expat mothers in Hong Kong. Even at play areas in public sports centres, you will have to pay for the use of the space and toys, and mind your kids both there and at a residents' club. The exception are play rooms provided by the Leisure and Cultural Services Department (www.lcsd.gov.hk/en/ls_fac_playroom.php). It's very difficult just to leave your child with someone while you go for a swim. So many expat families, like local Cantonese families, opt to pay for full-time help. Usually they live in, although some helpers prefer to live out.

There are around 220,000 foreign domestic helpers (FDHs) in Hong Kong, of whom over 53% came from the Philippines, 43% from Indonesia and 2% from Thailand. Currently, FDHs – variously called amahs, helpers, maids or nannies – earn a minimum wage of $3,580 a month for a six-day working week. The employer is responsible for providing accommodation and paying the domestic worker's health insurance, airline tickets and other costs incurred during the contract period – including pregnancy. Visit www.labour. gov.hk to obtain more information on employment legislation.

Many women resist getting a full-time helper in because of fears of sharing the house with a stranger, worries about theft or feelings of guilt. An argument also runs, of course, that you are providing a job to someone who can then support a family back home.

However, most women find the benefits far outweigh the disadvantages. Sue Dockstader, a British lawyer married to an American, lived in Hong Kong for over ten years – first as a single, then as a mother of two young children. She observes that 'the big difference I find to the States [where she had her kids before coming to Hong Kong] is here you can have a life, because you have a helper'. Ferrying your children round Hong Kong and even going shopping can be difficult, because of crowds, split-level shops with steps and escalators, supermarket aisles that aren't wide enough to manoeuvre strollers easily and car parks far from shops.

Even after children grow up and a helper is no longer needed for child-minding, there's still the cleaning, washing and cooking to do, and many find the convenience just too great to give up. According to Sharon Glick, a director of St John's Counselling Service, some expat women refuse point blank to leave Hong Kong, even if their husbands have lost their jobs, because they don't want to get by without a helper. However, plenty of single friends of mine, and some married friends, do not have one.

Part-time help
Although it's illegal to hire an FDH part-time, in practice many people do, paying a friend's amah for a few hours' cleaning per week or babysitting. Companies such as **Merry Maids** (www.merrymaids.com.hk) or **Home Easy**

(www.homeasy.com; tel. 2776 2900) can supply part-time cleaning and domestic help, or you may be able to find a local Chinese cleaner – rates usually start at $50 per hour.

Part- and full-time babysitting and nannying can be found at the expatriate-run **Rent-A-Mum** (12A Amber Lodge, 21–25 Hollywood Road; tel. 2523 4868) and **Mums R Us** (17B, Valley View Terrace, 68 Blue Pool Road, Happy Valley; tel. 2805 7559). Prices are roughly $100–130 per hour.

ADOPTING A CHILD

Adoption in Hong Kong is organized through the Social Welfare Department. Hong Kong residents can submit applications for adoption through the **Adoption Unit** office (4/F, Harbour Building, 38 Pier Road, Central, Hong Kong; tel. 2852 3107).

Prospective single or married adopters will need to be at least 25, prove that they are mature and healthy, have no criminal record, have an income sufficient to support a child and are eligible to stay in Hong Kong for a continuous period of 12 months. Couples should be able to show evidence of a stable marriage. Single expat women as well as expat couples have successfully adopted local children, including those past babyhood – especially special needs children. **Mother's Choice**, an organization providing foster care for babies and advice for pregnant women, gives an overview of the adoption and fostering process in Hong Kong, as well as details of support groups for adopting families, on its website, www.mchoice.org.

REGISTERING YOUR BABY'S BIRTH AND OBTAINING A PASSPORT

For UK citizens, a local Hong Kong birth certificate is sufficient for most purposes, including British passport applications. For a fee, you can register the birth of your child with the **British Consulate**, who then provide your child with a British-style birth certificate.

In any case, you must register your child with the Hong Kong government. Registration and birth certificate forms are available for downloading on the **Immigration Department**'s website, www.immd.gov.hk/ehtml/birth_1.htm. BNO and British citizen passports can be obtained by following the procedures outlined on the British Consulate's website (www.britishconsulate.org.hk). A similar process is necessary for other foreign nationals. Contact details of consulates are provided in Appendix 3.

SCHOOLS

Pre-schools and kindergartens

Many international schools, including **ESF** primary schools, have a kindergarten attached to them that acts as an unofficial 'feeder' to the primary, taking children from three or four years old. Another prominent group are the **Woodlands** pre-schools (www.woodlandschools.com), based in locations with large expat populations, that take children from two years upwards and includes Montessori-style teaching in some centres. A popular pre-school on the South side that doesn't advertise is the stand-alone **Montessori for Children at Stanley** (tel. 2813 9589). The school has a waiting list and takes children between two-and-a-half and six years old.

The **HKPPA** offers open play for 3–5 year olds on Monday, Wednesday and Friday afternoons at their centre in Mid-Levels, but children must be accompanied. At the same location is **City Kidz**, a class staffed by qualified supervisors and trainees studying to be kindergarten teachers. One or two parents are on volunteer duty every morning as assistants. Charges are around $2,500 per month if a parent helps on a rota basis or $3,300 per month if they do not – both very reasonable by Hong Kong standards. Other HKPPA-affiliated pre-schools include **Earlybirds** at Taipo, **Leapfrog** at Sai Kung (tel. 2791 1540) and the **Sai Kung Pre-School Group** (tel. 2791 7354), which offers classes for children between 18 months and five years old based on the learning-through-play philosophy. See www.hkwithkids.com/kindy.htm for other groups.

The **YMCA** in TST (www.ymcahk.org.hk; tel. 2899 2912) runs an English-language Toddlers World for children between three months and three years old and an International Kindergarten for children between 32 months and six years old. The kindergarten year starts in September and costs approximately $4,324–7,640 per month.

Tutor Time International Nursery and Kindergarten (www.tutortime. com.hk) has received praise from parents. There are pre-schools at Kowloon Tong (tel. 2337 0822) and Red Hill Plaza, Tai Tam (tel. 2529 1188). Benefits include exposure to Mandarin and a web facility allowing parents to check on their children from the office.

Pre-school support for children with special needs

Although Hong Kong does not have the same level of resources as a typical national health and education system has, there are places that parents can seek advice, support and help for their special needs children, especially younger ones. **Mathilda Child Development Centre** (http://mcdchk.com; tel. 2849 6138) is a non-profit-making centre that offers education for young children with learning difficulties. There are also parent counselling and training courses for pre-school teachers.

Quite a few expat mums are involved on a voluntary basis with **Watchdog Early Learning and Development Centre** in Borrett Road (www.watchdog.org.hk; tel. 2521 7364/5), which was set up to provide a pre-school programme for special needs children with cerebral palsy, hyperactivity, Down's syndrome, autism and learning difficulties. They advise parents and prepare youngsters for entry into the regular school system.

The HK Association for Parents of Gifted Children has details of courses and child development centres on its website (www.gifted.org.hk).

International schools

There is quite a large choice of private day schooling available in Hong Kong for parents who do not wish to put their children in boarding school. Over 50 international schools cater to the needs of expatriate communities, offering several different Western educational cultures. Schools include:

- **Hong Kong International School** – American curriculum;
- **Kellett School** – British curriculum;
- **Chinese International School** – International Baccalaureate curriculum;
- **French International School** – French and International Baccalaureate curriculum;
- **German Swiss International School** – German and British curriculum; and
- **The Carmel School** – the only Jewish day school in south-east Asia; teaches Jewish studies and Hebrew as a second language.

The **ESF** runs 20 schools, including the well-regarded **Island**, **Bradbury** and **Kennedy** schools, using the British curriculum and the International Baccalaureate at selected schools. It is popular with parents not only because of the good reputation of its schools, but also because its fees are lower than most other international schools due to local government subvention. This may change, as the government looks to trim its education spending, but there is a need for affordable English-language schooling for non-Chinese (Cantonese) speaking children, Hong Kong returnees and locals who do not wish to put their children into the local education system. More information about ESF schools can be found on their website, **www.esf.edu.hk/**. The Foundation also operates a corporate surety scheme to secure a place ahead of the family arriving in Hong Kong.

Smaller schools also exist, including the Christian **Norwegian International School** (http://nis.edu.hk) in Taipo, home to about 70 pupils.

An A–Z listing of international schools can be found in the *Guide to International Schools in Hong Kong* by Yoko Yamato and Sally Course, which can be ordered online from **www.paddyfield.com.hk**.

International schools are generally well run, properly accredited, staffed by excellent teachers and furnished with exceptional facilities. As well as considering reputation, fees and location when choosing a school, it is worth thinking ahead to where your child will be going after they leave Hong Kong and choosing a school that will prepare them for that step.

'The major challenge at the beginning was making friends at school which is very important for every child. So yes, they were very unhappy and sometimes did not want to go to school. For one of them (in P3), I had to speak to the teacher about it and she immediately took steps to rectify the situation by asking her classmates who played with her to report it to her each day. This strategy worked very well and she ended with so many friends, some of who are still friends with her till date.' (Mary Bodomo, working mother of two girls.)

Entry criteria

Each international school has its own entry requirements, which usually include an interview and/or consideration of past school records, and a test. Language proficiency is also an important factor for schools (such as the Chinese International School) that have a strong emphasis on Chinese. The ESF schools demand a certain level of English before they will accept students, as priority is given to expatriate children with foreign passports. In practice, however, more and more local children have joined ESF schools to opt out of the local education system, which is seen as over-competitive and high-pressured. The ESF also uses a zoning system for allocating students to schools based on a student's residential location.

It is advisable to book your child a place at your selected school well ahead of your arrival in Hong Kong. Individual schools can advise about waiting lists and application deadlines. Private companies such as ITS Tutorial School can offer advice and help with submitting applications to international schools. Their Hong Kong Education calendar (at www.tuition.com.hk/calendar.htm) shows application date deadlines, school holidays and other useful information.

Fees

The ESF currently charges $58,100 (primary) and $89,250 (secondary) per annum. There are no bursaries, but short-term financial assistance is offered to parents who experience 'sudden and unexpected changes' after their children join the school. This compares favourably with schools such as the Hong Kong International School, which charges approximately $125,200–145,100 plus an application fee and debenture – individually, $12,000 per annum. Debentures are (refundable) one-off payments or (usually non-refundable) annual payments that schools use to finance their development. Individual or corporate debentures are sometimes required. Since the economic downturn, many parents have had to seek alternatives to schooling, putting more pressure on ESF prices.

Other schools

Increasingly, the government is looking at ways to provide a useful alternative to the traditional state school system that divides students and schools into three bands according to academic merit at the tender age of 11. By introducing the Private Independent Scheme (PIS) and Direct Subsidy Scheme (DSS) for local schools, it is thought that parents and students will be offered more choice and schools will have more freedom to decide what to specialize in (including an emphasis on English language in the curriculum), fees and student intake. Expats hoping to give their children a taste of life in a local Chinese school will be disappointed unless children can demonstrate proficiency in Cantonese.

For students who can speak Cantonese, the options are greater. Local DSS schools with excellent academic reputations, such as **St Paul's Co-Educational College**, currently charge around $48,000 per year – considerably less than international schools. They also offer bursaries and financial aid. They follow the Hong Kong schools curriculum and students study for the Hong Kong Certificate of Education Examination (HKCEE) and the Hong Kong Advanced Level Examination (HKALE).

The **Sir Ellis Kadoorie Primary School** is a government primary school that caters specifically to Hong Kong's Indian community. English is the medium of instruction, with Hindi or Urdu as a second language.

Local or international?

Shelagh and Ethan Heath of Discovery Bay decided they would send their kids to a local kindergarten.

'Most people here send their kids to an ESF or international school; many commute by ferry to Island School, Bradbury, German Swiss, etc. and the mums take turns to ferry the kids in shifts. We were both interested in having our boys learn Chinese to a high level and the best way was to be educated in Chinese for a period of time. There's also the money issue – we pay about $462 a month for kindergarten (three hours a day, five days a week), compared with between $1,500-5,000 a month at an international kindergarten.'

Schools for children with special needs

The **Jockey Club Sarah Roe School**, an ESF school, provides for the special educational needs of up to 60 students aged 5–19 who have severe learning difficulties. Smaller schemes include **The Rainbow Project** (tel. 2179 5222), which runs a class to provide a bridge for children with autistic-related problems between kindergarten and primary, and the **Springboard Project** (tel. 2813 4508), which organizes classes for children aged 5–18 with mild to moderate learning difficulties.

The **Children's Institute of Hong Kong** (www.tcihk.org; tel. 2812 2144) was set up in 2003 to provide individualized learning opportunities for children with autism-related disorders who cannot benefit from education in a mainstream environment. It currently caters to English-speaking children aged 5–9. Mainstream international schools that can cater to the special needs of students within the regular curriculum include the Australian International, Chinese International, Bradbury Junior, Korean International, South Island, Clearwater Bay and Beacon Hill schools. A total of six ESF primaries and three secondary schools provide some kind of learning support.

InfoKids Academy of Excellence in Computer Education (www.infokids. com.hk; tel. 2504 2228) offers IT and multimedia literacy programmes based on Stanford University's Education Programmes for Gifted Youth.

LEISURE ACTIVITIES AND EXTRA-CURRICULAR CLASSES FOR CHILDREN

The most common providers of children's leisure activities are club houses in residential complexes and international schools, both of which regularly invite private companies in to offer classes such as aerobics, ballet, music, chess, foreign languages, computers and martial arts.

Those who are fortunate enough to belong to private clubs such as the **Aberdeen Marina Club** or the **American Club** – membership is often a perk included in overseas contracts – can make use of extensive children's facilities including playrooms, bowling alleys, an ice rink, play stations and video game rooms, a soft foam ball shooting gallery and a whole range of organized activities. The contact details of the clubs are in Chapter Nineteen, 'Sports'.

But even if you aren't a member of a private club, there are plenty of things for your kids to get involved in. The South Side of Hong Kong Island, for example, has excellent water sports facilities. Other outdoor activities such as horse riding, golf, rugby and sailing are a few of the many sports open to children on a pay-as-you-go basis. A useful resource in this respect is **Hong Kong with Kids** (www.hkwithkids.com), a website that has a comprehensive list of activities and classes for kids and plenty of useful information for parents. Local publications such as *The Parents Journal* will also have details of things to do.

Toys, games and children's products
Details of where to find toys, games, children's clothes, books and other products are provided in Chapter Seven, 'Shopping'.

Sports
ESF Educational Services (www.esf.org.hk), a member of the ESF, offers sports coaching through ESF schools and organizes inter-school leagues. **Play Sport Coaching** (www.playsport.com.hk; tel. 2818 9453) offers group and private lessons in golf, gymnastics, skating, football, tennis and other sports for kids at six venues around Hong Kong. **Multi-Sport** (www.

multi-sport.com.hk; tel. 2540 1257), founded in 1983, provides classes in basketball, action cricket, trampolining, aquarobics as well as other sports for children and adults. **Force One** (www.forceone.com.hk) offers kick-boxing for kids.

The best source of information on public sports facilities is the **Leisure and Cultural Services Department** (LCSD; www.lcsd.gov.hk). It lists facilities by sports type and location, including public swimming pools, and hosts web-links to the sites. It is possible to book playrooms, squash, badminton courts and other sports spaces through the Leisure Link for Facilities Booking and Programmes Enrollment (visit www.gov.hk and click on the link). Public riding schools are located at Lei Yue Mun, Pokfulam and Tuen Mun (www.hongkongjockeyclub.com/english/school/riding_index.htm).

The **YMCA** (www.ymcahk.org.hk; tel. 2268 7756) in TST provides many sports classes for youngsters. **Warehouse Teenage Club** in Aberdeen (www.warehouse.org.hk; tel. 2873 2244) runs skateboarding, handball and other sports courses and activities (in English and Chinese). Other options include:

▪ skateboarding (www.xskate.com.hk); and
▪ paintballing – **Paintball Headquarters** has 10,000 square feet and costs $250, including equipment rental and 100 rounds of paintball (11 Wang Chi Road, Kowloon Bay; www.paintballhq.com.hk; tel. 3106 02200).

Kwok's Kung Fu & Dragon Lion Dance (www.kwokslion.com.hk; tel. 9644 1999) offers kids the chance to learn kung fu, flag dance, drum array and the eponymous dragon and lion dances.

Details of other sports activities are provided in Chapter Nineteen, 'Sports'.

Arts
Art and craft
There are many private schools offering creative and performing arts classes for children. **Kids Gallery** is popular with kids and parents, and offers classes in visual, performing, digital and creative arts for children aged 3–12. They run four schools including those at 21/F, Coda Plaza, 51 Garden Road, Central (tel. 2501 4842) and 28 Cumberland Road, Kowloon Tong (tel. 2337 1001). Visit their website at **www.kidsgallery.com** to find details of courses, links to websites for kids to explore and a kids' posting section.

An exciting range of arts and crafts is also offered by **Colour My World** (Room 108, Aberdeen Marina Tower, 8 Shum Wan Road, Aberdeen; www. colour-my-world.com; tel. 2580 5028). Activities include drama and music, sculpture, clay, mixed media, and photography. They also offer drop-in workshops for children and classes for adults.

Arts Plus (G/F, 11 Tin Hau Temple Road; tel. 2807 0208) has a few art classes in English, and can also provide tailor-made courses for children. **The Pottery Workshop** (2 Lower Albert Road, Central; www.ceramics.com.hk; tel. 2525 7949) offers clay-making classes for 6–12 year olds.

In August, the Leisure and Cultural Services Department sponsors an **International Arts Carnival** for children and families, with a host of programmes including music, dance, drama, puppetry, acrobatics, film and theatrical arts, workshops and exhibitions.

Dance
Recommended dance classes for kids and teens include the **Southern School of Dance** (at venues in Happy Valley and Pokfulam; tel. 2872 6917) and the **DMR School of Ballet** (tel. 2987 4338) in Discovery Bay, both of which run ballet, tap and jazz dance classes. Recommended teachers include:

- Glenda Allen, who teaches ballet, jazz and tap (tel. 2987 7370);
- Victor Fung, who teaches jazz and tap (tel. 6851 4378); and
- Jamie Chung, who teaches jazz and tap (tel. 9059 0709).

Well-established schools include the **Jean M. Wong School of Ballet** (www. jmwballet.org) and the **Carol Bateman School of Dancing** (www.cbsdhk. com) or check www.hkwithkids.com/classes-dancing.htm.

Drama
Drama classes are often offered through school, but older children can also get involved with productions mounted by the **Hong Kong Youth Arts Festival** (www.hkyaf.com) and the **Faust International Youth Theatre** (FIYT; www.faustworld.com). The latter also offers classes in improvisation, live performance, make-up, masks, mime, movement, musical theatre, pantomime, puppetry, script-work, set design, stage-fighting and story-telling, and also has a choir. **Faust Educational Services** offers exams, tuition and creative writing workshops. The **Kely Support Group** (www.kely.org) runs a summer circus school which is very popular.

Music

Besides participating in school orchestras, young classical musicians can audition for the **Asian Youth Orchestra** (www.asianyouthorchestra.com), a six-week summer camp where young musicians get to rehearse together and then perform on tour for three weeks with international solo artists and conductors. The well-regarded Junior Music Programme at the **Hong Kong Academy for Performing Arts** (www.hkapa.edu) enrolls international and local students, and has orchestra rehearsals on Saturday mornings.

Music classes are advertised at music shops throughout the city, the largest being **Tom Lee** (Yamaha Music Programs; www.tomleemusic.com), or try finding a teacher through **www.hongkongstrings.com**, which is run by a classical musician.

PLACES TO TAKE KIDS

A nice website for families to browse is **www.hkwithkids.com**. It provides information about Hong Kong and suggests all sorts of activities to choose from. Another useful publication is *Fun Excursions in Hong Kong* by Sabina Wong. Below I have highlighted some of the popular places to visit and things to do for kids, but the list is nowhere near exhaustive. More information on places of interest is included in Part Three, 'Leisure in Hong Kong'.

Weather

Visit the **Hong Kong Observatory's** website to see what the weather's going to be like – **www.hko.gov.hk/contente.htm**.

Museums
Hong Kong Science Museum

- 2 Science Museum Road, TST East; www.lcsd.gov.hk/ce/museum/science/index.htm; tel. 2732 3232.
- Open 1:00–9:00 pm, Saturday and Sunday 10:00 am–9:00 pm. Closed Thursdays (except public holidays).
- Free admission Wednesdays.
- Screens nature films occasionally.

Hong Kong Space Museum

- 10 Salisbury Rd, TST; www.lcsd.gov.hk/ce/museum/science/index.htm; tel. 2721 0226.
- Open 1:00–9:00 pm, Saturday and Sunday 10:00 am–9:00 pm. Closed Tuesdays (except public holidays).
- Screens Omnimax film shows.
- A 24-hour Astropark, opened in 2010, showcases ancient Chinese astronomy and provides different star-gazing facilities (at Chong Hing Water Sports Centre, Sai Kung).

Hong Kong Heritage Museum

- 1 Man Lam Rd, Shatin, New Territories; www.heritagemuseum.gov.hk/; tel. 2180 8188.
- Open 10:00 am–6:00 pm. Closed Tuesdays (except public holidays).
- Free admission Wednesdays.
- This vast museum includes models and interactive exhibits on the arts, culture and history of Hong Kong.

Hong Kong History Museum

- 100 Chatham Road South, TST; http://hk.history.museum; tel. 2724 9042.
- Open 10:00 am–6:00 pm, or until 7:00 on Sundays and public holidays. Closed Tuesdays (except public holidays).
- Free admission Wednesdays.
- Popular exhibitions include *The Hong Kong Story*. Best for children 6+.

Hong Kong Police Museum

- 27 Coombe Rd, The Peak; www.info.gov.hk/police/english/museum/2-6-1.htm; tel. 2849 7019.
- Open Wednesday–Sunday 9:00 am–5:00 pm and Tuesday 2:00–5:00 pm. Closed Mondays and public holidays.
- Galleries include Narcotics and Triad Societies.

Hong Kong Museum of Coastal Defence

- 175 Tung Hei Rd, Shaukeiwan; www.lcsd.gov.hk/hkmcd/; tel. 2569 1500.
- Open 10:00 am–5:00 pm. Closed Thursdays.

- Free admission Wednesdays and for under-fours.
- This museum is beautifully landscaped and partly open-air. Exhibits include wartime video footage and children's corner programmes, which include tank and model-making workshops. An English translation service is provided – call 2569 1248.

Hong Kong Maritime Museum

- G/F Murray House, Stanley Plaza, Stanley; www.hkmaritimemuseum.org; tel. 2813 2322.
- Open 10:00 am–6:00 pm. Closed Mondays.
- Suggested for children five and older. Hands-on exhibits include driving an ocean liner and loading a container.

Hong Kong Railway Museum

- 13 Shung Tak Street, Tai Po Market; www.heritagemuseum.gov.hk/english/branch.htm; tel. 2653 3455.
- Open Monday and Wednesday–Sunday (including public holidays) 9:00 am–5:00 pm.
- Free admission.
- This small, open-air museum is located in the old Tai Po Market railway station, which dates from 1913. The exhibition includes a full-size model of an electric train compartment, as well as old coaches and photographs from the city's rail history.

Entertainment

Hong Kong Disneyland (hongkongdisneyland.com) opened in 2005 and, though considerably smaller than its US and European counterparts, has attracted hordes of fans. Accessible from downtown by bus, MTR and, soon, ferry, day tickets cost $170–350 depending on the day and the age of the Disney fan.

Madame Tussauds was recently refurbished at the Peak Tower and profiles Kung Fu Stars, Asian Stars and Fashion Icons, amongst others. Tickets cost $160 (adults); $90 (3–11 year-olds and seniors).

At **Cityplaza Ice Palace** (www.icepalace.com.hk) or **Festival Walk Glacier** (www.glacier.com.hk), you can go ice-skating or book a coach from the skating school. McDonald's, Pizza Hut and food courts are conveniently located nearby.

UA Cinemas are generally plusher than others in Hong Kong and are located at Pacific Place, Times Square, Festival Walk, Taikoo Shing, Shatin, Telford and Whampoa (the cheapest venue). Tuesday tickets are discounted. Showing times are advertised daily in the *South China Morning Post* or on the **Cityline** website (www.cityline.com.hk). This website also serves as a billboard for many cultural and artistic shows and events.

For more information on cinemas, refer to Chapter Eighteen, 'The Local Arts Scene'.

Hiking

Although Hong Kong is not famed for its natural environment, the territory has 23 beautiful **Country Parks**, most of which are open to the public. Lion Rock Country Park is home to over 2,000 wild long-tailed macaques.

There are more than a hundred hiking trails. Some, such as the **Maclehose**, **Pak Sin Leng** and **Violet Hill**, are quite strenuous; others, such as **Black's Link** (at the top of Wanchai Gap) and the **Peak Trail** on Harlech Road, are much less so. Details of popular trails can be found in the following places:

- **Hong Kong Tourism Association** (www.hkta.org);
- Agriculture, Fisheries and Conservation Department (http://parks.afcd. gov.hk/newparks/eng/index.htm); and
- *Hong Kong Hikes* by Christian Wright.

- **Kadoorie Farm and Botanic Garden**, Lam Kam Road, Tai Po, New Territories. www.kfbg.org.hk; tel. 2483 7200. Open 9:30–5:00. Check the website for information on closed days.
  Roam the nature trails and visit the farm to learn more about Hong Kong's fauna and flora and locally sustainable farming. Animals on the farm include wild boar and orphaned pigs, and exhibits include a Raptor Roost and Greenhouse. Wild animals such as civets and Chinese porcupines can be glimpsed in the further reaches of the property.

Beaches

Hong Kong's 41 public beaches are officially open between April and October, when they are manned by lifeguards – although a few remain open throughout the year. Beaches at risk of shark attacks – although the risk is minimal – are fitted with shark nets.

Giving more reason for concern is the cleanliness of the water. Water-testing is carried out weekly and the e-coli levels are published in the *South China Morning Post* and on the government's website (**www.epd.gov.hk**). Beaches consistently rated 'good' for their water quality include:

- Clearwater Bay Beach (both Number 1 and Number 2 beaches);
- Discovery Bay;
- Cheung Sha Upper and Lower Beaches (Lantau);
- St Stephen's; and
- Stanley Beach.

For lists of beaches and more information, visit **www.hkwithkids.com**. The LCSD's website has a map locating the beaches and water safety advice (**www. lcsd.gov.hk/swimhandbook/en/pbb.html**).

A popular outing for children and adults is to North Lantau to see the famous wild **pink dolphins** (*Sousa chinensis*). There are several tour operators organizing half-day trips – not all of them environmentally friendly – but one that I have been on and found excellent was **Hong Kong Dolphinwatch** (www. hkdolphinwatch.com; tel. 2984 1414). Prices are $360 for adults and $180 for children; there are discounts for seniors and students while under-threes travel free. The **YMCA** (1 Salisbury Road, Tsimshatsui; www.ymcahk.org. hk; tel. 2369 2211) occasionally runs special events, such as Squid Catching Nights.

Indoor Playrooms

A list of public indoor playrooms and toy libraries can be obtained at www. lcsd.gov.hk. Privately-run **Playtown** (www.playtown.com.hk) provides a 10,000 square foot themed indoor playground for children up to 12 years old. Kids can play all day ($80–$100), or drop by for Happy Hour in the evening (half-price). Shop 121–3, Podium Level 1, The Westwood, 8 Belcher's Street; Kennedy Town; tel. 2258 9558. Adults and children are required to wear socks.

Parks

Two animal and bird parks nestle between a forest of skyscrapers in Mid-Levels – **HK Zoological & Botanical Gardens** (Albany Road) and **Hong Kong Park** (19 Cotton Tree Drive). The former has some sad but interesting enclosures housing orang-utans, gibbons, a jaguar and flamingos, amongst other mammals and birds. Ten minutes' walk away, Hong Kong Park has a wonderful walk-through canopy aviary, beautiful fishponds and a children's playground. It also has a nice open-air restaurant. Avoid weekends and public holidays, when the park gets crowded.

Other large parks include **Victoria Park** in Causeway Bay and **Kowloon Park** in TST, both of which have public pools. Another green and pleasant place – usually very quiet, but somewhat out of the way – is **Victory Peak Garden** atop the Peak. It's the perfect hideaway for mother and baby.

Amusement parks
Victoria Peak
Visiting the Peak is a must with visitors and residents alike, not only for the gravity-defying journey up on the historic peak tram but also for the magnificent views of Hong Kong from the top. Entertainments for kids include:

- **EA Experience** – a virtual world where gamers can try their hand at Harry Potter, warfare, sports and much more; and
- **Madame Tussauds** – $160 for adults, $90 for children and senior citizens (www.madame-tussauds.com.hk).

All of the above attractions are open between 10:00 am and 10:00 pm. There are plenty of reasonably priced places to snack, including Pacific Coffee, DeliFrance, Häagen-Dazs and Movenpick Marche. There is also a children's playground in Mount Austin Road. For more information, visit **www.thepeak.com.hk**.

Ocean Park
Ocean Park, just the other side of the Aberdeen Tunnel (**www.oceanpark.com. hk**; tel. 25502 0291), is popular with children of all ages. In the lower sections of the park you can find the panda enclosure, Butterfly House and Kids' World, housing fun rides and conservation exhibits. The upper reaches of the park are accessed by cable car and are home to a host of adult rollercoaster rides, Ocean Theatre – which has performing dolphins and sealions – and a spectacular viewing tower. Other attractions include the Middle Kingdom, which has traditional Chinese buildings and characters in traditional dress, a Bird Paradise canopy enclosure and a Bird Theatre of performing birds. The park is open between 10:00 am and 6:00 pm daily and admission, which includes access to all the rides and shows, costs $185 for adults and $93 for children. For more than two trips a year, it's worth buying an annual pass.

Noah's Ark

Located in Ma Wan Park, this multi-media, sculpture and amusement park was built to promote social harmony and family values. Highlights for kids include the animal sculptures, tight-rope walking and rope tunnels. Reserve tickets online in advance (www.noahsark.com.hk).

Themed shopping malls

Teddy Bear Kingdom in The Amazon, the underground mall between the Space Museum and the Regent Hotel in TST, boasts a teddy bear museum home to more than 400 teddies and a teddy bear picnic area. There are also plenty of children's shops to browse. Admission is $50 for adults and $25 for children and senior citizens. **Snoopy's World** in Shatin New Town Plaza, near Shatin KCR station, has an outdoor *Peanuts* playground, canal canoe ride and eating area.

Party ideas

The UA Cityplaza cinema operates a **Director's Club**: two private auditoriums with 16 luxury seats each. If you book the whole auditorium, you get to choose the film. Soft drinks, hot dogs and popcorn are included. Individual tickets are $175; booking the whole auditorium costs $2,800. Call 2567 3111 for more information.

For younger kids, pizza and McDonald's still come out tops for food. **Pizza Hut** offers a 'Birthday Party' deal for ten kids or more at $39 per child. This includes invitations, party games, food and gifts, and the chance for the birthday boy or girl to make their own pizza (www.pizzahut.com.hk/kids_corner.html). **Pepperoni's** does children's parties and pizza-making parties at most branches. **Pizza Express** (www.pizzaexpress.com.hk; tel. 2850 7898) runs pizza-making parties for children at its Soho restaurant between 3:00 and 5:30 pm at $125 per child. They also can offer special prices for party catering and organize entertainment such as clowns, face-painting and magicians on request.

Trendy Toon Town (Shop B101, Basement 1, 1 Peking Rd, TST; tel. 2739 1318), a Disney-themed venue, offers party favours, invites, decorations, free popcorn or candyfloss, and a choice of two menus for children's birthday parties. It is available on Saturdays, Sundays and public holidays for two-and-a-half hours, and costs $138–150 per adult, $108–110 per child, plus a service charge. **McDonald's** (www.mcdonalds.com.hk) provides a decorated venue, invitations, gifts, games and food coupons for a surcharge of $12 per child based on a minimum of ten children at the party.

Other companies offering party-hosting and activities include fivestarasia. net, Gymboree.com.hk, littleacademy.com.hk (cooking parties for two-year olds and up), jwtkidsgym.com.hk, kindyroo.com.hk and rollypollies.com.hk. Babycakes Asia (www.BabyCakesAsia.com), provides cake-decorating parties for kids and a large play area.

There is a good selection of entertainment available if you are prepared to pay for it:

- **No Name Family Circus** has a good reputation (tel. 2982 0862);
- **Drum Jam** (www.drumjam.com.hk; tel. 2982 1846) will organize a drum jam session for children;
- **Zani** (http://topaz.hknet.com/~zani; tel. 9612 0502) provides make-up, magic and jugglers for children's parties; and
- **Abbott Leisure** (www.abbottleisure.com; tel. 2540 3982) offers a mixed programme of traditional entertainment such as clowning, magic, music or puppetry, face painting, kiddies disco and bubble machine.

Other vote-winners include the YMCA indoor climbing wall party (tel. 2268 7055), for up to 20 participants; a crazy golf party; a football party, organized by Play Sport; and a bowling party.

17. Railway Museum
Photograph taken by Stanley Ng

Chapter Nine

Looking after your Health

Life expectancy in Hong Kong runs to 79 years for men and 85 years for women, second only by a whisker to that bastion of the elderly, Japan, according to the United Nations. The public healthcare system is excellent and cheap and, barring the occasional outbreak of influenza, the city is by-and-large a healthy place, despite the high stress levels and air pollution everyone complains about. Since the SARS outbreak in 2003, Hong Kong has become fleet-of-foot in dealing with any new outbreak of avian flu, swine flu or other infectious influenza strains.

SARS acted as a wake-up call to the public at large, scientists, the Hospital Authority and the government, who are now much more alert to the possibility of 'flu epidemics in the city and how to control the spread of infectious disease in the densely populated urban environment. The threat of another SARS or avian (bird) 'flu outbreak is being actively managed through:

- the imposition of stricter controls on importing and testing of birds and animals;
- closer co-operation and information-sharing with mainland Chinese authorities; and
- increased monitoring of travellers.

Public education campaigns exhort people to clean their homes, wash their hands after using the toilet, wear masks if they have colds and open windows to improve air circulation. The message is reinforced by punitive fines for littering and spitting. Improved standards of hygiene in public areas, such as public toilets, have actually made Hong Kong a cleaner city.

ENVIRONMENTAL SAFETY

Typhoons and rainstorms

Whilst Hong Kong is fortunate not to lie on any earthquake-inducing faults, unlike its near neighbours China, Taiwan and Japan, the territory is battered most summers by occasional typhoons. There is a sophisticated modus operandi that comes into play when a severe typhoon is spotted approaching:

18. Mother and child at Clearwater Bay beach
Photograph taken by the author

schools, offices, hospitals and public buildings are closed; shops, taxis and restaurants close at their discretion; buses and ferries stop running (although the MTR stays open); and everyone is sent home in good time to batten down the hatches. Whilst typhoons rarely cause fatalities, they can wreak havoc on buildings, structures and parks, causing potentially dangerous situations when scaffolding and windows come loose.

Rainstorms can cause flooding and landslides, which accounts for the 'spraycreting' of banks thought to pose a risk. It's also during a rainstorm you find out whether the ceiling of your bedroom is sound or not. Typhoons and weather warnings are issued by the **Hong Kong Observatory** (www.hko.gov. hk; tel. 2926 8200) and publicized on TV and radio.

- A **Black Rain Warning** is issued when 100mm or more of rain is predicted to fall within two hours. People are advised to stay indoors. Amber and red signals are less severe, but signify heavy rain and flooding.
- **Typhoon Warnings** are issued when a typhoon (a severe tropical storm) is approaching. The warnings are graded. Signal 3 means that kindergartens are closed because strong winds are likely; if the warning is signal 8 and above, schools, government offices and most businesses close and people are advised to return home immediately and not go out. Winds can exceed 220 km/hr.

For explanations of other weather warnings, visit **www.hko.gov.hk/textonly/ explain/intro.htm**.

Air pollution

Air pollution tends to be one of the major complaints from expatriates in Hong Kong, and it is getting worse. Although Hong Kong has controls on vehicle and power emissions, a lot of the city's pollution blows in from the manufacturing hub of the Pearl River Delta in South China.

Air pollution indices taken from monitoring stations are broadcast daily on the TV and on the government website (**www.epd.gov.hk/epd**); visit the website of campaign group **Clear The Air** (www.cleartheair.org.hk) for more information. Pollution is worst in industrial areas such as Kwun Tong and Tuen Mun, and traffic hubs such as Causeway Bay.

Water

As could be expected in one of the busiest container ports in the world, the sea and river water is not exactly pristine. Marine refuse, insufficient sewage treatment systems and pollution of rivers and streams by live animal waste contribute to the pollution of the sea. That doesn't, however, deter thousands from swimming and relaxing on the beaches throughout the long hot summer. Water quality is monitored weekly during the swimming season, and the results are published in the *South China Morning Post* and on the website **www.info.gov.hk/epd/beach/index.html.** Swimming in the sea should be avoided after heavy rainfalls, when runoffs and sewerage overflows get washed into the sea.

Hong Kong's drinking water comes mainly from Dongjiang in Guangdong, supplemented by Hong Kong's reservoirs. It is treated and made safe to drink from the tap, but boiling and filtering are sensible precautions. If water runs yellow or brown from your kitchen tap, it could well be that the pipes that are rusty. Mineral and distilled water are popular alternatives. **Watsons** do both and can deliver dispensers (www.watsons-water.com; tel. 2660 6688).

Noise

One of the things constantly confronting you in Hong Kong is noise. Whether it is the perpetual stream of video advertising on buses, instructions in MTR stations, the barrage of people chatter in restaurants, or the eternal drilling and filling of Hong Kong that goes on day and night, chances are that you'll be affected. By law, contractors are not supposed to work on public holidays or at night in built-up areas. If your neighbours are playing their music too loud, you can call the police, who will give them a friendly warning.

Many people don't bother – whatever people may tell you about the communality of Chinese culture, it only goes so far in Hong Kong. The Cantonese are great believers in the right of the individual to do their own thing, providing it is not a physical threat to other people – hence the selfishness of mobile phone users in cinemas, who actually have *conversations* on their phone. The only places in Hong Kong that ban the use of mobile phones, incidentally, are private clubs.

Rubbish

Unlike other Asian countries such as Japan and Korea, Hong Kong does not have strict requirements for individual household disposal of rubbish, nor is illegal dumping heavily penalized. Beaches are strewn with rubbish after public holidays and there is little systematic recycling. Most MTR stations have paper-recycling bins, so at least you can dump your newspaper there.

when you've finished reading it. But what do you do with the plastic bag that was forced on you when you bought the newspaper? You can find your nearest waste separation bins and recycling collection points for aluminium, plastic and textiles on the **Environmental Protection Department**'s website (www.epd.gov.hk).

Most of Hong Kong's 5,956 tonnes of daily domestic waste is buried in landfill sites, but these are being filled up, whilst incineration is strongly opposed by environmental groups. For more information about current environmental issues in Hong Kong, visit the websites of the following groups:

- World Wide Fund for Nature (www.wwf.org.hk/);
- Civic Exchange (www.civic-exchange.org);
- Greenpeace China (www.greenpeace.org.hk/eng/); and
- Friends of the Earth (www.foe.org.hk).

Power

Electricity is supplied by two companies: **CLP Power Hong Kong** supplies customers in Kowloon, the New Territories and islands such as Lantau and Cheung Chau; **The Hongkong Electric Company** supplies electricity to Hong Kong Island, Ap Lei Chau and Lamma Island. The latter company owns the Lamma Power Station. The other power stations – at Castle Peak, Black Point and Penny's Bay – are owned by CLP Power, which also has an interest in Guangdong Daya Bay Nuclear Power Station, about 50 km north-east of Hong Kong. Another nuclear power station, Lingao, is located near Daya Bay. A thermal power station fuelled by natural gas is located at Black Point.

Towngas is manufactured at plants in Tai Po and Ma Tau Kok and distributed to domestic and commercial customers by The Hong Kong and China Gas Company. LPG is imported and stored at Tsing Yi.

The Daya Bay nuclear plant in Guangdong supplies a quarter of Hong Kong's annual power consumption.

Telephone hotlines for gas and electricity services are included in Chapter Five, 'Accommodation'.

Public hygiene

The **Food and Environmental Hygiene Department** (FEHD) is responsible for the obsessive road and pavement sweeping and hosing down that goes on round the clock to keep Hong Kong's streets clean. Recent government initiatives to get the community to take more responsibility for the environment have had some success, but that's not to say the abundant rat and cockroach populations have packed up and moved away. As a result of SARS, fines for spitting, littering and dog-fouling were raised to $1,500. Residents of public housing estates were also introduced to a scheme whereby dripping mops, illegal pets and other anti-social behaviour attracts penalty points, an accumulation of which can lead to eviction.

Smoking in public areas, including restaurants, schools, offices, beaches and parks, was prohibited in 2007. Exceptions include bars, nightclubs, mah-jong parlours and bath houses.

Food hygiene

Poor hygiene in some animal and food markets means that you need to be careful when buying meat and seafood. Most imported meat in supermarkets is thawed and should not be refrozen after purchase – there have been cases in the recent past of supermarkets unwittingly selling contaminated meat and seafood. Some doctors recommend that you don't eat local and other Asian seafood on a regular basis, as it is contaminated with heavy metals, particularly mercury. Imported fish is available at supermarkets. They also recommend that patients who drink milk should buy the imported Australian variety, as Chinese milk may be contaminated by pesticides in the cows' feed. Most of the fruit and vegetables for sale at street markets are grown in the mainland and should be thoroughly washed to remove pesticides – Chinese routinely peel fruit like apples and grapes, and rarely eat raw vegetables.

Take care when eating cooked food or snacks bought from street stalls. If you're in Hong Kong for any length of time, it's more than likely that you will succumb to at least one bout of food poisoning. Vegetarians are not immune.

FOOD LABELLING

Nutritional and genetically modified (GM) food labelling are in the pipeline, but consumers in Hong Kong are generally unconcerned about issues such as GM and imports from over the border, such as rice, have no GM restrictions. Many Chinese restaurants use monosodium glutamate (MSG) in their cooking, and if this bothers you, look for those that advertise themselves as MSG-free.

INFECTIOUS DISEASES

Malaria and rabies are both absent from Hong Kong, but are prevalent elsewhere in the region. Apart from the odd case of cholera, the largest number of infectious cases annually are caused by tuberculosis and chicken pox. Children in Hong Kong are immunised against tuberculosis, hepatitis B, poliomyelitis, diphtheria, tetanus, pertussis, measles, mumps and rubella, so the occurrence of vaccine-preventable infectious diseases among children is relatively low.

Before coming to Hong Kong you should ensure, at a minimum, that your TB and tetanus injections are up to date and that you have been vaccinated against hepatitis A and B.

For the latest information on recommended immunizations for those coming to Hong Kong, check the **World Health Organization**'s guidelines (www. who.int/ith/).

Dengue fever

One disease that tends to make the headlines is dengue fever, a mosquito-borne infection for which there is no cure. The symptoms are fever, coughs and chills, and Hong Kong records around 40–50 cases every year. For more information, visit **www.cheu.gov.hk/eng/index.asp**. To avoid contracting dengue fever, use mosquito repellents and wear long-sleeved clothing and trousers all day if you are out in country areas – unlike other mosquito-borne diseases, dengue fever is spread in daylight hours.

Avian 'flu

Avian (bird) 'flu H5N1 virus is a type of influenza known to be transmitted from infected live birds to humans. It can result in a high fever, chest infection, respiratory failure, multi-organ failure and death, and there have been documented outbreaks in Hong Kong and the Asia region since 1997. What is still unknown is whether avian 'flu will develop a strain allowing human-to-human transmission – a potentially deadly situation for crowded cities such as Hong Kong.

Many locals prefer to eat freshly killed chickens rather than frozen (or 'chilled') chicken, which they say has less flavour. However, in view of the health threats posed by birds, the government is considering whether to ban the sale and slaughter of chickens in Hong Kong. In the meantime, 'rest days' for poultry sellers have been imposed, when trading of live poultry is suspended for cleaning, disinfection and inspection of premises.

For more information on swine and avian 'flu, see **www.cheu.gov.hk/eng/ index.asp**.

AIDS

There were over 4,000 cases of reported HIV infections by the end of 2008. About 435 new cases of HIV infection were diagnosed in 2008 although it is difficult to know how accurate these figures are, as there is a strong stigma attached to the disease here. The Department of Health runs an interactive **AIDS Hotline** (tel. 2780 2211) that connects callers to information, voluntary counselling and HIV testing. Information is also available at **www.aids. gov.hk** and **AIDS Concern** (www.aidsconcern.org.hk).

Other common health problems

Asthma sufferers or people who have breathing difficulties could find Hong Kong inhospitable because of the air pollution. Other side effects can include headaches and nausea. Athlete's foot, swimmer's ear and skin infections are relatively common due to the humid climate.

DRUGS

According to counsellors and advisory services in Hong Kong, the drug scene here is similar to that in most developed countries, the exception being that heroin and opiate use has a long history here and so is perhaps more pure and more available. Ecstacy, ketamine and cannabis are the most common drugs, but solvent abuse by younger kids and alcohol abuse are significant problems. Two services that provide bilingual help for drug users or parents and kids with problems are the **Kely Support Group** (www.kely.org; tel. 2521 6890) and the **Community Drug Advisory Council** (tel. 2521 2880), both at 12 Borrett Road in Mid-Levels.

Kely runs outreach programmes to English-speaking students, including those at international schools. They also have a confidential hotline, 9032 9096, that anyone can call which operates from Monday to Saturday between 2:00 and 10:00 pm. According to Laura Bennett, a youth worker there, most expat teens know where to get drugs. Joe Pianpiano at CDAC, which provides advice and training, goes further: drugs, he says, are 'the ultimate network marketing company'. Most kids get their drugs from friends. Buying them isn't a problem, as most kids have adequate pocket money.

Concerned parents shouldn't ignore signs that their child may have a drugs problem. Pianpiano says to look for 'a cluster of changes' – changing friends, moods, grades, weight and so on, which could mean that 'there's something going on and drugs are a part of it.' He recommends the websites www. drugscope.org.uk and www.adf.org.au (the Australian Drug Foundation) to find out more about drugs. Drug statistics in Hong Kong and other information are available from the government's **Narcotics Division** (www. nd.gov.hk).

HEALTH INSURANCE

Expats working legally full-time in Hong Kong will generally be covered by an employer-sponsored health insurance plan, often with the option for employees to pay top-up fees to increase the level of cover. A basic insurance plan will cover the cost of GP consultation and outpatient treatment, hospitalization, and maternity care. Dental care is usually not included. Those working for multinationals, of course, may well be entitled to substantial private healthcare. Major health insurers include:

- **BUPA** (www.bupa.com.hk; tel. 2517 5175);
- **Manulife (International)** (www.manulife.com.hk; tel. 2108 1188);
- **Blue Cross** (www.bluecross.com.hk; tel. 2163 1333); and
- **AIA** (www.aia.com.hk).

HOSPITALS AND GP SERVICES

Anyone holding a Hong Kong ID card is entitled to subsidized treatment at a government clinic or hospital. A list of public hospitals and services can be found on the **Hospital Authority**'s website (www.ha.org.hk). The **Department of Health**'s website (www.info.gov.hk/dh/) lists registered private hospitals and institutions.

The standard of public healthcare in Hong Kong is high and teaching hospitals such as Queen Mary's on Hong Kong Island and Prince of Wales in Shatin have excellent reputations. Doctors, like dentists, whether in public or private practice, are Western-trained to a very high standard.

A visit to A&E at a public hospital will cost around $100; an outpatient visit $45–100. Public hospitals also offer a private service charged at market rates. In spite of this, some patients still prefer to see an expat, or private, GP. This may be because of communication difficulties or problems connected with follow-up. If you attend a government clinic and require follow-up treatment, you are unlikely to see the same doctor when you return. There is also an over-readiness by some doctors to prescribe drugs for minor ailments. Expect to pay around $600 for a visit to a private doctor and more for treatment. Use word-of-mouth recommendations from friends and colleagues.

Comprehensive health checks such as the 'Well Woman' package are competitively priced by private hospitals.

SPECIALISTS

Chiropodists and podiatrists
German Brunhilde Ng at German Footcare Centre (Yu To Sang Building, 37 Queen's Rd, Central; tel. 2522 6413) can help your bunions and rough skin. In the same building you can find Koo Footcare (Room 901–2; www.foot.com.hk; tel. 2522 0897).

Chiropractors
The **Chiropractic Doctors' Association of Hong Kong** (www.cda.org.hk; tel. 8108 5688) has members practising all over the territory. Clinics include the **Chiropractic Centre** (Room 601, Baskerville House, 13 Duddell Street; tel. 2973 0353) and the **Hong Kong Chiropractors' Clinic** (26 Des Voeux Road; tel. 2522 7998).

Maternity hospitals and services
For full details, see Chapter Eight, 'Having and Raising Children'.

Physiotherapists
Physiotherapists include:

- **Physio-Central** (Unit 2104, 2YF Universal Trade Centre, 3–5A Arbuthnot Road; tel. 2801 4801); and
- **Byrne, Hickman & Partners** (various locations; tel. 2526 7533).

Dentists

There is no government dental care provided for the general public in Hong Kong except an annual check-up for primary school children. However, civil servants – including teachers – do have dental care provided under the terms of their healthcare plans. If you do not have private health insurance, expect to pay about $500 for a check-up at a private dentist before treatment.

The **Dental Council of Hong Kong** (www.dchk.org.hk/) provides a list of registered dentists. Recommendations are usually word-of-mouth from friends and colleagues.

Opticians

Opticians will provide a free eye test if you are buying glasses or contact lenses from them. A full range of hard, soft and disposable contact lenses are available in Hong Kong, and solutions can be bought at opticians or most pharmacies. Shop around to get the best deal on glasses and be prepared to bargain – details of optical shops are included in Chapter Seven, 'Shopping'.

Chemists

Most Western over-the-counter and prescription drugs are available in Hong Kong and can be purchased at pharmacy counters in branches of **Mannings** and **Watsons**, and at dispensaries such as **Victoria Dispensary** (Theatre Lane, Central).

Traditional Chinese medicine

TCM is slowly gaining official recognition in Hong Kong and is now offered via clinics at several public hospitals – visit www.ha.org.hk for details. Common treatments include acupuncture, acupressure, moxibustion and herbal medicines. Some drugs found in Chinese medicine, such as ephedra, are legal in Hong Kong, despite being banned in other parts of the world. A list of registered Chinese Medicine practitioners is available from the **Chinese Medicine Council of Hong Kong** (www.cmchk.org.hk). Again, word-of-mouth helps here, but Cecilia The at **Vitality Centre** comes recommended (www.vitalitycenter.com.hk; tel. 2537 1118).

For acupuncture, try Helen He at **Holistic Central** (16/F, Hing Wai Building, 36 Queen's Road, Central; tel. 2523 8044). Other English-speaking acupuncturists work out of the **Quality Chinese Medical Centre** (Unit A, 5/F Jade Centre, 98 Wellington Street, Central; tel. 2881 8267) and **Holistic Central**

(16/F, Hing Wai Building, 36 Queen's Road, Central; tel. 2523 8044). **OT&P** (www.otandp.com; various locations) uses acupuncture, holistic practice and functional medicine, which includes herbs, to treat stress, eczema and breathing-related difficulties.

STRESS

Not everyone is suited to working abroad and the stresses of coping with a new climate, food, culture, lifestyle and work environment will make themselves felt quite quickly. Before you accept a job in Hong Kong, it may be sensible to undergo a self-assessment to see whether you – and, if applicable, your family – stand a reasonable chance of being happy and successful here. That is, if you have any choice in the matter. General 'ideal' qualities for those going to live overseas that have been identified by psychologists include a sense of adventure, curiosity, open-mindedness, ability to cope with ambiguity, a strong sense of self and a keenness to communicate and become part of the host culture.

Although Hong Kong is very comfortable for Western expats when compared with other destinations in Asia, it is unforgiving to those who can't keep up with six-day working weeks, frequent overseas travel and the combined pressures of the fast pace of life, volume of people and cramped space. In Hong Kong, it's a given that you'll be at the end of a mobile phone or an e-mail away most hours of the day and night. Hong Kong people spend more time on mobile phones than virtually anyone else in Asia. Because of the costs associated with bringing out foreign employees, employers are expecting much more in terms of personal investment from their expat staff: Hong Kong is no longer a junket.

Partners and children experience other stresses. Partners who may not have wanted to come in the first place, and may well have had to put their own careers on hold as a consequence, may be reluctant to accept responsibility for the family's emotional and social adjustment. While one of you may have a demanding job you enjoy, the other one is stuck at home with nothing to do. This can be potentially isolating and lonely, and it's extremely important to establish a group of friends as soon as possible. Throughout this book, I've suggested ways of finding groups of like-minded people, support groups and different ways to make the most of life in Hong Kong. Hiring a helper to assist with daily chores can provide a vital support to homemakers, especially those whose partners are away on business often (see Chapter Eight, 'Having and Raising Children').

For extra help and support you could think of using a **relocations service** to help with adjustments – social, professional and cultural. They will also assist, of course, with the logistics of getting you and your family and home out to Hong Kong and back again. Details of relocations services are provided in Chapter Five, 'Accommodation'.

COUNSELLING SERVICES

Many counselling services offer a sliding fee scale, including the **YMCA** in Salisbury Road (tel. 2783 3360, appointments only), **ReSource The Counselling Centre** in Central (www.resourcecounselling.org; tel. 2523 8979) and the non-denominational **St John's Counselling Service** (www.stjohnscathedral.org.hk/counselling.htm; tel. 2525 7207/8). St John's staff offer counselling on a range of issues, including relationship difficulties, problems adapting to life in Hong Kong, grief, trauma, eating disorders, sexuality and substance abuse. They also run a popular Skilled Helping Relationships (SHR) experiential course that focuses on personal growth.

Harmony House (www.harmonyhousehk.org) offers refuge to victims of domestic violence. **Soul Talk** (www.soultalk.org; tel. 2525 6644) is a support network for women in emotional crisis and provides advice as well as a safe house. The website also has a useful listing of support groups for men, women and children. **The Samaritans** (www.samaritans.org.hk; tel. 2896 0000) offers a 24-hour hotline and e-mail service in English.

Support groups include:

- **Cancer Link Support Centre** (tel. 3667 3000);
- **Alcoholics Anonymous** (www.aa-hk.org; tel. 2522 5665);
- **Overeaters Anonymous** (tel. 2899 0823);
- **Remar Association** (drug-related issues; tel. 3193 4919); and
- **Horizons Lesbian & Gay Hotline** (www.horizons.org.hk; tel. 2815 9268).

Other psychologists can be contacted at **Therapy Associates** (www.talhk.com; tel. 2869 1962).

ALTERNATIVE AND COMPLEMENTARY HEALTH

The website **www.holisticasia.com** publishes details of forthcoming workshops, lectures, meditations and so on, as well as a useful services directory that includes details of where to find aromatherapy, life coaching, astrology, auras, numerology, crystals and much more. **Heartbeat** (www. heartbeat.com.hk) lists information and services offered by natural health practitioners, and provides details of seminars and links to other useful sites such as the **Natural Health Organisation** (www.naturalhealth.org.hk).

Other shops and organizations offering alternative and complementary health medicines include:

- **The New Age Shop** (7 Old Bailey Street, Soho; www.newageshop.com. hk; tel. 2810 8694) hosts visiting and resident psycho-spiritual practitioners, as well as selling a range of New Age books and health-related products.
- **Vitality Center** (801 Commercial House, 35 Queen's Road, Central; www. vitalitycenter.com.hk; tel. 2537 1118) offers a range of health services, including homeopathy, aromatherapy, nutritional therapy, cranial sacral therapy and reiki.
- **Wholistic Centre** (2202 Causeway Bay Plaza 1, 489 Hennessy Road; tel. 2882 2703; www.wholistic-centre.com) provides hypnotherapy services, past life therapy, qigong and reiki.
- Balance and wellness-focused **Zama** (Unit 1006 Kinwick Centre, 32 Hollywood Road; www.zamaint.com; tel. 2850 6400) offers detox, clinical nutrition, food allergy testing, iridology and counselling services and training.
- The **Raja Yoga Centre** (17 Dragon Road, Tin Hau; www.rajayoga.com.hk; tel. 2806 3008) offers meditation practice and teaching.
- **Optimum Health Centre** (2/F, Prosperous Commercial Building, 54–58 Jardine's Bazaar, Causeway Bay; www.naturalhealing.com.hk; tel. 2577 3798) provides homeopathy, oxygen therapy, foot reflexology and colon hydrotherapy.
- **HydroHealth Colon Hydrotherapy** (Central and Causeway Bay; www. hydrohealth.com.hk) is another reputable colon health centre.

PHYSICAL FITNESS

Hong Kong has a number of affordable health and fitness clubs equipped with comprehensive gyms, personal trainers, exercise classes, juice bars, steam and sauna rooms and beauty/spa services, etc. These include:

- **Pure Fitness** (32 Hollywood Road; Langham Place and IFC2; www.pure-fit.com; tel. 2970 3366);
- **Fitness First** (check website www.fitnessfirst.com.hk for locations);
- **California Fitness** (check website www.californiafitness.com for locations);
- **Seasons Sports Club** (3/F, Citibank Plaza; tel. 2878 6288). This club can boast that rare thing – an indoor pool;
- **Fightin' Fit** (2/F, World Trust Tower, 50 Stanley Street; www.fightinfit.com.hk; tel. 2526 6648). The club offers a combination of exercise gym, martial arts and massage. They also have a gym on Lamma (Island Gym).

Exercise and training food supplements are available from gyms and at the **American Nutrition Company** (23 Lyndhurst Terrace, Central and Discovery Bay Plaza). More information on sports and fitness activities is included in Chapter Nineteen, 'Sports'.

Yoga

As in other cities, physical yoga has really taken off in Hong Kong in the past few years, and many dedicated yoga centres now offer hot yoga, hatha, iyengar and ashtanga yoga at competitive rates. Yoga centres include:

- **Planet Yoga** (20/F, Silver Fortune Plaza, 1 Wellington Street, Central; www.planetyoga.com.hk; tel. 2525 8288). A very full programme of classes running throughout the day includes several different types of yoga, cosmic dance, mantra and meditation, and kids' yoga;
- **Yoga Central** (4/F, 13 Wyndham Street, Central; www.yogacentral.com.hk; tel. 2982 4308). Mainly hatha yoga;
- **Yoga Limbs** (3rd Floor, Dot Com House, 128 Wellington Street; www.yogalimbs.com; tel. 2525 7415). Includes Mom & Baby and One-to-One sessions;
- **Pure Yoga** (www.pure-yoga.com; tel. 2971 0055). Hot yoga, power yoga and yin yoga.

More information on yoga is available from **The Yoga Society of Hong Kong** (www.yogahongkong.com).

Tai chi

Join a free outdoors tai chi class at **Victoria Park** (Causeway Bay), **Hong Kong Park** (Admiralty – see http://contemporarytaichi.com for details) or the piazza of the **Hong Kong Cultural Centre**, TST (call the Hong Kong Tourism Board Visitor Hotline on 2508 1234 for more information).

SPA AND BEAUTY

Western-style spas

There are several luxurious city spas offering body pampering and skin beautifying treatments. New spas often offer special opening deals, or you can get a facial, manicure and pedicure as a practice model, at $80 per treatment, at **The International Spa and Beauty College** (10/F, Silver Fortune Plaza, 1 Wellington Street, Central; tel. 2526 8818). **The Beautiful Skin Centre** (Shop 344, Pacific Place; tel. 2877 8911) and **The Well-Being Centre Kowloon Club** (24 Salisbury Road, TST; tel. 2269 7833) offer grooming including Brazilian waxing, body sculpting and the irresistible-sounding 'Heaven on Earth' spa experience.

The **Elemis Day Spa** (9/F, Century Square, 1 D'Aguilar Street, Central; tel. 2521 6660) offers facials, 'spa rituals' for couples and individuals, nail buffs and massages – try their famous 'Hawaiian Wave Four Hands Massage'. **The Frederique Spa**'s body worship includes 'Body Oil Ceremony', 'The Sea Glow' and 'Self-Heating Mud Booties' (4/F, Wilson House, 19–27 Wyndham Street, Central; tel. 2522 3054). Visit these spas and others at www.paua. com.hk.

Other well-regarded spas include **Ellespa at The Repulse Bay** (www. ellespa.com; tel. 2537 7736), which offers services including massage for mums-to-be, Indian head massage, hot stone treatments, oxygen facials, simultaneous manicure and pedicure and reflexology. Downtown, **Retreat at the Firm** (15/F, The Centrium, 60 Wyndham Street; tel. 2525 6696) offers 'pamper parties' for between two and twenty people, where you get to choose the treatments, 'Hair Miles' and a treatment 'that honours self-love and worthiness'. Nearby **Ziz Skincare** (5/F, Hang Shun Building, 10–12

Wyndham Street; www.ziz.com.hk; tel. 2111 2767) caters specifically to men.

Hair salon **Zucoma African Salon** in Gold Shine Tower, 9/F, Queen's Road, Sheung Wan (tel. 2544 7188) specializes in cuts for black hair, corn braids, etc.

Chinese massage

There are many Chinese masseurs operating in Hong Kong, and massage parlours in Mongkok, Central, Wanchai and Causeway Bay charge a fraction of what you pay at Western-style spas. These places generally score low on ambience, with no chirruping bird calls and rose petals, but high on value for money. Note, however, that you may need to ask Cantonese-speaking friends or colleagues to help you book. For details of trained blind masseurs, contact **The Hong Kong Society for the Blind's Career Support and Development Centre** (tel. 2778 8332).

Foot reflexology and massage

Centres providing foot reflexology as well as body massage include **The Only Herbal Steam** (17–19 Percival Street, Causeway Bay; tel. 2572 2223) and **Zhong Yi Guan** (30 Yik Yam Street, Happy Valley; tel. 2832 9339). Expect to pay around $180 for a 50-minute foot massage and $200 for a 50-minute body massage. Cheaper options for foot massage (under $100 for 45 minutes) include the **Heartlink Therapeutic Reflexology Centre** (Unit 802, 8/F, Wellable Commercial Building, 513–517 Hennessy Road, Causeway Bay; tel. 3962 8422) and the **Blessing Leisure Centre** (1/F, Tai Kun Mansion, 452 Lockhart Road, Causeway Bay; tel. 2572 8192). All of the above can speak *some* English.

Over the border in Shenzhen, it costs from $30 an hour for a back massage, $25 an hour for a foot massage and extra for pedicure. One place that gives a reasonable service for the price quoted above is **Xinghe Lie Fallow Center**: tel. 6551 2289 to arrange an appointment from Hong Kong or 0755 2629 1513 for a complimentary pick-up from Lowu station – they can drop you back at the railway station when you've finished. Again, you need to be able to speak Cantonese or Putonghua for booking.

FACIAL SURGERY AND INVASIVE TREATMENTS

Clinics offering more invasive treatments such as Botox, peels and intense pulsed light treatment include:

- **The Face Magic Haven** (2B, 30/F, The Centrium, 60 Wyndham Street, Central; tel. 2524 6565);
- **Neoface Clinic** (Room 430, Prince's Building, Central; tel. 2530 2338; www.neofaceclinic.com); and
- **Bella Skincare** (Room 1722, Tower 1, New World Tower, 16–18 Queen's Road, Central; tel. 2526 6352).

Chapter Ten

Saving and Spending

They say money talks, and Cantonese is its mother tongue. Water is to a thirsty man what money is to this trading port. It's no surprise that Cantonese slang for money is 'sui' – water. 'Mo sui' means 'I don't have any money'. 'Sui' is also the other half of feng shui ('wind water') and sentiment and superstition continue to have a significant influence on the city's finance in all manner of bizarre ways. Financial analysts have noted that whenever soap star Adam Cheng appears in a TV series, the Hang Seng Index drops. This has been measured and correlated over the last 12 years. It even has a name – 'the Adam Cheng effect'.

PART OF THE PLAN

It was only after I came to Hong Kong that, for the first time in my life, I found myself with money left over in the bank each month. Over time this money started to accrue and demand some thought about what to do with it. Other women I've talked to have found themselves in a similar situation. One of the first challenges you will face in Hong Kong is managing your money, especially if you are single or a divorced woman who left the money side of things to your husband. Force of circumstance will drive you to find out what sort of financial vehicles for saving and investments are available if you hadn't bothered or needed to bother before.

With no tax on investments and a flat 17% salary tax (2009–10), Hong Kong represents a tremendous opportunity to build serious wealth compared with Europe, Australia and New Zealand. For young or middle-aged couples, Hong Kong is part of the plan – a desirable career move with huge potential for savings when accommodation and education allowances are provided by the company. For older couples, Hong Kong can provide an opportunity to secure a nest egg that will see them through retirement.

Whichever stage of your savings plan you're at, Hong Kong can provide a wealth of financial planners and advisors to assist you. They'll be beating a path to your door in no time. But beware – Hong Kong is not as well regulated as

38. Sights such as this are becoming rare due to massive redevelopment
Photograph taken by Stanley Ng

places such as the UK and Australia, and investors should proceed warily, as detailed below.

The significance of the 'dollar peg'

The Hong Kong dollar is pegged to the US dollar at HK$7.78 and one Hong Kong dollar is worth just more than 1 Renminbi. This means that the Hong Kong dollar broadly follows the same ups and downs as the US$. It also contributes to the expensiveness of Hong Kong as a place to do business, when compared with other de-linked Asian currencies in the region. If the Hong Kong dollar loses its peg to the American dollar – and financiers speculate that at some time, although no-one knows when, it may need to in order to reduce costs in Hong Kong, which are being kept artificially high due to the peg – then it could devalue by about a third. Another scenario sees the Hong Kong dollar merging with the Chinese yuan when that currency becomes fully convertible. Chinese yuan deposits can be made at most banks in the city.

BANKS

Personal banking is offered by all major banks, including:

- Hongkong and Shanghai Banking Corporation (HSBC – www.hsbc.com. hk);
- Hang Seng Bank (www.hangseng.com);
- Bank of China (www.bochk.com);
- Standard Chartered Bank (www.standardchartered.com.hk); and
- Bank of East Asia (www.hkbea.com).

Other retail banks include **Citibank** (www.citibank.com.hk) and **Dao Heng Bank** (www.daoheng.com). Non-retail branches of British banks in Hong Kong include **Barclays International Banking** (42/F, Citibank Tower, 3 Garden Road, Central; tel. 2903 2000) and **Lloyds TSB Bank** (Suites 3901–04, Two Exchange Square, Central; tel. 2847 3000).

Business banking services are mentioned in Chapter Thirteen, 'Work'.

Banking hours

Banks are open from Monday to Friday between 9:00 am and 4:30 pm, and on Saturdays from 9:00 am to 12:30 pm. Cashpoints (ATMs) are available at all times. You should avoid banks at lunchtime unless you have a lot of time to queue.

Banking services

All banks in Hong Kong provide product information and account statements in English and Chinese. Major banks offer the same services you would normally expect from a bank with international standing:

- savings and current accounts;
- time deposit accounts;
- foreign currency accounts (with no restriction on the inflows and outflows of currency);
- money transfers;
- standing orders;
- direct debits;
- currency exchange (free for account holders, but restricted to certain branches);
- credit; and
- a range of investment and insurance services.

Most banks provide insurance quotes online, as well as contextual information regarding the Hong Kong stock market, types of investment vehicles and financial planning basics. You can plan the cost of your wedding, house move and much more with their online models.

The HSBC and Hang Seng banks share free-to-use ATM facilities, as do many of the Chinese banks with Standard Chartered. ATM facilities for these banks in Macau are also accessible to Hong Kong-based account holders. HSBC offers Hong Kong customers savings and deposit services at its branches in Shenzhen and Shanghai. The Bank of China offers a specially tailored service for overseas Chinese clients.

American Express cardholders can use Jetco ATMs and can withdraw cash and travellers' cheques at Express Cash ATMs. MasterCard and Visa holders can withdraw money from HSBC ATMs.

Bank charges

Many Hong Kong banks charge customers for the following:

- if you close your account within three months of opening it;

- if your account is inactive for a year with less than $2,000 in it (charged every six months);
- telegraphic transfer (outward remittances); and
- amendment of standing order instructions.

Beware of credit card plans that were free to join but then start to charge you (without notice) after the first year, and 'relationship banking' plans that impose hefty charges if your balance drops below a fixed level.

Setting up a bank account

You will need to call into a bank branch in person to open an account, bringing along your Hong Kong ID card or passport, proof of address, and a minimum deposit amount of around $1,000. No-frills current and savings accounts are available, but the trend is for banks to hook their customers into a 'one-stop shop' account that links all your accounts to one card. Preferential services including priority when queueing and higher credit limits are given to customers joining more expensive service plans.

Cheques are still used in Hong Kong to a large extent, so it is useful to set up a cheque/current account with a cheque book. An **EPS** card functions as a debit card when you're out shopping. Supermarkets, chain stores and department stores take EPS cards, although restaurants, small shops and travel companies generally do not.

You can leave your Hong Kong bank account in place after you leave and you don't have to be a resident in Hong Kong to open an account.

Telephone banking

Telephone banking offers a time-efficient alternative to effect transactions such as opening an account, money transfers between your accounts, checking your balance, reporting lost credit cards, ordering a cheque book, checking deposit interest rates or obtaining information from bank staff. Most services, except money transfers to foreign currency accounts, are available 24 hours. You will usually be asked if you want telebanking services, which are free and come in addition to normal bank services, when setting up your account.

E-banking

These days, banks are encouraging their customers to go online to complete transactions such as tax and bill payments, transfers and so on. The service is free and additional to normal bank services.

Paying bills

Tax, water, electricity and gas bills can all be paid via the Jetco payment terminals at banks. Alternatively, you can set up a direct debit ('autopay') arrangement with your bank, pay PCCW phone bills at Hong Kong Post Offices or 7-Eleven shops or post a cheque to the relevant authority.

PPS is a service which facilitates automatic payment from your bank account to over 150 merchants, including credit card companies, charities, universities and telecom services, through phone or Internet. To open a PPS account, visit www.ppshk.com.

Obtaining credit cards

Obtaining credit cards is generally an easy business in Hong Kong if you have a good credit record and a regular salary coming in. Card incentives include annual fee waivers and free gifts. Credit cards offered by major banks generally charge a very low rate of interest. Many credit cards have tie-ins with other bonus point schemes such as 'Asia Miles' or can give discounts on major Hong Kong brands – HSBC is good in this respect. Cards generally accepted in Hong Kong include Visa, Mastercard and American Express.

Credit cards are accepted at most large shops and restaurants, but not at smaller Chinese restaurants (including some of the seafood restaurants on the Outlying Islands) or low-cost service providers such as the dry-cleaning firm Clean Living.

MONEY CHANGERS

Money changers in Hong Kong charge commission, so visitors staying for only a short time should shop around for competitive rates. Shops recommended by the Hong Kong Tourist Association include **First International Resources**, which has branches centrally located at Shop 42, G/F, Mirador Mansion, 54–64 Nathan Road, TST (open 9:00 am–6:00 pm) and Shop 12, Unpaid Concourse, Kowloon Tong KCR Station, Kowloon Tong (open 7:00 am–7:00 pm). Banks offer their account holders commission-free exchange.

FINANCIAL PLANNING

Even if you have a rudimentary understanding of the different investment vehicles offered to you in Hong Kong, it makes sense to seek professional

advice from a reputable financial advisor who you will be able to go back to as
your circumstances change and you need to adjust your plans. When choosing a financial advisor, Melanie Nutbeam, Director of International Financial
Planning with financial planning company ipac, recommends that you:

- get a referral from someone, but do your homework;
- check whether you match the advisor's client type;
- check whether they are regulated, and the longevity and track record of
  the institution;
- check the advisors' qualifications;
- check that they disclose information about charges up front; and
- don't do nothing – 'don't let uncertainty freeze you into inaction'.

There are several different local bodies acting as regulators of the financial
industry – the **Securities and Futures Commission** (SFC), the **Insurance
Authority**, the **MPF Authority** and the **Monetary Authority** which regulates the banks. The SFC regulates most financial planners in Hong Kong,
and their website, www.sfc.hk, has a list of approved advisors.

As with the regulation of the financial services industry worldwide, however,
regulation is not a guarantee. Even though a company may be regulated,
not all of the products it is selling may be authorized for sale: in Hong Kong,
a huge number of unregulated funds are sold on a private placement basis.
Most financial advisors work on commission, but it is possible to find those
who charge a fee for advice. Generally, reputable advisors do not charge a fee
for a first meeting.

If you are unhappy about the financial planning advice you have received,
put your complaint in writing to your advisor first. If they do not address the
complaint, then lodge a complaint with the SFC (8/F, Chater House, 8 Connaught Road, Central; tel. 2840 9222).

If you are being employed by a company, your financial planning should start
ahead of your arrival in Hong Kong with the effective structuring of your financial package. Take tax advice to ensure you maximize the tax advantages open
to you in Hong Kong; for example, if your employer pays your rent, holiday
allowance and children's education fees rather than including them in your

salary, you can avoid these components being taxed at the standard salary tax rate. You should also inform the Inland Revenue Department of your home country that you are leaving for Hong Kong.

More information is provided in Chapter Thirteen, 'Work'.

INVESTMENTS AND SAVING

If you plan to return to your home country, most financial advisors recommend saving in that currency, especially if you plan to buy property back home. Hong Kong is a sophisticated financial market with a range of investment options for expats based here. The following are widely available through the major banks and can often be activated by phone/Internet as well as from inside a bank:

- mutual funds;
- online no-load trading;
- the Tracker Fund – a fund that follows the benchmark of the Hang Seng stock exchange;
- IPOs;
- bonds;
- hedging; and
- currency trading.

According to Andrew Eden, Managing Director of the independent financial advisory company Ernest Maude, 'Having witnessed and experienced the chaos in financial markets over the last few years, there is a return to more conservative planning and core investments such as property. Many expats were sold long-term savings and multi-currency mortgage facilities', he adds, commenting that it is still a case of 'buyer beware' in the city. He recommends taking two or three different opinions and maintaining flexibility by not getting into long-term commitments beyond the next five to ten years.

Expats should also check out interest rates on term deposits with their own banks for deposits in their home country's currency. Interest rates on term deposits of these currencies may be higher than those offered by local banks.

Property

Property is expensive in Hong Kong. Real estate went up 20 per cent in 2009 and looks to rise a further 20–30 per cent in 2010. Purchasing property is not something undertaken lightly by non-permanent residents. When buying, equity of 30% is commonly required and it can be difficult to get a mortgage from the bank if you are an expat rather than a permanent resident. Banks are generally unsympathetic to those with no track record of income in the territory. In this case, it may be better to go through a financial advisor who has already developed a relationship with a bank and to whom they refer their clients. If you plan to buy property in Hong Kong or elsewhere in Asia, for example Bali or Thailand, it goes without saying that you should consider the tax implications before you buy.

For more information on mortgages, see Chapter Five, 'Accommodation'.

Wills

Debbie Annells, Director at Equity Trust, recommends expats reconsider their wills when coming to Hong Kong:

> A will that's valid in your home country may not be valid here and you need to take into account your changing assets. If you die, your relatives may not be able to just come and take your children home; they should be appointed as guardians in your will.

Just as useful, make a list of all your assets – including life insurance if you have it. In the event of your death, your next of kin will be able to track down the insurers, who otherwise won't come calling. Also, appoint someone to be your power of attorney so that they can access your bank account if you become incapacitated.

Tax and inheritance

Another thing to bear in mind if you come from a common law country such as the UK is the possibility of complications arising from marriage to someone from a civil law country such as the Philippines or the US. Annells says:

> In the event of your demise, and if you have a wife and children that hold a passport from the Philippines, all of your assets will pass into the hands of that family in the Philippines. If you marry a US citizen and bequeath your assets to him or her and then you die, you can get the worst of all worlds as your assets may be liable to US tax.

If you are domiciled in a country other than Hong Kong, you may inherit tax exposures – even though you are living in Hong Kong. Similarly, if you are still using a credit card from your home country, the money you remit back to pay off your credit card debts may fall into the tax net of your home country.

FINANCIAL NEWS AND EDUCATION RESOURCES

Hong Kong-based publications with extensive financial news include *The Asian Wall Street Journal*, the *Far Eastern Economic Review* and the Money pages of the *South China Morning Post* and the *Standard*. Overseas publications such as *The Ecomonist* are available at Central/Admiralty news-stands and magazine booths, including those on the Star Ferry concourse.

The **Hong Kong Electronic Investors Resource Centre** website (www. hkeirc.org) aims to help potential investors learn about investing, locate key facts and carry out research. The **SFC** website (www.sfc.hk) includes a register of licensed institutes and products, as well as a Q&A section and downloadable factsheets. Another popular resource is **Quamnet** (www.quamnet. com).

Chapter Eleven

Staying Safe

CRIME

Hong Kong is generally a safe place to live, work and bring up a family. The 24-hour nature of the city means that there are people of all ages on the streets till all hours. Taxis are ubiquitous so it's never difficult to find one to take you back home; nightbuses also run between Hong Kong and Kowloon.

Hong Kong is definitely one of the safest places for women in Asia. That said, indecent assault is alarmingly common – a survey once reported that about 60% of women had been indecently assaulted on public transport. I count myself in this statistic. Petty thievery and apartment break-ins have also happened to friends of mine. If you are a victim of crime, report it as soon as possible to your local police station. I have found the police efficient and friendly.

Triads won't bother you if you don't bother them: avoid black spots such as Mongkok and Sham Shui Po late at night. Mongkok, by day the busiest part of Hong Kong – its name means 'busy corner' – is overrun with markets and has a wonderfully colourful, bustling atmosphere. But police activity, drugs, gambling dens and prostitution make parts of the neighbourhood unsafe after dark.

Call tel. 2860 2000 to locate the nearest police station.

Since late 2008, there have been a small number of acid attacks around the city, including Mongkok and busy pedestrian areas. The culprit/s have yet to be apprehended.

RELIGIONS

Hong Kong's colonial history and freedom of religion means that there is a profusion of religious communities operating in this quintessentially materialist culture. Although their impact on politics and governance in the territory is difficult to assess, the former head of the Catholic Church in the

39. Market stall on Cat Street

Photograph taken by Stanley Ng

city, Bishop Zen, was outspoken in his defence of democracy, whilst Buddhist leaders are often seen shoring up Beijing's influence. Somewhat ironically for the secular mainland, 'Buddha's birthday' was officially made a public holiday in Hong Kong after the 1997 handover.

An estimated one third of the Hong Kong population practise a form of Taosim which includes elements of Confucianism and polytheism. Ancestor worship is common – public holidays twice a year are given over to grave-sweeping and burning paper money, etc. – as is seeking the blessings of popular gods thought to protect fishermen, businesses or family/fertility. Small red shrines adorned with jaffa oranges and joss sticks are common in the homes of the older generation, and are often observable at outdoor sites, too. The Chinese almanac is also important when it comes to choosing lucky dates for business, marriage and the compatibility of partners.

Larger religious groups in Hong Kong include Buddhists (600,000), Protestants (300,000) and Catholics (250,000):

- **Christian.** Protestant denominations include Baptist, Lutheran, Adventist, Anglican, Methodist and Pentecostal. Two weekly publications, *The Christian Weekly* and *The Christian Times*, are published in Hong Kong. The *Sunday Examiner* is the local English language magazine published by the Catholic church. Church notices and times of services appear in the Saturday edition of the *South China Morning Post*.
- **Jewish.** Hong Kong's Jewish community includes three main congregations: the Ohel Leah (Orthodox in the Sephardic tradition), the United Jewish Congregation (Reform/Conservative) and the Chabad Lubavitch. More information is available from the Jewish Community Centre (www.jcc.org.hk; tel. 2801 5440).
- **Muslim.** There are about 80,000 Muslims in the city. The largest masjid is the Kowloon Masjid and Islamic Centre on Nathan Road in TST. Other masjids include Jamia Masjid on Shelley Street and the Masjid Ammar and Osman Ramju Sadick Islamic Centre in Wanchai.
- **Hindu.** The Hindu temple in Happy Valley functions as the centre for Hong Kong's 15,000-strong Hindu community.
- **Sikh.** The Sikh temple in Wanchai serves the Sikh community.

Other religious communities include the Mormons (22,000), Russian/Greek Orthodox Church and Jehovah's Witnesses.

THE POLITICAL SYSTEM

Under the Basic Law agreed with Britain prior to the handover in 1997, Hong Kong is supposed to enjoy a high degree of autonomy and to suffer no drastic changes in the way its government is run. In practice, Beijing has the power to interpret grey areas of the Basic Law and overturn decisions made by Hong Kong's **Legislative Council** (LegCo), as happened in the infamous 'Right of Abode' case.

The LegCo has about 60 members, of whom 24 are democratically elected members of geographical constituencies. Thirty other members are elected from functional constituencies with a limited electoral base – 'functional constituencies' here roughly translates as 'business sectors'. A further six members are hand-picked by an Election Committee of 800 people. The Chief Executive is also chosen by the Election Committee, which in turn is elected by about 163,500 voters, including corporate voters. Unsurprisingly, then, Hong Kong's political elite are often criticized as being out of touch with the grass roots – or as one commentator put it:

> a government behaving as if its only constituency were Hong Kong tycoons.

Major political parties include the **Democratic Party**, the **Democratic Alliance for the Betterment of Hong Kong** and the **Liberal Party**.

Beijing has yet to promise full democratic elections, or even an election for Chief Executive, but has hinted at 2017 as a possible date for the latter.

Chapter Twelve

Getting Married and Bereavement

MARRIAGE

Whether you plan to marry in a registry office or a church, the first thing you need to do is to give a written **Notice of Marriage** in advance at a marriage registry – see **www.immd.gov.hk/ehtml/bdmreg_4.htm** for details. The cost for this is $305. If you plan to get married in a marriage registry, you can make your *Appointment Booking for Giving of Marriage Notice* online at **http://marriage.esd.gov.hk/eng/default.htm** (if you book online, you can choose your date up to three months and fourteen days in advance). Otherwise you must go to a marriage registry in person. The *Notice of Marriage* will be exhibited for a minimum of 15 days, after which time a marriage can take place.

When filing a 'Notice of Marriage', one or both of you will be required to submit identity cards and passports for inspection. If your intended spouse is out of Hong Kong, a photocopy of their passport will be sufficient at this stage, although the original passport will need to be shown before the marriage date. Spouses do not need to be resident in Hong Kong to marry here, but they do need to be over 21 – or 16, with consent. After a 'Notice of Marriage' has been given, the marriage must take place within three months.

Visit **www.lcsd.gov.hk/wedding/en/index.php** to find a list of marriage registries and other public worship venues licensed to celebrate marriage, lucky dates for marriage, and tips on wedding arrangements and planning. Popular marriage registries include Cotton Tree Drive Marriage Registry in Hong Kong Park and City Hall Marriage Registry in Central. For these two registries, a 'Notice of Marriage' must be given at the Hong Kong Marriage Registration Office, 3/F, Queensway Government Offices, Low Block, Admiralty.

The ceremony at the registry office is short – 15 minutes – during which time the bride and bridegroom and witnesses sign the marriage certificate. You are permitted to include your own readings and wedding vows in the ceremony as long as you don't over-run your allotted 15 minutes. You can also bring a CD to be played during the ceremony. Confetti is not allowed to be thrown

40. Legislative Coucil Building, Central
Photograph taken by the author

inside the registry but may be thrown outside, as long as it is cleared away afterwards. The price of the ceremony is $715–1,935, depending on the day and time.

Arrangements for a marriage in church should be agreed with the church concerned.

BEREAVEMENT

In Chinese culture, burial is considered essential to bring good luck to future generations, but the city has run out of places to bury the 40,000 people who die each year. A recent report commented that there were 34,630 urns on the government's list awaiting accommodation in a niche or columbarium.

Deaths from natural causes where the deceased was attended by a registered medical practitioner must be registered within 24 hours at the registry of the district where the death occurred. If the deceased is to be buried outside Hong Kong, a permit for the removal of the body should be obtained. If they are to be cremated, a relative of the deceased should approach the Department of Health and the Food and Environmental Hygiene Department.

More information on procedures, location of registries and fees is available at **www.immd.gov.hk/ehtml/bdmreg.htm**.

Part Two

Working in Hong Kong

Chapter Thirteen

Working and Networking

The Grant Thornton International Business Report 2010 found that Hong Kong private businesses reported the biggest drop worldwide in stress levels in the last three years. The reason, according to one tax partner at the company? 'In the last decade Hong Kong's privately held businesses have been facing one historic up and down after another. These business owners learnt and became proficient in coping with the adverse effects brought by the economic downturn from their continuous experiences; and today, they will not exhaust themselves on any unnecessary worry and stress anymore.'

BUSINESS ENVIRONMENT

Compared to other cities in Asia, Hong Kong is an easy place to do business as an expat. A free trade environment (low profits tax and an unrestricted flow of capital and foreign exchange), the rule of law, an excellent infrastructure and a skilled workforce are often cited as the main competitive advantages enjoyed by businesses that operate out of Hong Kong. The widespread use of English and low-cost telecom systems are other important factors.

Expatriate entrepreneurs running their own small and medium-sized enterprises (SMEs) rave about the connectedness of the business community here – 'networking in the true sense of the word'. Although expats constantly joke that they are in Hong Kong 'for the sunshine and the money', many are enthusiastic about the work they do here and choose to stay long-term to build a career. Melanie Nutbeam, Director of International Financial Planning with financial planning company ipac, has been here for more than fifteen years and loves it. She says:

> Hong Kong provides opportunities for people to carve out their own niches – and for people who are hard working, they'll find these opportunities. Especially for professional women, Hong Kong is an accepting community because it's a business community. People take women in business seriously. Networking is important – business is based on contacts and spheres of influence. If I go to a cocktail party on a Thursday night, it's understood that I'm there as a woman who's networking.

41. Night view – Hong Kong Island
Photograph taken by Stanley Ng

173

It doesn't bother Melanie when the distinctions between private and profes-sional life become blurred. She says:

> *Your professional style becomes incorporated into your lifestyle. People socialize with those they do business with.*

She also notes that Hong Kong

> *... is a very giving community. If you're looking for work, you can ring the MD and nine out of ten times they will say 'come and have a coffee'. And because I experienced that, I do that for people who are new in town. We appreciate that people who arrive in Hong Kong have got the guts to get up and go and we're happy to support and encourage this.*

Simon Scott, who offers international consultancy services on legal matters via his own company, Scotts, arrived in Hong Kong in 1987 and his enthusi-asm for the territory has never wavered. He's in good company. 'There are a relatively large number of hard-core, long-term professionals in Hong Kong. In fact I think that the days of a 2/3/5 year rotation are long gone and such persons are a minority or simply do not like Hong Kong …The growth of China is actually bringing higher standards of work and more opportunities, so my son's generation of aspiring investment bankers are all looking at Hong Kong as the place to be, and then maybe in Shanghai.'

EXPATRIATE EMPLOYMENT SECTORS

The opportunities in Hong Kong for expats range from junior to medium and high-end executive positions, although increases in the local talent pool mean that some sectors are heavily localized. And of the international com-panies which have a presence in Hong Kong, 90 per cent will have branches in mainland China and will recruit locally, if at all possible, to fill positions there. Putonghua, therefore, has become a much more critical skill than it was, even five years ago.

The main sectors of work for expats are finance, accountancy, sales and mar-keting, IT, human resources, legal, telecommunications, and industrial (lo-gistics, engineering, etc.). Although Hong Kong is renowned for its high-end expat salaries, with luxury accommodation, private healthcare and private education for children thrown in, since the global economic downturn, some of these perks have been trimmed.

REQUIREMENTS

Expats looking to work in Hong Kong need to be able to demonstrate a high degree of professionalism, experience and specialist knowledge. Increasingly, language proficiency in Cantonese and Mandarin/Putonghua is desirable, especially now that the mainland has become a key focus of growth for most international companies and as Hong Kong responds to political pressure from the north. According to Anthony Behan, Managing Director of The Communication Group, a consultancy specializing in corporate language and business skills training, expats in Hong Kong need to know enough Cantonese 'so you can order your favourite dishes at a restaurant and to show that you have a connection'. If you can learn some Cantonese to get by, you're effectively 'in the circle' rather 'out of the circle', otherwise, says Behan, 'you're not going to be able to fit into society as it's evolving.' English and Putonghua are the most useful languages in Hong Kong.

A guy I know has just been made Regional Head of a head-hunting firm and he's desperate to learn Mandarin. He's going into China on a regular basis and it's being able to break the ice, basic 'getting around' – and foreigners are expected to have some knowledge of Putonghua.

This is particularly true for professionals working in specific areas on the mainland. Mr Behan has received several queries recently from golfers:

A golf professional I know used to work in China a lot, but now all the top golf courses in China, if they're recruiting from overseas, the players must have Putonghua.

In practice, though, most expats still have limited Chinese language skills.

Being able to develop a 'cultural affinity' for Hong Kong, China and the Asia region in general is also regarded as important for a successful adjustment to the lifestyle, society, mores and way of doing business here. According to Anthony Lewis, it is often an inability to fit in with the culture and adjust working styles, or the 'trailing spouse's' adjustment problems, that causes some expats to come to grief, as most are 'well thought out' before they arrive.

VISAS

If you are not a permanent resident in Hong Kong, you will need a visa to work here. An ID card is the next prerequisite. Anyone permitted to stay in Hong

Kong for more than 180 days needs to apply for an ID card within 30 days of arrival. Forms and more details are available at www.immd.gov.hk. A work visa application should be made before you come to Hong Kong and is usually sponsored by the company that has offered you a job.

Dependent visas permit spouses to work.

There are two main types of work visa: the **employment visa** and the **investment visa**.

Employment visa

This shows you have been given permission by the Hong Kong government to be employed in Hong Kong. Companies sponsoring you as their employee usually submit your application, although you may have to get the paperwork together and do it yourself. An employment visa can take between four to six weeks to process. If you are in Hong Kong when the work visa is granted, you are required to go in person to collect your work visa from the Immigration Department in Wanchai and pay the $135 fee. Otherwise your company will put it in your passport for you.

The sponsoring company will have to prove that you have the skills necessary for the job and that a local worker could not fill the position. When granting work visas, the Department will consider the applicant's educational background, relevant experience and professional knowledge, amongst other things. Intra-company transfers are possible for employees who have worked for over 12 months in an overseas office and also meet the strict criteria above.

An application for a work visa can be made after (or preferably before) entry to Hong Kong – UK residents are allowed a visa-free stay for three months. Employment should not officially start until the visa has been obtained. Employment visas are not transferable from one company to another, so if you quit a job in Hong Kong you will need to apply for another visa and start the process all over again. A sponsoring employer must notify the Immigration Department if a sponsored employee leaves.

Work visas are usually granted for a year in the first instance, and on renewal can be extended by one, two or three years, depending on criteria such as the specified length of a contract. Continuous periods of employment and tax payment in Hong Kong totalling seven years is one of the grounds on which to apply for permanent residency status. More information is available on the **Immigration Department**'s website (www.immd.gov.hk).

Business immigration specialist Stephen Barnes at Emigra Asia (www.emigra.com.hk) can offer immigration consulting and support, and handles visa law compliance for companies operating in Hong Kong, as well as those seeking to enter the markets in China, Taiwan and Macau.

Investment visa

An investment visa is for self-employed people. Before you apply, you will need to complete a hefty amount of paperwork detailing your educational background, professional experience and knowledge, and provide details of proposed business activities, capital and promises of work. There are no official guidelines regarding how much monthly income a business needs to make in Hong Kong to be deemed viable, but $20,000 upwards per month is a figure that gets bandied about. It's also important to show how your business will benefit Hong Kong, whether you are providing a unique service, whether you will employ local people, and so on.

When applying for an investment visa based on your sole proprietorship, you need to have a permanent resident sign for you to undertake to pay your deportation fees, should that become necessary. You will also need to obtain a Business Registration Certificate. This is a straightforward procedure – see below.

Further information is available on the Immigration Department's website (www.immd.gov.hk). The website www.investhk.gov.hk has a downloadable investment guidebook and key statistics and facts.

Side-line employment

If you plan to undertake work outside the scope of your existing visa – for example, for another employer – you should apply for permission to take up side-line employment. This is handled in the same way as when you apply for a normal work visa. You should apply four weeks in advance, completing a visa application form from the Immigration Department. You should also submit your ID card and passport, a copy of the work you have been contracted to do, and a letter from your current work visa sponsor giving permission for you to take up the work.

JOB SEARCH

Recruitment agencies

Large international recruitment agencies specializing in topflight executive searches for multinational clients include:

- **Hiedrick & Struggles** (54/F, Bank of China Tower, 1 Garden Road, tel. 2103 9318);
- **Egon Zehnder International** (Level 8, One Pacific Place, 88 Queensway; tel. 2525 6340);
- **Russell Reynolds Associates** (24/F, Central Tower, 28 Queen's Road, Central; tel. 2523 9123); and
- **Korn/Ferry International** (2102–6 Gloucester Tower, Landmark, Central; tel. 2971 2700).

Mid-market recruitment specialists such as **Michael Page** (tel. 2530 2000), **Robert Walters (HK)** (tel. 2525 7808), **Ambition** (www.ambition.com.hk) and **Executive Access** (tel. 2842 7136) recruit from junior executive level up.

Recruitment agencies Michael Page and Robert Walters have salary surveys available online, as does **www.investhk.gov.hk**, that allow you to check the going market rate for positions in different industries in Hong Kong.

Newspapers and magazines

The *South China Morning Post* is the main English-language source of job advertisements and the Saturday edition publishes a compendium of all advertisements placed that week, listed by industry. Other advertisements appear in the *Standard*, the *Far Eastern Economic Review*, the *Asian Wall Street Journal* and *HK Magazine*. Trade magazines also sometimes advertise, for example *Hong Kong Lawyer*, *FinanceAsia*, *Asia Money*, *Computer World HK*, *Capital Asia* and *HK Industrialist*.

Websites

The *South China Morning Post*'s website **www.classifiedpost.com.hk** has the most comprehensive English language listing of jobs in Hong Kong. Other websites that allow you to search for jobs, post your CV and apply online – although they are limited to industries such as HR, admin, marketing, IT, engineering and the legal profession – include **www.jobmarket. com.hk**, **www.bestjobshk.com**, **www.jobsdb.com** and **www.monster. com.hk**. Monster also has finance, and sales and marketing messageboards and employer profiles. *Career Times* online (**www.careertimes.com.hk**) includes articles posted by industry insiders as well as advice on preparing CVs, networking and job hunting. The government's **Interactive Employ-ment Service** (www.jobs.gov.hk) offers job search and free job vacancy posting by employers.

EMPLOYMENT CONTRACTS

Most expats employed in Hong Kong are on full-time contracts. The simple reason for this is that living in Hong Kong is not otherwise an economically viable proposition unless, of course, you have family or friends here. That said, it is entirely possible to juggle several part-time jobs to make a decent income, which is commonly the case with English teachers.

Overseas contracts

If you are coming to Hong Kong via a company internal transfer or are being employed from abroad, it is definitely worth taking financial advice and consulting an accountant or lawyer over your contract structure, particularly with regard to tax. It is usually beneficial to have employers meet all ancillary costs rather than pay cash equivalents. For example, if your moving expenses are paid for by the employer, this avoids the same sum included in the employee's pay packet being liable to salary tax. Contracts also commonly include substantial private health cover including dental insurance, membership to private sports clubs, bonuses or an end-of-service gratuity. Although extravagant expat packages still exist, companies are increasingly keeping costs down by proposing basic remuneration plus bonus.

Time-in, time-out

If your job involves extensive business travel, then you may be able to claim time apportionment of income for your work inside and outside Hong Kong, so that you are only taxed for the time when you are actually in the city – that is, only the portion of income related to services performed in Hong Kong is taxable. In this case:

- the employer must be incorporated outside Hong Kong;
- the employment contract must be negotiated, signed and executed outside Hong Kong, and must not be governed by Hong Kong law unless you can provide a reason for it; and
- the employee must have regional responsibility.

Rental reimbursement

Housing receives specialized treatment from the tax authorities in Hong Kong. According to Fergus Tong of US Asia Tax (www.usasiatax.com; tel. 2851 8049):

> Usually it is beneficial to separate out part of your remuneration as housing

allowance on your employment contract, even if your employer is not paying a separate housing allowance. That way, you will normally be charged a lower taxable income rather than the entire housing allowance, provided that you actually spend the money on rental and you enter into an official lease agreement with a landlord.

A steady increase in the cost of high-end rentals ($70,000–100,000 per month) over the past few years has impacted on the value of housing packages.

Other items
Children's education allowance is taxable, as is home leave passage.

Local contracts
Expats who pitch up in Hong Kong to look for work, or who switch jobs locally, are unlikely to be employed on an overseas contract but may be offered a 'local contract'. Civil service contracts, including those for teachers, are usually offered on a fixed-term basis for two years with the option to renew. Companies operate on a month-by-month basis. Besides offering a salary, local contracts may also offer accommodation and education allowances.

A concise guide to legal aspects of a local contract as stipulated by the **Employment Ordinance** can be found at www.labour.gov.hk. Hong Kong-specific items include:

- **Extra payments.** A contract should specify any end-of-year payments – a 'thirteenth month' discretionary payment is common in Hong Kong at Christmas or Chinese New Year – or end-of-contract gratuities, common in civil service/teaching contracts.
- **Public holidays.** Employees are entitled to 17 public holidays.
- **Annual leave.** An employee having been employed under a continuous contract for not less than three months is entitled to holiday pay. Annual leave varies – the statutory minimum for 12 months' continuous work is 7 days, and 15 days or less is common.
- **Maternity leave and pay.** Companies are bound to provide 10 weeks' maternity leave for employees who have been in continuous employment for 40 weeks immediately before the commencement of maternity leave. Leave pay is four-fifths of the employee's normal wages.

In Hong Kong, it is common to work from Monday to Friday and a half day on Saturday. There is no minimum wage, except for foreign domestic helpers – see Chapter Eight, 'Having and Raising Children'.

TAX

Salary tax

Tax is not deducted at source, so employees need to complete a tax return annually with details of total salary earned for the fiscal year end of 31 March, often provided by the employer, and profits earned or losses incurred. The self-employed can elect personal assessment. You may not get your first tax bill for up to 18 months, depending on when your Hong Kong employment began. When you are presented with a bill that includes not only tax for the preceding year but also the estimated provisional tax for the following year, it can come as quite a shock. An assessment notice is usually sent out by the Inland Revenue Department (IRD) in the autumn with the sum due. The first payment on the balance of the preceding year's tax plus 75% of the provisional tax is usually due between January and March, and the second payment – the remaining 25% of the provisional tax – is due three months later.

When your tax return is issued, information in English describing how to complete it should be enclosed (see also www.ird.gov.hk for more information, or telephone 187 8022). An automatic salary tax computation service is also available on the IRD's website.

It is important to keep the IRD up to date with changes to your address and to tell them promptly if you require special permission to delay payment, as a surcharge of 5% is automatically added to late payments. Banks offer tax loans to help defray the expense, or you can save for your tax by purchasing **Tax Reserve Certificates** on a monthly standing order (see www.ird.gov.hk/eng/tax/trc.htm). These are then offset against tax when it is due.

Total tax is currently limited to 17% of salary. Allowances are made for single parents, married people, dependents, etc.

Residents from the UK are not subject to UK income tax on their worldwide income.

Other tax

There is no tax on capital gains, interest, dividends and offshore profit or income. Property tax on renting out property owned in Hong Kong and profits tax on unincorporated business is 15% for 2009–2010; corporate profits tax is 16.5%.

For more detailed information about tax issues, contact the IRD (www.ird. gov.hk/eng/tax/index.htm; tel. 187 8088).

Mandatory Provident Fund

All full- and part-time employees and self-employed people aged between 18 and 65 and earning more than $5,000 per month are required by the government to pay into an MPF (Mandatory Provident Fund). This is a privately managed fund that functions as a government retirement scheme. Schemes are administered by designated insurance companies or banks in Hong Kong.

Every month, employees must pay 5% of their monthly salary or $1,000 – whichever is less – into an MPF. The sum is matched by an employer contribution. The employees' mandatory contributions, subject to a maximum of $12,000 annually, are tax-deductible. You may be exempted from MPF payments if you have an overseas pension or similar plan. You can redeem your MPF before you reach 65 if you leave Hong Kong. For more information, browse the Authority website at **www.mpfahk.org**.

Leaving Hong Kong

All tax bills need to be settled before leaving Hong Kong. Your employer will notify the IRD that you are leaving, and will withhold your last month's salary until you have paid your tax and been issued with a 'Letter of Release'.

SETTING UP A COMPANY

If you're not an investment banker, running your own business is one of the main ways to make a small or big fortune in Hong Kong, according to Debbie Annells, a director at trust and fiduciary services company Equity Trust:

> People don't make a lot of money on investments, by and large, unless they're special. Most people make most money on starting a business, and there's a whole variety – bars, manufacturing, trading with China … they find a niche and they do very well.

In fact there are hundreds of SMEs (small/medium enterprise) run by expats in Hong Kong in a wide variety of industries, including financial services, accounting, IT, recruitment, consultancy, building, architecture, house maintenance and repair, education, executive training, security, clothing, leisure,

recreation, sports, dining, pet care and healthcare, as well as creative industries such as the arts, antique promotion and sales, interior design, publishing
agency work, marketing, editing, writing, book selling, life coaching, image
and fashion consultancy, graphic design and web design. Although the fixed
costs are reasonably high – rental, deposits, staffing costs and regulation and
compliance costs – these disadvantages are compensated for by the excep-
tionally favourable tax conditions.

Which business vehicle?

There is a choice of business vehicles available to those running their own
business – including *sole proprietorship*, *partnership* and *limited company*.

All businesses carried out by individuals (sole proprietors) or as a partnership
should register first with the **Business Registration Office** (4/F, Revenue
Tower, 5 Gloucester Road, Wanchai; tel. 187 8088), from which you can
obtain a 'Business Registration Certificate'. Processing time is a day and a
one-year certificate costs around $2,600. You should apply for the certificate
within a month of starting your business.

- **Sole proprietorship.** If a business is carried on by an individual, Form 1(a)
  should be completed (specimens available at www.ird.gov.hk/eng/tax/
  bre_abr.htm). The form should be submitted together with a photocopy of
  the proprietor's ID card or passport. Separate arrangements must be made
  if the sole proprietor does not reside in Hong Kong.
- **Partnership.** In the case of a partnership, Form 1(c) should be completed
  (specimens available at www.ird.gov.hk/eng/tax/bre_abr.htm). The form
  should be submitted together with photocopies of all the partners' ID
  cards or passports. Separate arrangements must be made if the partners do
  not reside in Hong Kong.
- **Company.** Incorporating limited companies and registering branches of
  overseas companies is very common in Hong Kong. A new limited company should first register at the **Companies Registry** (14/F, Queensway
  Government Offices, 66 Queensway; tel. 2867 2600/2234 9933), where
  Articles of Association, Memorandum of the company, declaration of
  compliance and proforma name and contact details will be required. The
  process takes six days and costs $170–1,720. An application for a Busi-
  ness Registration Certificate should be made within a month of the date
  of incorporation or registration with the Companies Registry. Form 1(b)
  (specimens available at www.ird.gov.hk/eng/tax/bre_abr.htm) should be

submitted with a photocopy of the Certificate of Incorporation or Certificate of Registration of Overseas Company issued by the Companies Registry. **Branch businesses** should also register at the Companies Registry, submitting documents such as company constitution, accounts, particulars of directors, etc. The process takes 22 days and costs $1,740. The business must also apply for a Business Registration Certificate within a month of its commencement. Form 1(d) should be completed.

Alternatively, you may prefer to buy a **shelf company** from a reputable accountant and save yourself a lot of red tape.

Business licensing

The **Support and Consultation Centre for SMEs** (M/F, Trade & Industry Department Tower, 700 Nathan Road, Kowloon; www.success.tid.gov.hk; tel. 2398 5133; fax 2737 2377) is a one-stop service run by the government. It provides information on all licences, permits and certificates necessary for business operation in Hong Kong (for example, Food and Beverage, Animals, Education, etc.)

Managing your tax

Generally, all expenses that have been incurred in the production of chargeable profits are tax deductible. Examples include interest on borrowed funds and office supplies bought to use in producing profits. Losses can be carried forward and offset against future profits. Allowances are given with regard to capital expenditure incurred on construction costs and expenditure incurred for the purpose of producing chargeable profit. In the case of capital expenditure on plant and machinery, depreciation allowances are given. An immediate 100% write-off is allowed for capital expenditure on plant and machinery specially related to manufacturing, and on computer hardware and software – except capital expenditure incurred under a hire-purchase agreement.

Big accountancy firms operating in Hong Kong include **Pricewaterhouse-Coopers** (www.pwchk.com), **Deloitte Touche Tohmatsu** (www.deloitte.com) and **Ernst & Young** (www.ey.com; tel. 2846 9888). Depending on the complexity and size of your company, you could also consult one of the many competent smaller accountancy firms. Accountants such as Millie Shing at **MSP Shing & Co.** (tel. 2881 1992; e-mail millie.shing@mspshing.com) can help with auditing, tax, accounting, company formation and business consultation.

BANKS

There are 145 licensed banks in Hong Kong and the banking system here is well-regulated, efficient and automated. Banks can offer a whole range of international standard services to customers, including foreign currency accounts, and there are no restrictions on remittances in and out of Hong Kong. The major banks serving businesses in Hong Kong include:

- HSBC (www.hsbc.com.hk);
- Bank of China (www.bochk.com);
- Hang Seng Bank (www.hangseng.com); and
- Standard Chartered Bank (www.standardchartered.com).

HSBC's website is one of the most comprehensive and easy to navigate. Amongst other things, it provides a profile of doing business in China, including a brief introduction to Labour Management and Advertising Law, Taxation and Banking on the mainland. The locations of dedicated Business Banking Centres are also listed on the website.

Unlike the UK, it can be difficult to get a bank loan for a start-up and most banks will only lend against assets (that is, property) held in Hong Kong.

Details on personal banking services are included in Chapter Ten, 'Money'.

SETTING UP AN OFFICE

Office space

Rental on business units is still high, despite the decline in the property market in Hong Kong in recent years. When setting up an office, check the operating hours of the air-conditioning (which may operate between fixed hours, for example 9:00 am to 6:00 pm), the usable space, the wiring for broadband access, telephones and computers, management fees, and rates. Two useful sites for checking out office rental, power and utilities charges are **www.investhk.gov.hk** (under their 'Investment Guidebook' link) and **www.gov.hk/en/business/**. When leasing, be prepared to bargain hard. Most offices are leased as bare shells, meaning that the tenant will have to equip the space with partitions and install electrical and lighting systems, carpeting, fittings and furniture. A rent-free period is sometimes given whilst the office is being set up.

Serviced offices

These days, 'serviced offices' are often preferred, but you'll need to shop around to get a reasonable deal. Companies such as **Regus** (www.regus.com; tel. 2824 8888), **LevelOne Central** (39/F, One Exchange Square, 8 Connaught Road, Central; tel. 3101 7200) and **Servcorp** (www.servcorp.net; tel. 2251 1888) can provide short- and long-term leases, fully furnished and wired office spaces, secretarial staff and call answering, photocopying and fax services. Costs vary depending on the size, location, view, lease term and service plan, but expect to pay around $5,500–15,000 a month for 55–120 square feet.

Virtual offices

Companies providing serviced offices also commonly offer virtual offices – particularly useful for sole proprietor companies. The virtual office can include services such as a business address and post box, call answering and forwarding, IT Helpdesk, and use of meeting rooms from around $600 a month.

Telecommunications

A comprehensive range of SME business communications packages are offered by companies such as **PCCW** (www.pccw.com). Packages include call plans, Internet services and communication equipment. A price list is available on their website, or call 1000. China-based services and products are also available (tel. 2883 0906).

For more information on telecommunications service providers, refer to Chapter Five, 'Accommodation'.

GOVERNMENT SUPPORT FOR BUSINESSES

Trade departments and offices

The Hong Kong government provides support to all companies doing business in Hong Kong via its **Trade and Development Council** (SME Service Station, Trade & Industry Department Tower, M/F, 700 Nathan Road, Mongkok; www.tdctrade.com; tel. 1830 668; fax 2787 3092). The TDC website provides a business contacts database and hosts a sourcing guide and business matching service. Other information links include credit checking, tendering and procurement, transport and logistics, trade fairs, customs and trademarks. Papers on economic issues affecting the region and tender notices for mainland China projects are also viewable. A free, web-based video conferencing service is provided at the **TDC Business Information Centre** (Hong Kong Convention and Exhibition Centre, Wanchai; tel. 1830 668).

Other government-sponsored agencies that can provide advice and information include:

- **Invest Hong Kong** (15/F, One Pacific Place, Queensway; www.investhk. gov.hk; tel. 3107 1000; fax 3107 9007). This provides an overview on the advantages of doing business in Hong Kong; a breakdown of business set-up procedures; the market outlook for different sectors; cargo, container and freight forwarding logistics; and links to detailed finance, sales and labour statistics.
- **Business and Trade** (www.gov.hk/en/business/) is a government portal with extensive information on business facilitation, doing business with the mainland, filing e-forms , taxes, market information etc.
- **Hong Kong Trade and Industry Department** (Room 908, Trade & Industry Department Tower, 700 Nathan Road, Kowloon; www.tid.gov. hk; tel. 2392 2922; fax 2787 7422). Besides disseminating trade policy information, forms, industry circulars and so on, the Department also provides information on funding for SMEs (**www.success.tid.gov.hk**) and an electronic database, reference library and mentorship programme.
- **Hong Kong Productivity Council** (HKPC Building, 78 Tat Chee Avenue, Yau Yat Chuen, Kowloon; www.hkpc.org; tel. 2788 5678; fax 2788 5900). The Council provides training, news and support to maximize businesses' productivity.

China trade initiatives

Since 1997, China has taken steps to boost Hong Kong's business by making it easier for the city to benefit from the huge developing market on its doorstep.

- Developing over the past twenty years into a major manufacturing hub, the **Pearl River Delta Economic Development Zone**, located around the Macau/Hong Kong/Guangzhou triangle in southern China, is likely to be a vital artery for Hong Kong's future economic success. The government is endeavouring to establish a pivotal role for Hong Kong in servicing the needs of the hub through management, logistics and professional services. Building a bridge to connect Hong Kong to Macau and Zhuhai is underway to aid export and logistics. More information is available at www. investhk.gov.hk.

- The **Closer Economic Partnership Arrangement** (CEPA) came into effect on 1 January 2004. It is designed to expedite trade in services, goods and investment between Hong Kong and China by abolishing tariffs on selected exports from Hong Kong, permitting involvement in distribution on the mainland and making it easier for Hong Kong companies to invest in service sectors on the mainland. A pact signed in 2010 marked the first formal agreement on co-operation between Hong Kong and Guangdong recognized by the central government. The plan states the central government's determination to turn Hong Kong, Macau and Guangdong into an international metropolis, through further economic integration. A $66.9 billion high-speed railway linking Hong Kong to Guangzhou is under construction.
- Since 2004, mainland **tourists** from Beijing, Shanghai and all of Guangdong have been allowed to visit Hong Kong individually, rather than as part of a tour group as was previously required. Mainlanders form the largest number of visitors to Hong Kong (29.5 million in 2009) and are some of the biggest spenders.
- Major local banks now offer **Renminbi** (RMB) deposit, remittance, credit card transactions and foreign exchange services. This is seen by many as testing the waters for future full convertibility of RMB worldwide.
- Mainland trade accounts now for almost 50 per cent of Hong Kong's total trade. Hong Kong's stock market, Asia's second largest after Tokyo, has thrived from huge profits earned from listing mainland companies in some of the world's biggest-ever initial public offerings (IPOs).
- **CCPIT** (China Council for the Promotion of International Trade; www.ccpit.org), based in Beijing, has extensive information on doing business in China and can provide business services. Advice, reports and services are also offered by the accountancy firms Ernst & Young, Deloitte and PricewaterhouseCoopers (details above).

IT INFRASTRUCTURE

Hong Kong has caught up fast with other Asian countries such as Taiwan and Korea in its adoption and application of technology in business, particularly in the B2B domain. According to Christine Petersen, Managing Director of Time Technology Solutions, the volume of e-mail traffic is as high as in places such as the US, and knowledge management and leverage through technology are well developed although secretarial manpower is heavily entrenched. A significant advantage here is the widespread availability of broadband.

Government initiatives so far include:

- **Cyberport** (www.cyberport.com.hk), billed as 'Hong Kong's IT flagship', is a hi-tech $15.8 billion multimedia hub that is being developed in conjunction with private enterprise. Located in Pokfulam, the Cyberport comprises four office buildings housing a five-star hotel, a retail entertainment complex and a deluxe residential development.
- **Hong Kong Science and Technology Park** (www.hkstp.org) is Hong Kong's answer to Silicon Valley: a 22-hectare state-of-the-art corporate campus at Tolo Harbour waterfront in Pak Shek Kok, New Territories. It is designed to house large and small corporations, with shared IT, business, IC Design and R&D services.
- The governent's **'Digital 21 – Information Technology Strategy'** is designed to promote advanced technology in Hong Kong. Initiatives include the inauguration of an Applied Science and Technology Research Institute and a $5 billion contribution towards an Innovation and Technology Fund.
- Installation of free government wi-fi premises around the city (see www. gov.hk).

CHAMBERS OF COMMERCE

Local chambers of commerce have a key role in Hong Kong as networking forums. They offer various services to businesses and are open to members of all nationalities involved in all types of enterprise. Members can obtain referrals of work, publicize business opportunities and advertise products and services. They can also gain access to local business news, obtain business advice and enjoy round table luncheons, speaker events, conferences and professional development, as well as social events.

Key chambers include:

- **American Chamber of Commerce** (www.amcham.org.hk; tel. 2526 0165; fax 2810 1289). 'AmCham' is the largest international chamber in Hong Kong, but considered expensive by many SMEs. It publishes useful titles such as the *China Business Directory* and *Who's Who in Hong Kong Communications*.

- **British Chamber of Commerce** (www.britcham.com; tel. 2824 2211; fax 2824 1333). 'BritCham' is influential and proactive, and has about 1,000 members. It publishes *The British Directory*, a guide to British companies doing business in Hong Kong and the Asia region. Individual membership is available to professionals under the age of 30 ($4,000).
- **Hong Kong General Chamber of Commerce** (www.chamber.org.hk; tel. 2529 9229; fax 2527 9843). A significant chamber in Hong Kong.
- **Australian Chamber of Commerce** (www.austcham.com.hk; tel. 2522 5054; fax 2877 0860). Favoured by many SME owners as being reasonably priced and excellent for networking and socializing.
- **Canadian Chamber of Commerce** (www.cancham.org; tel. 2110 8700; fax 2110 8701).
- **Chinese General Chamber of Commerce** (www.cgcc.org.hk; tel. 2525 6385; fax 2845 2610).
- **Indian Chamber of Commerce** (www.icchk.org.hk; tel. 2523 3877; fax 2845 0300).
- **New Zealand Business Association** (www.nzhkba.org.hk; tel. 2526 7898; fax 2810 9068).
- **Taiwan Trade Association** (tel. 2721 7636; fax 2721 3470)

A list of other trade associations and chambers appears on the AmCham website at www.amcham.org.hk/contacts/hongkong.html.

OTHER BUSINESS CLUBS AND NETWORKING ORGANIZATIONS

- **The Foreign Correspondents' Club** (2 Lower Albert Road, Central; www.fcchk.org/; tel. 2521 1511) provides a watering hole and networking gossip nexus for those in business, diplomacy and the media. It frequently hosts speaker events and lunches featuring international opinion formers and news-makers.
- **The Entrepreneurs Club** (www.entrepreneurs.com.hk) aims to provide existing and would-be entrepreneurs with a regular monthly forum for intellectual exchange.
- **The Women Business Owner's Club** (www.hkwboc.org; tel. 9158 7263) aims to support the owners of existing businesses and encourage those who aspire to own their own business through professional development activities and networking. Membership is around 200 strong. Men are welcome.

- The **International Association of Business Communicators** is a global network of PR and marketing professionals. The Hong Kong chapter (www.iabchk.com) meets regularly for informal drinks and speaker meetings.
- Expatriate doyenne **The Hong Kong Club** (1 Jackson Road, Central; tel. 2525 8251) and sparring partner **The China Club** (13–15/F, Old Bank of China Building, Bank Street, Central; tel. 2521 8888) cater to the wealthy elite of Hong Kong, although most people wind up at a function there at some time or another. Newer contender, the **Kee Club** (6/F, 32 Wellington Street, Central; tel. 2810 9000), is a funky, younger lounge/restaurant/bar club.
- The **Hong Kong Toastmasters Club** (www.toastmasters.org.hk), founded in 1954, gives members a chance to practise their public speaking skills, as well as running workshops and presentations led by guest speakers.

Details of other networking organizations are provided in Chapter Fourteen, 'Professional Women in Hong Kong'.

Smart tips from SME owners in Hong Kong

Carry name cards with you wherever you go. You can get them printed cheaply within 24 hours at copy shops such as Output Express, to whom you can e-mail the file (www.outputexpress.com). Go bilingual – English on one side, Chinese on the other. Present and receive a name card with both hands. Never write on or tear up a name card you are given.

Join a networking group for support and mentoring, volunteer to go on committees and offer to speak at events. As well as the chambers and small business organizations, the Productivity Council has forums and committees that are good platforms from which to advertise your services.

Use a service such as **CSL's 1010 Concierge service** (tel. 2988 1010), which can liaise on your behalf with Cantonese-speaking clients, book rooms and restaurants, etc. It's cheaper than a secretary and available 24 hours.

Learn a few phrases in Cantonese to use with clients – it makes a big difference.

Chapter Fourteen

Being a Professional Woman in Hong Kong

Professional women in Hong Kong enjoy high levels of esteem and responsibility, and many are SME owners and directors. The Grant Thornton International Business Owners Survey, published in 2006, showed that 35% of Hong Kong companies employ women in senior management positions, a figure significantly higher than in the UK, Canada, France and Germany.

Rehana Sheikh, who advises clients on relocation issues, comments:

> *Here, you're treated like a person; lots of women have remarked on that. Here, you're doing business with men who treat you normal, not like, 'Oh, a woman doing business', being patronizing or condescending. I think people are very pleasantly surprised.*

Jacquelyn, an Australian who found work in the environmental section of a multinational engineering company, is equally upbeat:

> *It's easier for women to get ahead here. Despite the fact that I've had resistance, I've also had opportunities. My career had stopped. I came to Hong Kong and picked it up and put it back where it should be.*

Many expat women decide to start their own business after coming to Hong Kong and discovering opportunities exist to provide a service or product that is currently unavailable or under-resourced. Setting up your own business from scratch is a challenge and a risk – even more so in a foreign country. However, in Hong Kong, the procedure of setting up a business is relatively simple and inexpensive, and the tax system is straightforward. Being part of a small business community is a distinct advantage when it comes to networking and obtaining referrals. Things get done quickly here and business operates almost 24 hours a day, seven days a week, allowing you to make the

42. Women entrepreneurs address a meeting of the WiPS, Hong Kong
Photograph taken by the author

most of opportunities. But at the end of the day, it can be about pushing the boundaries. As one woman said:

> Having my own business has helped to make me feel more confident in my abilities. I've experienced difficulties and been able to cope with things in new ways.

STORIES

One of the challenges mentioned by some expat entrepreneurs is language. Kay Ross, a freelance editor and marketing consultant (kayross@hkstar.com), says:

> Not speaking or writing the language enough makes it very difficult to communicate effectively, especially with secretaries and service providers. I'm sure I'd be a lot more marketable if I had fluent Cantonese and Mandarin.

Kay went into business by herself after spending several years as the Listings Editor for the South China Morning Post. She says:

> It wasn't necessarily because I had a dream of building a multi-million dollar company. It was simply that I thought I was unlikely to find a full-time job, since I spoke almost no Cantonese. I had developed lots of contacts so I decided to go freelance, and a sole proprietorship was the obvious and easiest business structure. The bottom line: establishing a business, even a very small one, offers significant tax advantages – every paper clip is tax deductible. Maybe it's also just my personality – I like the freedom, the flexibility and the variety of freelancing, and I like being my own boss.

Laurie Lemmlie-Leung, originally from the US, helps her husband in the family cotton terry garments business started by her father-in-law in the 1960s. The company handles all aspects of the customer's requirements, including design, manufacturing, testing and quality control. The last few years have been difficult:

We have faced the same economic challenges that everyone has had in the last few years. When I came to work in the business we were doing hotel amenities supply. When the hotels went into a slump, so did our business. We have changed our industry completely; our products are primarily for the retail market now. The change has been a real challenge.

She recommends that you 'join a group like the Women Business Owners' Club – it is great for support and motivation, especially when things are not going well.'

Australian Christine Petersen was 54 when she came to Hong Kong in 2004 to set up her company Time Technology Solutions. An experienced business-woman with international experience, Christine had joined the Austra-lian Chamber of Commerce prior to coming to Hong Kong and used it as a resource to locate IT services when she was setting up her company:

If people are well-organized, they can have a database of suppliers and service providers within a matter of weeks.

British IT expert Roz Beste set up Crystal Computer Services in 1999. She found it difficult to get an investment visa, but not impossible. Although she says it's 'simple and cheap to do business here', she also advises that you 'make sure you have enough money in the bank for the first six months when you may not make a profit.'

Depending on the nature of the business, the Immigration Department can take time to grant approval. Mary Bodomo, originally from Ghana, had been in Hong Kong ten years and was working as an English lecturer when she decided to start Hong Kong's first black hair salon. 'Setting it up was logisti-cally okay. However, there were plenty of hurdles with the immigration – it took one reject and a whole year to get an employment visa approved for my hairstylist to come from Ghana (because I'm a full-time teacher and can't juggle the two) and all the while I had to pay rent for the premises without income from the business. The only reason I got at the end was that this was a new case for the Immigration Department.'

Another Brit, Vanessa Bird, set up in business in 2000 as the exclusive distributor in Hong Kong and Macau of Tisserand Aromatherapy products from the UK. She had to learn everything from scratch, and made between $20,000–30,000 per month. She suggests that you do very thorough and realistic market research, and insist on a proper shareholders' agreement if you have a business partner:

> Set up clear procedures from day one and don't cut corners on IT – it won't pay off in the long run. Understand your accounts and agree a strategy with your accountant. Plan your exit strategy from the beginning, if you think you may not stay in Hong Kong forever.

Fiona Meighan, who specializes in human and technology interaction, found work falling into her lap, although monthly income was erratic:

> My overheads have been almost zero – I had to buy malpractice insurance and travel insurance, but had a computer at home. I work from home, so I don't need an office, and my clients supply laptops and mobile phones.

Hong Kong has provided her with an interesting angle on cross-cultural working practices, which she plans to research further:

> Hong Kong people treat a mobile phone like a commodity – we call it a three-month cycle [they buy a new one every three months]. In Australia, people buy a new phone every two years; as a consequence, Australian telecommunications companies use a strategic way of working, whereas local companies go for tactical advantages. There are lots of conflicts. The local companies have no understanding of why strategy is necessary. They're not interested in getting engaged with the project team until the product is nearly ready to sell.

On the other hand, she says the US and Australia:

> … don't understand the pressure and tight margins that people are working with in Hong Kong. The Chinese are very collectivist and no-one wants to fail and lose face. They work by committee. It's difficult to get people to commit. They will say 'we endorse this', not 'we approve'.

She has been in meetings where she believed everything had been resolved and agreed upon, 'then after the meeting his secretary has come up to me and said, "no, we don't want this, we want this, this and this". It threw me.' But Meighan has no regrets. 'I'm so glad I came. I wouldn't have traded coming here for anything.'

Entrepreneurs may also need to guard against becoming a victim of their own success. Nurse and mother-of-two Chris McGuigan, who ran a lucrative business teaching English, Speech and Drama for over five years, found the time had come to step back. Although she enjoyed the work and made a good living from it, she said, 'I'm captured here. I work all the time – and I don't want to do that.' She decided to leave Hong Kong, partly for family reasons – she missed her family back in New Zealand and she wanted her daughters to experience life back there – but also because money was losing its appeal:

> *Hong Kong offers an experience that everyone should have an opportunity to enjoy. We've become comfortable compared to the way we lived in New Zealand, but I'm not interested in sticking around to make more money.*

SUPPORT ORGANIZATIONS

There are a number of expat-oriented networking organizations that offer support to women in business.

- The **Hong Kong Association of Business and Professional Women** (HKABPW – www.hkabpw.org) aims to promote the interests of business and professional women, and organizes professional development training, round table luncheons and alternative seminars and workshops. They also have a book club and a mentoring programme, and collaborate with local university students. Men are welcome. Membership stands at around 140.
- The **Women in Publishing Society, Hong Kong** (WiPS – www.hkwips. org) aims to promote the status of women in all areas of publishing and provide a forum for discussion and the sharing of information and expertise. Monthly meetings include writing workshops, author panels and networking events. The organization publishes an *Imprint* journal annually, to which members are invited to contribute. Membership stands at

around 130 and includes writers, editors, designers, publishers, teachers and professionals from many other industries. Men are welcome to attend events.

- The **Women's Forum** (www.womensforum.com.hk) is described by founder Liz Murrihy as 'a female old boy's network'. It has a membership of around 3,000 women and hosts monthly informal networking meetings and mixers.
- The **WITI (Women in Technology International) Hong Kong Regional Chapter** was started at the end of 2003. It aims to help women by providing access to, and support from, other professional women working in technology. Visit **www.witi.com/center/regionalchapter/hongkong** to learn more about upcoming events.

43. Royal Hong Kong Yacht Club
Photograph taken by the author

Chapter Fifteen

Teaching English

There are between six and ten thousand expatriate English teachers currently working in Hong Kong, mostly from Australia, New Zealand, the UK and North America. Proficiency in the English language has retained its importance in Hong Kong, despite the increased resources and provision for Putonghua/Mandarin teaching since the handover in 1997.

TRENDS IN ENGLISH TEACHING IN HONG KONG

The Hong Kong government's linguistic ambition is to have the populace literate in English and Chinese, and trilingual in Cantonese, Putonghua and English. Over the past few years, the government has started various initiatives to bolster the level of English in schools and the workplace, but people still gripe about the standard of English.

The fact is, though, that as a non-Chinese speaker, it's very easy to get around, make yourself understood and do business in Hong Kong precisely because of the very serviceable standard of English in most areas of social life and business. Foreigners and international trade are such a fundamental part of Hong Kong's history that there remains a strong social bias in favour of English, with little of the post-colonial backlash that other places have experienced.

Hong Kongers are nothing if not pragmatic – people who know English get higher salaries and enjoy better job prospects. That does not, however, automatically equate to large swathes of motivated English learners filling the classroom. Exams are what gets bums on seats. Primary school students often need the Cambridge Young Learners exams to show to their prospective secondary school. Another Cambridge exam – the IELTS (International English Language Testing System exam) is now recommended by the government as a graduate exit test of English. This in turn creates a need for IELTS examiners and preparatory IELTS course teachers.

Because English is very much in the public eye, schools, students and their parents have a lot of say in what they expect and what they want. Recent

44. Students
Photograph taken by the author

legislation has reversed the push for 'mother tongue' teaching, allowing schools to elect to be English-medium. Parents generally prefer their children to be taught by expatriate English teachers rather than local teachers. Students expect to be involved and entertained in their English class and older students expect an egalitarian, friendly teacher. They're not studying English for love of the language; mostly they're doing it to get the necessary credits as part of their degree and they want to protect their grade point average (GPA).

DO I NEED TO BE QUALIFIED TO WORK AS AN ENGLISH TEACHER IN HONG KONG?

The brief answer is, generally, yes. As in the rest of Asia, where demand for English teachers outstrips supply, there are still private language schools in Hong Kong that will cut corners and take on unqualified teachers, usually on lower than average pay. For full-time primary and secondary teaching positions, a degree plus PGCE, or education degree and experience of teaching English, are prerequisites. For tertiary full-time teaching, a Masters in Applied Linguistics/TESOL is preferred. For part-time teaching, a first degree, a TEFL Certificate and teaching experience are desirable. The academic year runs from September to June, so most full-time recruitment happens between February and April.

The English-as-a-foreign-language (EFL) world is a small world in Hong Kong. Jobs usually travel by word of mouth and it's worth developing a network of contacts in order to hear about teaching jobs or related work, such as radio or voice-overs, as there are no recruitment agencies for teachers. Unlike the USA, Canada, the UK or Japan, there is unfortunately no English language teacher's association in Hong Kong.

SALARY AND WORK VISAS

Many English teachers prefer to work at tertiary institutions because the working conditions are good, and the salary is higher than in private language schools – typically, $400–500 per hour for part-time teachers. Tertiary Language Centres commonly use a mix of full- and part-time teachers.

Full-time

Full-time tertiary English teachers are usually sponsored by their institutions, who do the paperwork for their work visas, and enjoy basic health insurance, generous periods of leave and sometimes a gratuity of 10–15% paid at the end of their contracts. Full-time salaries vary, usually between $28,000 and $50,000 a month, and currently match civil service pay scales.

Many full-time staff are hired locally these days. The difference between 'local contracts' and 'overseas contracts' is becoming less marked as institutions seek to cut costs in an effort to reach government savings targets.

Part-time

Part-time teachers can register themselves as a business and seek to obtain an 'investment' visa – see Chapter Thirteen, 'Work' – or may be sponsored by their host institution if they have sufficient hours. First-time visa applicants are usually granted a single-year visa, but on renewal, the visa may be extended for one, two or three years. Anecdotally, many teachers have commented that a lot is left to the individual immigration officer dealing with your case and his interpretation of the guidelines. The important thing is to make sure you have all your papers in order. More information on work visas can be found on the government's immigration website (**www.immd.gov.hk**).

Teacher's story

Diana Cox, a British English teacher, taught variously at the Polytechnic University, the British Council, Hong Kong University's School of Professional and Continuing Education (HKU SPACE), the Hong Kong Academy for the Performing Arts and the Hong Kong Examinations Authority for seven years before moving to Spain in 2004:

> *It wasn't exactly a rags-to-riches story, but in 1996 I moved into an empty flat on Lamma Island without a stick of furniture. I went around a building site and picked out bricks and crates. By 2003, I had a flat full of furniture and a wonderful life. I have a DVD player and a television, everything material I could want. I've bought a house*

for cash in Granada, put a lot into a pension and acquired a Masters degree. I can't think of anywhere else in the world where a teacher could achieve that in this space of time.

By 2006, Diana was back in Hong Kong.

EMPLOYMENT SECTORS

Below is an overview of the different sectors in which to seek employment.

Government primary and secondary schools

The government offers incentives to qualified overseas English teachers to take up posts in local primary, secondary and special needs schools under its NET (native-speaking English teacher) scheme. In 2010, there were 484 primary and 414 secondary NETs employed in schools all over Hong Kong Island, Kowloon and the New Territories. Duties for NETs vary enormously:

- functioning as an independent English teacher with responsibility for a set number of classes;
- teaching conversation classes only; and
- being an adjunct to a local teacher.

Exam preparation often dominates class time, as students gear up to taking their HKCEE (Hong Kong Certificate of Education Examination) at 15 and HKAL (Hong Kong Advanced Level Examination) at age 18. There is often limited opportunity for teachers to explore creative approaches to teaching and NETs frequently bemoan the way that English is taught in local schools. More information is available from the **Native English Speaking Teacher's Association** (www.nesta.com.hk).

NET teachers generally enjoy an attractive salary and benefits package that, depending on experience and qualifications, ranges from $17,000 to $46,000 plus a monthly allowance of $13,000 covering passage, medical insurance and relocation. Contracts are for two years and can be renewed with the mutual consent of the teacher and their school. The application deadline is January. More information can be obtained from the Education and Man-power Bureau's website, **www.netscheme.org.hk**.

If you are not fortunate enough to be offered a full-time NET contract at a primary or secondary school, private companies such as **G-Set** and **Speak-**

Easy (details below) supply long-term and temporary NET teachers to schools around Hong Kong. Alternatively, try the 'Classified' section of **www. scmp.com** or **www.jobs.gov.hk/eng/**.

International schools

Other well-paid full-time and supply teaching jobs for qualified and experienced teachers exist in international schools at kindergarten, primary and secondary level. For more information about primary and secondary international schools, please refer to the 'Schools' section in Chapter Eight, 'Having and Raising Children'.

Vocational/technical colleges

Vocational and technical colleges employ English teachers to teach secretarial and business English to students aged 15 and over. They include the **Caritas Francis Hsu College** (www.cfhc.caritas.edu.hk), the **Vocational Training Council** (www.vtc.edu.hk); the **HK Shue Yan University** (www.hksyu.edu) and the **Hong Kong Management Association** (www.hkma.org.hk).

Tertiary institutions

There are ten tertiary institutions in Hong Kong, each of which has a dedicated languages department or English language centre. For details, please refer to Appendix One. The language centres provide English language training to full-time students of all majors. Courses range in scope from general English communication courses to English for engineers, English through film, etc. Positions are advertised on the institutions' websites and in the *South China Morning Post* (www.scmp.com), as well as in the Chinese press.

Continuing education

Many of the universities also operate profit-making continuing education arms. Again, English teaching is a lucrative source of income. Most hire their own teachers separately from the university and teaching is usually in the evenings and/or at weekends. These include:

- **HKU SPACE** (Admiralty, Hong Kong Island; http://hkuspace.hku.hk/);
- **Poly University's CPBE** (Centre for Professional and Business English – www.cpbe.polyu.edu.hk);
- **School of Continuing Studies, Chinese University** (www.scs.cuhk.edu. hk); and
- **Hong Kong Baptist University's School of Continuing Education** (www.sce.hkbu.edu.hk/).

Private language schools

Below is a selection of some of the larger private language schools currently operating in the city. Hourly rates for teaching vary considerably from $100 to $300 per hour.

- **The British Council** in Admiralty (www.britishcouncil.org.hk) employs full- and part-time staff. Courses taught include Early Childhood English, Young Learners, General English, Business, etc.
- **Berlitz** (www.berlitz.com.hk) sponsors new teachers and trains them to teach English the Berlitz way. This can be an easy way into the local English teaching job market, but in return teachers earn lower-than-average wages and classes can take place at any time between 7:00 and 9:00 pm, with long gaps in between. Most classes are one-to-one.
- **G-Set** (www.gset.com.hk; tel. 2877 7688/2525 2545) wins contracts from primary and secondary schools around Hong Kong and then recruits teachers to do the work. They also run courses on their own premises. Teaching often includes Saturdays.

Other private language schools include **Speak Easy** (tel. 2730 3813/3843), **Language Key** (tel. 2517 7725) and **Venture Language Training Centre** (tel. 2194 1468).

Private teaching

Private teaching can be a lucrative source of income if properly managed, but is often inconvenient and you may find yourself teaching three-year-olds. Teachers usually charge $200–500 per hour. Again, word-of-mouth is the usual avenue for requesting English teachers.

Examining

The IELTS has made significant inroads in the past two years and is now recommended by the government as a graduate exit test of English. This in turn creates a need for **IELTS examiners**, a well-paid role that is organized via the British Council or IDP Australia. The **Hong Kong Examinations and Assessment Authority** (www.hkeaa.edu.hk) also hires examination paper markers, oral English examiners and exam paper writers.

EFL publishing

Some teachers move into English language teaching publishing as freelance materials writers or editorial staff. Key employers include **Oxford University**

Press China (www.oupchina.com.hk) and **Pearson Education** (www. pearsonedasia.com), both located in Quarry Bay.

Voice work and acting

English teachers who are interested in doing voice work and have some experience can contact **David Pope** (dpope@netvigator.com), a freelance educational audio producer working for Longman (Pearson Education). Professional actors and voice talent should contact broadcasters **Star TV** and **Cartoon Network** directly for work. The agency **Word-of-Mouth** (tel. 2809 2710) books voice talent, mostly for advertising and commercial work. A CD demonstrating a range of voices and accents should be sent to them first. Occasionally, actors can find work as extras or are given speaking roles in movies being shot in Hong Kong.

Chapter Sixteen

Developing yourself Professionally

Below are some of the courses and training available leading to further qualifications or skills development.

EXECUTIVE AND LIFE COACHING

Life, career and executive coaches offer services to help clients maximize success and satisfaction in their careers, lives and companies. Well-regarded life and executive coaches include **Angela Spaxman Business and Career Coaching** (www.spaxman.com.hk; tel. 2918 0785), **OI Partners** (www.oi-partnershk.com) and **Charlie Lang** (www.progressu.com.hk; tel. 9199 2019). Most coaches will offer a one-to-one free initial session. The **Hong Kong Coaching Community** (www.coachinghk.org) can provide more information on coaches working in the city and how to qualify as a coach.

UNDERGRADUATE AND POSTGRADUATE STUDIES

Ten tertiary institutions in Hong Kong (see Appendix One) offer undergraduate and postgraduate qualifications in a range of disciplines and a variety of formats. Full- or part-time courses, a choice between distance learning or lecture-supported distance learning and the ability to complete courses online are some of the options on offer. Most programmes operated solely by local universities are taught in Cantonese supplemented with English materials, so check the language of instruction if it is not stated.

The HK University of Science and Technology's business school was recently ranked within the top 10 for MBA programmes by the *Financial Times* (2010).

Distance learning programmes offered by British universities via the **British Council** (www.britishcouncil.org.hk) include Building Management and Services Engineering, Business and Finance, Education, Law, Nutrition Science, Procurement Management, Psychology and English Language Teaching/Applied Linguistics.

45. Taking Notes
Photograph taken by the author

A Bachelor's degree in Fine Arts is offered by the Art School with the RMIT in Australia at the **Hong Kong Arts Centre** (www.hkac.org.hk/).

A complete list of courses offered by non-local institutions in Hong Kong is available from the **Non-Local Higher & Professional Education Courses** government website (www.edb.gov.hk).

CONTINUING EDUCATION

Continuing education providers in Hong Kong have built their public course offerings rather haphazardly and creatively, with the result that short courses, foundation level courses, certificate and diploma level courses, and under-graduate and postgraduate courses are bedfellows across a vast spectrum of disciplines. Floral design co-exists with PRC taxation for foreigners, yoga with a master's degree in criminal justice, introduction to the Internet with MBAs.

HKU SPACE (http://hkuspace.hku.hk; tel. 2559 9771) is the largest provider of continuing education in Hong Kong and provides a pick'n'mix assortment of short and long courses in everything from children's writing to Chinese medicine or music. International partners include Monash University, Curtin University of Technology and the University of Greenwich. SPACE also handles the administration of and applications for the University of London's external programmes, including the LLB, LLM and MBA in International Management. Other major providers of continuing education include the Open University of Hong Kong, City University and Polytechnic University.

TRAINING

The **British Council** runs the Cambridge suite of teacher training qualifications: CELTA (Certificate of English Language Teaching to Adults); CELTYL (Certificate of English Language Teaching to Young Learners) and the TEFL Diploma.

The **Frederique School of Beauty and Wholistic Health** (4/F, Wilson House, 19–27 Wyndham Street, Central; tel. 2522 3053) offers UK-accredited courses in international beauty therapy. The **International Spa and Beauty College** (10/F, Silver Fortune Plaza, 1 Wellington Street, Central; www.isbc.com.hk; tel. 2526 8818) offers holistic and complementary diploma and certificate courses. **Asia-Pacific Aromatherapy** (6/F, San Kei Tower, 56–8 Yee Wo Street, Causeway Bay; www.aromatherapyapa.com; tel. 2882 2444) offers a diploma in holistic aromatherapy as well as introductory and certificate courses.

Isofit (8/F, California Tower, 30–32 D'Aguilar Street, Central; www.isofit.com.hk; tel. 2869 8630) teaches courses in Pilates and Gyrotonic exercise methods designed for fitness and rehabilitation professionals, whilst **One Pilates Studio** (21/F, Winsome House, 73 Wyndham Street; www.onepilatesstudio.com; tel. 2147 3318) offers teacher certification programmes in Pilates.

LANGUAGE COURSES

There are many private language schools catering to expats who wish to learn Chinese or other foreign languages. Many advertise in the back of *HK Magazine*. Prices vary, so be prepared to shop around. Several universities offer part-time day and evening courses, including the **Chinese University** (www.cuhk.edu.hk/clc/ssp_regular.htm) and **HKU SPACE** (http://hkuspace.hku.hk). Cantonese is also offered by the British Council. An enjoyable alternative-style Cantonese class is offered by **Happy Jellyfish People's Democratic Language Bureau** (http://happyjellyfish.com/web), run by Norwegian Cecilie Gamst Berg, a long-time resident. Cecilie combines learning Cantonese with becoming better acquainted with the Hong Kong pub scene and Chinese card games.

European languages courses on offer include French at the Alliance Française (www.alliancefrancaise.com.hk), German at the Goethe Institut (tel. 2802 0088) and Italian (www.conshongkong.esteri.it).

GENERAL SHORT COURSES FOR SELF-DEVELOPMENT

Other organizations offering courses include:

- the **YWCA** (http://esmd.ywca.org.hk), which offers skills development courses, including computer courses in *PowerPoint, Photoshop, FrontPage,* Internet and e-mail.

More information on classes and hobbies is provided in Chapter Twenty-One, 'Classes'.

46. The Hong Kong Convention and Exhibition Centre
Photograph taken by Stanley Ng

Chapter Seventeen

Volunteering

The Ho-sum Organization (www.ho-sum.org; tel. 2549 2010) is a non-profit, independent organization which acts as an online matchmaker between would-be volunteers and charities requiring help. It's free for charities to post projects and for volunteers to register. Details of over 4,000 vounteer projects have been posted, including PR, fundraising, after-school care and translation.

Manager Clare Chan has seen a shift in attitudes to voluntary work:

> *People changed after SARS. This one big disaster made people realize it was time to help each other. It was a trigger point to prompt people to volunteer.*

For some, it's the opportunity to give back to the community, whilst others get involved to make friends or to boost their self-esteem. Volunteers can log work hours and earn Volunteer Recognition Certificates. Motivation isn't important, according to Chan:

> *You can't say there's a good volunteer or a bad volunteer. The important thing is to have a good heart.*

Recently, 'virtual volunteering' has begun to take off. Volunteers can choose to work online or by phone, offering PR and marketing advice, translation services and website design. Contact Ho-Sum or any of the other charities listed below if you are interested in volunteering.

ANIMAL WELFARE

- The **SPCA** (www.spca.org.hk; tel. 2802 0501) is headquartered at 5 Wan Shing Street, Wanchai and has centres around Kowloon, the New Territories and the Outlying Islands. Volunteers aged 16 and over are welcome to register for a range of work, including dog-walking, clerical support, assisting vets and kennel keepers, and socializing the animals.

47. Vegetable farming
Photograph taken by Stanley Ng

■ The **Hong Kong Alley Cat Watch Society** (www.hkalleycats.com) is always interested in permanent and temporary homes for rescued cats.

CONSERVATION

■ The **World Wide Fund for Nature Hong Kong** (www.wwf.org.hk; tel. 2523 2316) focuses on conservation and environmental education. They need volunteers for a range of activities, including film-making, web design, copywriting and office work.

■ **Friends of the Earth** (www.foe.org.hk; tel. 2528 5588; e-mail foehk@ foe.org.hk) offers opportunities for English speakers to help with editorial work and promotional material for campaigns, tree-planting every spring, and the solar cart race which is in November.

■ **Greenpeace** (www.greenpeace.org.hk) seeks volunteers to help with campaigns, fundraising, outreach activities and publications.

Some of the many local projects include 'Save Our Harbour' and 'Clear The Air' campaigns – visit **www.cleartheair.org.hk** for details.

COUNSELLING AND SUPPORT

■ **The Samaritans** (www.samaritans.org.hk/volunteer.htm; tel. 2896 0000) recruits English-speaking volunteers to man their English hotline. Volunteers are given a training course.

■ **Prisoner's Friends Association** (www.pfa.org.hk; tel. 2601 0129; e-mail info@pfa.org.hk) recruits penfriends or prison visitors for inmates who have requested a visitor. Prisoners' friends are matched to prisoners with whom they speak a common language. Meetings and training sessions are held periodically.

INTERNATIONAL HUMANITARIAN

■ **Oxfam** (17/F, China United Center, 28 Marble Road, North Point; tel. 3120 5284; e-mail volunteer@oxfam.org.hk) runs a number of fundraising, education and advocacy activities throughout the year. Volunteers are needed for office administration, translation, typing and web design.

- **Médecins Sans Frontières** (www.msf.org.hk; tel. 2338 8277) recruit field and office volunteers and fundraisers.
- **Crossroads International** (2 Castle Peak Road, Tuen Mun, NT; tel. 2984 9309; e-mail volunteer@crossroads.org.hk) is an organization which redistributes quality used goods to people around the world. They need volunteers to help with fundraising, Internet research, data entry, handy-man tasks, sorting and packing of clothing and household goods, furniture repair and container loading.

LOCAL ISSUES

- **AIDS Concern** (www.aidsconcern.org.hk; tel. 2898 4411; e-mail aidscon@netvigator.com) recruits volunteers to work in one of five areas – Office Team, Event Team, Cross Border Travellers Team, Ride Concern Transport Team and Helpline Group.
- **Mother's Choice** (42B Kennedy Road, Mid Levels; www.motherschoice.com; tel. 2524 4310) welcomes regular part-time or full-time volunteers to care for babies and children and to teach English, arts and crafts, drama, computer skills and pre- and post-natal workshops. Part-timers should be willing to commit to a minimum of three hours per week at the same time each week.
- **China Coast Community** (www.chinacoastcommunity.org.hk; tel. 2337 7266) volunteers assist with leisure activities for elderly English-speaking residents, offer classes and lead outings.
- **The American Women's Association of Hong Kong** (www.awa.org.hk; tel. 2527 2961/2) has strong links with several local charities and organizations, including Riding for the Disabled, Helpers for Domestic Helpers and the Hong Kong Society for the Blind.
- The English Speaking Members Department of the **YWCA** (3/F, 1 MacDonnell Road, Mid-Levels; www.esmdywca.org.hk; tel. 3476 1340; e-mail esmd@ywca.org.hk) seeks volunteers to help in the office for half a day on a weekly basis and periodically with mailings, bazaars and bake sales.
- **Hands on Hong Kong** (http://handsonhongkong.org/) require volunteers for dog-walking, refugee and asylum-seekers, elderly residents and making handicrafts, etc.

- **English-speaking volunteers** are also needed to lead social activities, games and so on by organizations including the **Hong Kong Society for the Protection of Children** (www.hkspc.org).

Part Three

Having Fun in Hong Kong

Chapter Eighteen

Getting Involved in the Local Arts Scene

Hong Kong has a small but vibrant arts scene, comprising music, dance, film, theatre and visual arts. Future developments to bolster the role of the arts include a twenty-four billion dollar West Kowloon cultural district. The district will feature a purpose-built opera house, theatres, museums and other cultural facilities as well as offices, shopping and dining venues.

One of the most enterprising undertakings in recent years has been the Hong Kong Youth Arts Foundation (established by the charismatic Lindsey McAlister). The Foundation offers opportunities to all children and young people aged 8–25 to get involved in a broad range of public performances and creative projects each year, boasting 800,000 participants.

Details of performances and events around Hong Kong are listed daily in the *South China Morning Post*, weekly in *HK Magazine* (out each Friday) and monthly in *BC Magazine*.

For a complete listing of local arts groups, visit **www.hkadc.org.hk**.

ARTS FESTIVALS

The main international arts events of the year are the **Hong Kong Arts Festival** (www.hk.artsfestival.org), which runs from early February to March, and the **Hong Kong International Film Festival** (www.hkiff.org.hk), which runs during April. The Arts Festival features opera, ballet, multimedia, music, drama and performance arts from local and internationally renowned groups. The Film Festival features several hundred films from all over the world screened through the day and well into the night.

Smaller-scale film festivals (German, French, Australian, British, Jewish, Gay and Lesbian, etc.) run at other times of the year and are publicized in the local media.

48. Art jam
Photograph taken by the author

CLASSICAL MUSIC CONCERTS

Of all the Western art forms performed in Hong Kong, Western classical music is probably most prevalent. Whilst English language theatre is thin on the ground, there are year-round classical concerts featuring the local professional orchestras – the **Hong Kong Philharmonic Orchestra**, the **Hong Kong Sinfonietta** and the **City Chamber Orchestra**.

In the past, the city has played host to concerto performances and recitals by Yuri Bashmet, Hilary Hahn, Lang Lang, Garrick Ohlsson, André Watts, Vladimir Spivakov and Elmar Oliviera, as well as to internationally famous conductors such as Taadaki Otaka, Gunter Herbig and Libor Pesek. Musical programmes are available at kiosks in the Cultural Centre and City Hall, as well as from other arts venues around town.

Chinese classical music concerts are held regularly by the **Hong Kong Chinese Orchestra** (www.hkco.org). For the uninitiated, this is so much more than 'Chinese opera': the haunting melodies of the erhu (a two-stringed instrument held upright and bowed on the knee) and the bright notes of the zheng, pipa, the sheng and dizi (Chinese flute) are just some of the beautiful instruments showcased in concerto or solo performances. Chinese opera concerts are staged at venues around Hong Kong – visit **www.lcsd.gov.hk** for details.

The **Hong Kong Academy for Performing Arts** (1 Gloucester Road, Wanchai; www.hkapa.edu) holds regular student and guest recitals, many of which are free to members of the public. Popular public programmes include the Monday lunchtime concerts in the First Floor Foyer, where food is available. Register by e-mail to receive a monthly diary of events.

Wednesday lunchtime recitals are held at **St John's Cathedral** on Garden Road. The **Cultural Centre** in TST hosts free musical performances every Saturday afternoon and on Thursday evenings between 6:00 and 7:00 pm in the foyer.

Brioso, a professional trio, offers music for hire (www.briosohk.com; tel. 9329 4761).

POP CONCERTS

Cantopop artists dominate the music scene in Hong Kong and Asia. Andy Lau, Twins, Leon Lai, Sammi Cheng and Karen Mok are some of the local icons.

Western artists still swing by Hong Kong on their international tours: recent visitors have included Robbie Williams, Dionne Warwick and Brian Ferry. There have also been government-sponsored large-scale music festivals featuring big-name acts such as the Rolling Stones, José Carreras, Prince and Santana.

A summer pop concert, which debuted in 2009, is planned as a permanent fixture, starting 2010 at the Hong Kong Coliseum (August).

JAZZ

There are few dedicated jazz venues, although jazz bands play regularly at **The Blue Door** (5/F, 37 Cochrane Street, Central; tel. 2858 6555) and the **Fringe Club** (2 Lower Albert Road, Central; tel. 2521 7251). Most bands play in bars and restaurants around the city, including **Gecko** (tel. 2537 4680), **Bohemian Lounge** (3–5 Old Bailey Street, Central, Tel 2526 6099), **San Marzano Pizza Express** (21 Lyndhurst Terrace, Soho; tel. 2850 7898) and **Grappa's Country** (Basement, Jardine House, Connaught Road, Central; tel. 2521 2322).

DANCE

Hong Kong has a vibrant dance scene, with local companies including the **Hong Kong Ballet** and **City Contemporary Dance Company** staging productions throughout the year at major arts venues around Hong Kong. The Hong Kong Academy for Performing Arts showcases student dance productions in ballet, modern and Chinese dance each semester.

Musicals are especially popular and hits that have migrated from London or Broadway to Hong Kong over the years include *Riverdance*, *Miss Saigon*, *Fame*, *Umoja* and *Mamma Mia*.

THEATRE

There is plenty of Cantonese theatre around, and professional companies such as the **Hong Kong Repertory Theatre** and **Springtime Productions** stage classics from the Chinese and Western repertoire as well as contemporary plays. As far as English-language theatre goes, the quality is variable and performances few and far between, although the Fringe Club and Arts Centre (see 'Major performance venues' below) host occasional performances.

The Indian restaurant **Viceroy** (2/F, Sun Hung Kai Centre, 30 Harbour Road, Wanchai; tel. 2827 7777) hosts monthly stand-up comedy staged by the **Punchline Comedy Club** on the last Friday of the month (www.punchlinecomedy.com/hongkong/index.html).

Grappa's Country (see above) hosts regular Sunday performances, many of which are for children.

MAJOR PERFORMANCE VENUES

The major government-owned performing arts venues in Hong Kong include the the **Hong Kong City Hall** in Central, **Hong Kong Cultural Centre** in TST, **Kwai Tsing Theatre** in Kwai Chung and **Sha Tin Town Hall**. Other large-scale venues popularly used for concerts and spectaculars include the **Hong Kong Coliseum** (Hung Hom) and the **Wanchai Convention and Exhibition Centre**.

The Fringe Club (www.hkfringeclub.com) in Central acts as a meeting point and venue for many of the English and European language performances. The Club hosts jazz nights, contemporary international theatre, stand-up comedy, poetry jams and photographic exhibitions on a regular basis. The venue has a bar with low-priced drinks, and a roof terrace and restaurant that can be hired for social evenings, BBQs, etc. The club also hosts an annual **City Festival**.

The Arts Centre in Wanchai is equipped with theatres and a cinema and hosts theatrical productions, film screenings, art installations and photographic exhibitions.

Tickets

Tickets to events held at the Hong Kong Convention and Exhibition Centre, the Hong Kong Academy for Performing Arts, the Arts Centre and the Fringe Club are sold through **Hong Kong Ticketing** at box offices in the venues listed (www.hkticketing.com.hk; tel. 3128 8288). Venues managed by the Leisure and Cultural Services Department sell tickets through **URBTIX** (www.lcsd.gov.hk/CE/Entertainment/Ticket/en/index.php; tel. 2734 9009).

FILM

Cinema-going is a popular pastime and a cheap form of entertainment. Tickets to UA cinemas and affiliates can be bought via **Cityline** (www.cityline.com; tel. 2317 6666); tickets to **Broadway Circuit** cinemas via www.cinema.com.hk (tel. 2388 3188). Tickets to **MCL** (Multiplex Cinema Limited) theatres can be bought via www.moviesuper.com/big5/.

Cinemas mainly frequented by expats and showing English- or European-language films include **UA Pacific Place**, **Palace IFC** and **CineArt** in Wanchai. Shop around, as ticket prices vary depending on theatre location. On Tuesdays, tickets are discounted at many cinemas. The larger venues supply shawls if you find the air-conditioning too strong – just ask. Some theatres, for example UA Cityplaza and Windsor House, have smaller theatres that can be hired for a private screening.

The Hong Kong Film Archive in Sai Wan Ho was established in 1999 and offers lectures and regular film screenings of Cantonese, Chinese and international films.

Omnimax films are screened at the **Hong Kong Space Museum** in TST (www.lcsd.gov.hk/CE/Museum/Space/Sitemap/e_index.htm). The **Agnès B Cinema** in the Arts Centre shows non-commercial films; tickets are available for purchase at www.hkticketing.com.

CHINESE CULTURAL ACTIVITIES

The **Ko Shan Theatre** (www.lcsd.org) and the **Hong Kong Academy for Performing Arts** regularly stages Chinese operas. The **Bun Festival**, held every May in Cheung Chau, is also the place to see traditional Chinese musical performances.

EUROPEAN CULTURAL ACTIVITIES

The Hong Kong Arts Centre houses the **Goethe Institut** (www.goethe.de/hongkong), which offers German-language classes from beginner to advanced level. Wanchai is also home to the **Italian Consulate**, which provides information on Italian-themed social events and Italian classes (www.conshongkong.esteri.it). The nearby **Alliance Française** (www.alliancefrancaise.com.hk)

has a French-language library, holds French classes and sponsors exhibitions, film screenings and talks involving French writers and artists. *Le French May* (www.frenchmay.com) annual festival showcases dance, music, film and other performances and work from France.

VISUAL ARTS

The **Hong Kong Art Museum** (http://hk.art.museum) hosts the largest collection of fine art in the city, including collections of Chinese art and calligraphy. Above the Hong Kong Park, the **Hong Kong Visual Arts Centre** (7A Kennedy Road; tel. 2521 3008; closed Tuesdays) and **Hong Kong Design Centre** (28 Kennedy Road; www.hkdesigncentre.org; tel. 2522 8688) host occasional exhibitions.

BROWSING ART GALLERIES

Most art galleries hosting exhibitions of fine art are located on and around Hollywood Road – details can be found in Chapter Seven, 'Shopping'. Details of special exhibitions, many of which are free and open to the public, are published daily in the *South China Morning Post* Listings column and weekly in *HK Magazine* (out Fridays) or browse www.aziacity.com/hk or www.hongkonggalleries.org.

To discover more about contemporary Chinese art, visit the **Asia Art Archive** (Room 208, Wah Koon Building, 181–191 Hollywood Road, Sheung Wan; www.aaa.org.hk; tel. 2815 1112). There is also an e-library at **State of the Arts Gallery** (G/F, 36 Pottinger Street, Central; www.sotagallery.com.hk; tel. 2526 1133).

One enjoyable annual event launched a few years ago is Art Walk, an unguided tour of contemporary art galleries in Central and Sheung Wan with food laid on by well-known local restaurants. Proceeds go towards helping victims of AIDS. Details can be found at www.hongkongartwalk.com.

Public art is slowly but surely making inroads and can be seen on office walkways in Taikoo Place, in shopping malls such as Times Square and Pacific Place, on art corners in Hong Kong Park, and at MTR stations. Some would argue that the city's best art is its public advertising, as seen in the head-turning advertising billboards and moving video ads on skyscrapers in Central and Causeway Bay.

BOOKS

Although the Hong Kong public is not usually considered a book-reading public, a dedicated book-loving community gathers together for literary events. The week-long English-language **Hong Kong International Literary Festival**, established in 2000, is held annually in March and creates a frisson amongst aspiring writers and literary fans. Past speakers have included Yann Martel, Maxine Hong Kingston and Gish Jen. Local literary journal *Dim Sum*, produced by leading literary light Nury Vittachi, is available at local bookstores.

Throughout the year, literary events are promoted by:

- the *South China Morning Post*, which also holds an annual short story competition;
- the **Foreign Correspondent's Club** (www.fcchk.org); and
- the **Women in Publishing Society, Hong Kong** (www.hkwips.org), which also publishes *Imprint*, an annual journal.

The **British Council** is another organization that occasionally hosts literary events featuring visiting British writers – Louis de Bernières and Alexander McCall Smith visited in 2010. You can sign up for notification about new events at http://registration.britishcouncil.org.hk/en/newsletter/.

Hong Kong public libraries worth visiting include the modern, well-equipped **Hong Kong Central Library** (66 Causeway Road, Causeway Bay; www.hkpl. gov.hk/hkcl; tel. 3150 1234) and **City Hall Library** (Central).

Details on where to buy books appear in Chapter Seven, 'Shopping'.

Current Exhibitions

For up-to-date information on current exhibitions, visit www.hongkongex-tras.com

Chapter Nineteen

Playing Sports

SPORTING EVENTS

Hong Kong's best-known sports icon, the Olympic and world champion windsurfer Lee Lai-Shan, is a local legend and rightly cherished in a city not known for its sporting prowess. Sports venues, training and opportunities for professionals are limited, although for amateurs and enthusiasts there is plenty of choice.

The city plays host to some important international sporting events – January brings the **Hong Kong Ladies Challenge** tennis championship to Victoria Park and in March, the famous **Hong Kong Rugby Sevens** attracts fans from all round Asia for three days of rugby and merry-making. The Hong Kong Jockey Club hosts the **Hong Kong International Races** each December, attracting punters from all round the world. Other competitions include the **Cathay Pacific Hong Kong Squash Open**, the **Hong Kong Open Windsurfing**, **Cricket Sixes** and the **Hong Kong Marathon**.

SPORTS CLUBS AND ASSOCIATIONS

There are amateur associations for most sports, including archery, athletics, badminton, basketball, baseball, martial arts, cricket, cycling and dragon boating, as well as associations for disabled athletes.

The easiest way to book squash, badminton, tennis courts and other sports spaces is through www.gov.hk, featuring the Leisure and Cultural Service Department's online information and booking system.

Many of the associations and sports clubs below provide training for adults and children. *Action Asia* (www.actionasia.com), a monthly magazine published in Hong Kong, details travel, sport and adventure activities in the Asia region.

Information on gyms, fitness clubs and yoga classes is included in Chapter Nine, 'Looking after your Health'.

49. Dragon Boating
Photograph taken by Stanley Ng

Athletics

- South China Athletic Association (www.scaa.org.hk; tel. 2577 6932).
- Hong Kong Triathlon Association (www.triathlon.com.hk).

Aviation

- Hong Kong Aviation Club (Sung Wong Toi Road, Kowloon City; www.hkaviationclub.com.hk; tel. 2713 5171).

Basketball

- Hong Kong Basketball Association (www.basketball.org.hk; tel. 2504 8181). Please note that this website is mostly in Chinese.

Bowling

- Kowloon Bowling Green Club (123 Austin Road, Jordan, tel. 2368 7733).
- Hong Kong Lawn Bowls Association (www.hklba.org).

Boxing

- DEF boxing (www.def.com.hk; tel. 2840 0162).
- Boxing/Kick boxing at The One Martial Gym (www.fightinfit.com.hk).
- K-1 Thai Kickboxing and Fitness (2/F, Yen Men Bldg, 98–108 Jaffe Road, Wanchai; tel. 2865 1608).
- Kontact MMA Training Centre (http://kontact.com.hk).

Cricket

- Hong Kong Cricket Club (137 Wong Nai Chung Gap Road, Happy Valley; www.hkcc.org; tel. 2574 6266).
- Kowloon Cricket Club (10 Cox's Road; www.kcc.org.hk; tel. 2367 4141).

Cycling

- Hong Kong Cycling Association (www.cycling.org.hk; tel. 2504 8176).

Diving

- Hong Kong Underwater Club (www.hkuc.org.hk).
- South China Diving Club (www.scdc.org.hk).
- Splash (www.splashhk.com; tel. 9047 9603).

Fencing

- HK Amateur Fencing Association (www.hkafa.org.hk). The South China Athletic Association (see above) also offers fencing classes.

Golf

- City Golf Club driving range, opposite Kowloon MTR station, has 180 bays (tel. 2992 3333).

A full list of golf clubs in the region is at the end of this chapter.

Hockey

- Hong Kong Hockey Association (www.hockey.org.hk).
- Hong Kong Football Club (www.hkfc.com.hk).
- Valley RFC (www.valleyrfc.com).
- Unicycle Hockey (www.unihk.org; tel. 9203 1505).

Horse riding

- Hong Kong Equestrian Federation (www.hkef.org; tel. 2464 2800).
- Pokfulam Public Riding School (tel. 2550 1359).
- Lo Wu Saddle Club (www.lowusaddleclub.org; tel. 2673 0066).

Ice hockey

- Women's Ice Hockey Organization (www.icehockey.com.hk).
- Hong Kong Amateur Hockey Club (www.hkahc.com).

Lacrosse

- Hong Kong Lacrosse Association (www.hklax.org; tel. 8107 6636).

Martial arts

- The South China Athletic Association (see above) offers classes in kung fu, judo, karate, tai chi, etc.
- Hong Kong Kendo Association (www.hongkongkendo.com; tel. 2504 8145).
- Karate (www.karatehk.com; tel. 2956 2868).

Motorbiking

- Classic Bike Club (tel. 9130 4536).
- Motocross Club (info@mxclub.com.hk; tel. 2659 8159).

Mountain biking

- The Hong Kong Mountainbike Association (www.hkmba.org). For an index of mountain bike trails and information on applying for a permit, visit www.afcd.gov.hk.

- Adventure Plus (www.adventureplus.com.hk; tel. 3480 4895).

Mountaineering and rock climbing
- Hong Kong Mountaineering Union (tel. 2504 8125).
- Information on rock climbing at www.hongkongclimbing.com.

Netball
- Hong Kong Netball Association (tel. 2504 8208).

Orienteering
- Orienteering Association of Hong Kong (www.oahk.org.hk; tel. 2504 8111).

Paragliding
- Hong Kong Paragliding Association (www.hkpa.net/).

Pool
- **The Foreign Correspondents' Club** (2 Lower Albert Road, Central; www.fcchk.org/; tel. 2521 1511) plays competitive pool.

Rowing and dragon boating
- Hong Kong Island Paddle Club (www.hkipc.com).
- The Hong Kong Dragon Boat Association (www.hkdba.com.hk).
- Stanley Residents' Association (www.dragonboat.org.hk).
- Hong Kong Amateur Dragon Boat Association (www.dragonboat-hk.org).
- Hong Kong China Rowing Association (www.rowing.org.hk).

Rugby
- Hong Kong Football Club (www.hkfc.com.hk).
- Hong Kong Cricket Club, previously Aberdeen Rugby Club (tel. 9179 5844).
- Hong Rugby Football Union (www.hkrugby.com; tel. 2504 8311).
- Kowloon Rugby Football Club (www.kowloon-rugby.com).
- Valley RFC (www.valleyrfc.com).

Running
- Hong Kong Runners (www.hkrunners.com). The website includes links to hashes around Hong Kong.
- Ladies Hash House Harriers (www.hkladieshash.com; tel. 2881 0748).
- Ladies Road Runners (www.hklrrc.org.hk).
- Athletic Veterans of Hong Kong (www.avohk.org).
- Babes Hash (http://babeshash.blogspot.com/). Girls-only Hash.

There are also jogging tracks at Victoria Park, Happy Valley Race Stadium, Harlech Road (The Peak), Bowen Road (Mid-Levels) and Kowloon Park.

Sailing
- Hong Kong Yachting Association (www.sailing.org.hk; tel. 2813 1784).
- Yachting Ventures (www.yachtingventures.com).
- Sailing Adventure (www.lcsd.gov.hk for more details).

More information can be found below under 'Private yacht clubs and marinas'.

Shooting
- Hong Kong Shooting Association (www.hkshooting.org.hk).
- China Gun Club (www.chinagunclub.com.hk; tel. 2915 0088).
- Hong Kong Gun Club (tel. 2493 0514).
- Hong Kong Rifle Association (www.hkra.org; tel. 2744 2283).

Skiing and snowboarding
- Slope Infinity (www.slope8.com; tel. 2107 4567).

Soccer
- Hong Kong Football Club (3 Sports Road, Happy Valley; www.hkfc.com.hk; tel. 2830 9502).
- Hong Kong Football Association (www.hkfa.com; tel. 2712 9122).

Softball
- Hong Kong Slo-pitch Softball Association (www.hongkongsoftball.com).

Squash
- Hong Kong Squash Centre (www.hksquash.org.hk; tel. 2521 5072).
- Public squash courts:
  - Queen Elizabeth Stadium, Wanchai (tel. 2591 1331);
  - Victoria Park (tel. 2570 6186);
  - Shatin (tel. 2604 7647);
  - Sai Kung (tel. 2792 6459);
  - Kowloon Tsai Park (tel. 236 7878);
  - Lai Chi Kok Indoor Games Sports Hall (tel. 2745 2796); and
  - Morse Park (tel. 2338 3047).
- Hong Kong Cricket Club (see above for details).
- Hong Kong Football Club (see above for details).
- Island Squash Rackets Club (tel. 2868 4885).

Swimming

- Hong Kong Amateur Swimming Association (www.hkasa.org.hk).
- Indoor heated public pools open all year round include Morrison Hill and Kowloon Park. Open-air public pools, which are closed from mid-October to the end of April, include Victoria Park and Kennedy Town.
- The YWCA, YMCA and South China Athletics Association (see above) also have pools for members' use.

Surfing

- Simon Chau (tel. 93681415; e-mail simonkc@netvigator.com) heads up the Hong Kong Surfing Association and gives lessons at the weekends. He recommends that beginners begin by renting a boogie board at Big Wave Bay beach in Shek O, which costs about $50 rent plus $100 deposit. Other beaches for surfing include Tai Long Wan in Sai Kung. Daily weather forecasts for windsurfing hotspots can be found at www.hko.gov.hk/sports/windsurf.htm.

Tennis

- Hong Kong Tennis Association (www.tennishk.org; tel. 2504 8266).
- Public tennis courts:
  - Hong Kong: Quarry Bay Park (tel. 2513 8499), Victoria Park (tel. 2570 6186), Bowen Road (tel. 2528 2983) and Wong Nai Chung Gap Road (tel. 2574 9122);
  - Kowloon: Morse Park (tel. 2338 3047) and King's Park (tel. 2385 8985); and
  - New Territories: Shatin (tel. 2605 3622) and Sai Kung (tel. 2792 6459).

Wakeboarding

- Sea Dynamics (www.seadynamics.com; tel. 2604 4747).
- Tai Tam Wakeboarding Centre (www.wakeboard.com.hk; tel. 3120 4120).
- Wakeboard Camp (www.wakeboardcamp.com.hk).

Waterskiing

- Hong Kong Waterski Association (www.waterski.org.hk).

Windsurfing

- Windsurfing Association of Hong Kong (www.windsurfing.org.hk; tel. 2504 8255).
- Government water sport centres offering training can be found at www.lcsd.gov.hk/watersport/en/index.php.

PRIVATE SPORTS AND SOCIAL CLUBS

The sports and social clubs listed below are generally extremely expensive to join and may have a waiting list for entry. Many require individual or corporate debentures, which are sometimes advertised for sale in the *South China Morning Post*. However, a concessionary entry fee and accelerated entry is offered to serious sportsmen and women. The clubs have a range of splendid recreational, social and leisure facilities geared towards families. These often include swimming pools, tennis courts, squash courts, sports coaching, exercise classes, children's activities and camps, a choice of restaurants, and evening entertainments.

Hong Kong Island

- American Country Club (28 Tai Tam Road; www.americanclubhk.com; tel. 2813 3299). Connected to the American Town Club in Central.
- Craigengower Cricket Club (188 Wong Nai Chung Road, Happy Valley; www.ccc1894.com; tel. 2837 1820). Tennis and lawn bowls; no cricket.
- Dynasty Club (7/F, South West Tower, Convention Plaza, 1 Harbour Road, Wanchai; www.dynastyclub.com.hk; tel. 2824 1122).
- Hong Kong Country Club (188 Wong Chuk Hang Road, Deepwater Bay; tel. 2552 4165).
- Hong Kong Cricket Club (137 Wong Nai Chung Gap Road, Happy Valley; www.hkcc.org; tel. 2574 6266).
- Hong Kong Football Club (3 Sports Road, Happy Valley; www.hkfc.com.hk; tel. 2830 9502).
- Hong Kong Jockey Club (Shan Kwong Road, Happy Valley; www.hongkongjockeyclub.com; tel. 2966 1333). Other club houses are located in Shatin and Kam Tsin.
- Victoria Recreation Club (Sai Kung and Deepwater Bay; www.victoriarecreationclub.com.hk; tel. 2812 2565).
- World Trade Centre Club (38/F, World Trade Centre, 280 Gloucester Road, Causeway Bay; www.wtcchk.com; tel. 2577 9528/2808 2288)

Kowloon

- Club de Recreio (20 Gascoigne Road, Kings Park; tel. 2388 8194).
- Hilltop Country Club (10 Hilltop Road, Lo Wai, Tsuen Wan; tel. 2412 0201).
- Kowloon Cricket Club (10 Cox's Road; www.kcc.org.hk; tel. 2367 4141).

- Kowloon Tong Club (113A Waterloo Road, Kowloon Tong; www.kowloontongclub.org; tel. 3652 7878).
- Pacific Club (Harbour City, 5 Canton Road, TST; www.pacificclub.com.hk; tel. 2118 1802).
- United Services Recreation Club (1 Gascoigne Road, Jordan; www.usrc.org.hk; tel. 2367 0672).

Private yacht clubs and marinas
- Aberdeen Boat Club (www.abclubhk.com; tel. 2555 6216).
- Aberdeen Marina Club (www.amchk.com.hk; tel. 2555 8321).
- Clearwater Bay Marina Club (www.cwbgolf.org/public/marina_boat_yard_services.aspx).
- Discovery Bay Marina Club (www.dbmc.com.hk) and Discovery Bay Yacht Club (www.dbyc.net).
- Gold Coast Yacht and Country Club (www.goldcoastclub.com.hk; tel. 2404 2222/3229).
- Hebe Haven Yacht Club (www.hhyc.org.hk; tel. 2719 9682).
- Hong Kong Hobie Club (www.hobie.com.hk; tel. 2813 5003).
- Hong Kong Marina (www.hkmarina.com.hk; tel. 2792 1436).
- Royal Hong Kong Yacht Club (www.rhkyc.org.hk; tel. 2832 2817).

GOLF

Public courses
There are six golf courses in Hong Kong. The only public course, designed by Gary Player, is **The Jockey Club Kau Sai Chau Public Course**, Kau Sai Chau in Sai Kung (www.kscgolf.com; tel. 2791 3388). No membership is required. The green fees for ID card-holders over 21 start at $600 for a full course. Non-cardholders are permitted.

Private golf clubs (see below) admitting visitors include:

- Fanling (Monday–Friday);
- Deepwater Bay (Monday–Friday);
- Clearwater Bay (Tuesday and Friday); and
- Discovery Bay (Mondays, Tuesday and Fridays).

Public golf driving ranges include the **Tuen Mun Golf Centre** (tel. 2466 2600) and the **Wo Yi Hop Road Sports Ground** in Kwai Ching (tel. 2426 3269).

Golf coaches can be found at **Central Golf** (www.centralgolf.com.hk; tel. 2140 6633); **Tuition Swing Club** (tel. 2530 0875) and, for ladies, **JJ Golf** (www.jjgolf.com; tel. 2517 6736).

Private clubs and courses

- **Clearwater Bay Golf & Country Club**, Sai Kung (www.cwbgolf.org; tel.2358 0564).
- **Discovery Bay Golf Club** (www.discoverybay.com.hk; tel. 2987 7273).
- **Hong Kong Golf Club Fanling** (www.hkgolfclub.org; tel. 2670 1211).
- **Hong Kong Golf Club Deep Water Bay** (www.hkgolfclub.org; tel. 2812 7070).
- **Shek O Golf & Country Club** (tel. 2809 4458).

South China golf clubs

Twenty more golf clubs in Southern China are within easy reach of Hong Kong (less than two hours by ferry). More information on these clubs can be found at **www.hkprogolf.com** and **www.china-golf.com**.

Top clubs include:

- The **Chung Shan Hot Spring Golf Club** in Zhongshan City, Guangdong (tel. 2521 0377), which has courses designed by Arnold Palmer and Jack Nicklaus.
- The **Mission Hills Golf Club** in Shenzhen, which features four championship 18-hole golf courses designed by Jack Nicklaus, Jumbo Ozaki and Nick Faldo, and has a five-star resort hotel (www.missionhills.china.com).
- The **Lotus Hill Golf Resort** in Panyu, which offers an 18-hole course designed by Bernhard Langer in a 'walking game' style – not a golf cart in sight (www.lotushillgolf.com; tel. 2882 1811).
- The **Royal Orchid Golf Club** in Guangdong, which has 18 holes designed by Nick Faldo (www.royal-orchidgolf.com; tel. 2377 2368).
- The **Sand River Golf Club** in Shenzhen, which has 27 holes, including 18 championship holes designed by Gary Player in the style of a British seaside links course (tel. 2865 1739).
- The **Macau Golf & Country Club, Coloane Island** (tel. 2803 0811).

Chapter Twenty

Finding Interest Groups

ASIAN INTEREST

The **Royal Geographical Society Hong Kong** (www.rgshk.org.hk; tel. 2583 9700) is a large and active society with around a thousand members, and holds lectures, dinners, field trips, quiz nights and social balls. Standard membership is $400 a year. The **Hong Kong Branch of the Royal Asiatic Society** organizes lectures, visits to sites of historical interest and Asian trips as well as social activities (www.royalasiaticsociety.org.hk; tel. 2813 7500). Standard membership is $475 a year.

The **University of Hong Kong Museum Society** supports the university's museum and art gallery (www.hkums.com; tel. 2241 5500). Members can join lectures on the appreciation of Chinese art, walks and other cultural activities. Societies connected to the Chinese University include **Friends of the Art Museum** (www.cuhk.edu.hk/ics/friends), which sponsor lectures, study groups and tours to places of interest in Hong Kong and throughout Asia, and the **Hong Kong Anthropological Society** (www.cuhk.edu.hk/ant/others/anthro.htm).

Free lectures on Chinese culture are held monthly at the **Hong Kong City Hall** in Central. Details are published in the *South China Morning Post*.

The **Kwang Hwa Information and Cultural Centre** (40/F, Pacific Place, Tower One; www.taiwaninfo.org; tel. 2523 5555) hosts events promoting the culture and arts of Taiwan.

FRIENDS OF THE ARTS

Many of the arts organizations and venues around the city offer 'Friends' schemes entitling members to reduced price tickets, shopping discounts, arts classes and other benefits. They include:

▓ **Friends of Hong Kong Ballet** (www.hkballet.com/). Standard membership is $150 a year.

50. Kassia Women's Choir 'Disco Divas'
Taken by Katterwall Ltd.

- **Friends of the Cultural Centre** (see www.lcsd.gov.hk/). Standard membership is $150 a year.
- **Club Bravo**, supporting the Hong Kong Philharmonic Orchestra (tel. 2721 2030). Standard membership is $480 a year.
- **Fringe Club** (www.hkfringe.com.hk). Membership includes invitation to special exhibitions, lunch and drinks discounts, rent-free exhibition and performance facilities, and a cover charge waiver at M at the Fringe. Standard membership costs $300 for an annual subscription, plus a $300 joining fee.

AMATEUR THEATRE GROUPS

Join a group of very talented actors, singers, directors and choreo-graphers at the **Hong Kong Singers** (www.hksingers.com), the **American Community Theatre** (www.acthongkong.com) or **Hong Kong Players** (www.**hongkongplayers**.com). All three companies are regularly looking for new acting talent, singers, dancers, stage crew, directors and choreographers for their shows. Auditions are usually advertised in the *South China Morning Post*'s Listings column.

CHOIRS

There are a number of choirs active in Hong Kong, comprising expat and local singers. The **Bach Choir** (www.bachchoir.org.hk) has more than 80 members and performs a variety of classical repertoire. Weekly rehearsals usually take place at the Cultural Centre in TST. Subscription for each season, which runs from September to June, is $600, or $300 for students. **Hong Kong Voices** (www.hkvoices.org) focuses on masterpieces from the twentieth century to the present. Rehearsals usually take place on Wednesday evenings at the Hong Kong University campus, Mid-Levels. **Nova**, the Hong Kong Women's Choir (www.thkwc.org) performs all over the city.

Smaller choirs include **St John's College Chorale** (sacred music), the **Kassia Women's Choir** (popular jazz and musical theatre), **The Cecilian Singers** (who focus on unaccompanied smaller-scale classical works) and **The Catch Club** (eating, drinking and singing). Details of these are given on the website **www.katterwall.com**. **Soho Collective** (see same website) offers a choir-for-hire.

FILM BUFFS

Broadway Cinematheque (Prosperous Garden, 3 Public Square Street, Yaumatei; www.cinema.com.hk; tel. 2332 9000) screens current and classic movies throughout the year. Members have access to the film library, Sunday screenings, discounts on tickets and other benefits.

WRITERS

The **Society of Children's Book Writers and Illustrators** (www.scbwi.org; tel. 2471 7332; e-mail suemark@hknet.com) organizes workshops and readings. Writers' groups such as the **HK Writer's Circle** (www.hkwriterscircle. com) hosts writing crits, social events and online forums and publishes *Wild East* magazine. **Outloud** (poetry group) meet at the Fringe club to exchange poetry (e-mail madeleine@so-net.com.hk). The **Women in Publishing Society Hong Kong** (WiPS) regularly holds writing, marketing and editing workshops (www.hkwips.org).

OTHERS

- The **Philosophy Café** meets regularly in Kowloon and Hong Kong to debate philosophical and ethical issues. Register to find out more at www.hkbu.edu.hk/~ppp/HKPC.
- The **YWCA** runs mah-jong and bridge groups.
- There is also the **Hong Kong Gardening Society** (www.gardeninghongkong. com). Gardening enthusiasts should look out for the annual Flower Show, which is held in May in Victoria Park, and azalea-viewing dates at Government House gardens – see press for details.
- Rotary Club of Hong Kong.

WOMEN'S CLUBS

The clubs below welcome all nationalities:

- **American Women's Association of Hong Kong** (www.awa.org.hk; tel. 2527 2961 between 9:30 am and 3:30 pm) is one of the largest and most active women's associations. Membership costs $750 a year and includes subscription to *Aware*, a monthly magazine. Activities include community service and fundraising, travel and local tours, interest groups, dining groups, book clubs and sports programmes.

- **The Helena May Ladies Club** (35 Garden Road Central, Hong Kong; www.helenamay.com; tel. 2522 6766) is located in its own very attractive early twentieth-century building and is well-positioned for those living and working in Central or Mid-Levels who want a social/dining venue. It also has an extensive library.
- The **Ladies' Recreation Club** (10 Old Peak Road, Mid-Levels; www.lrc. com.hk; tel. 2522 0151) offers a range of sports facilities for families, children's activities and socializing and dining options.

Other women's associations include:

- the British **Women's Corona Society** (tel. 3476 1340), which meets in TST every Monday morning;
- the **Spanish Speaking Ladies Club** (www.amhh.org.hk; tel. 2592 4105);
- the **German Speaking Ladies Club** (www.gslg.de; tel. 2264 0762);
- the **Italian Women's Association** (www.iwa.org.hk; e-mail associazionedonneitaliane@hotmail.com);
- the **Hong Kong Indian Women's Club** (tel. 2526 6889);
- the **Indian Kowloon Ladies Group** (tel. 2602 8898); and
- the **Kowloon Women's Club** (tel. 2693 4425).
- the **Hong Kong Indian Women's Club** (tel. 2574 4079).

COUNTRY ASSOCIATIONS

- **The Australian Association** (www.ozhongkong.com; tel. 2530 4461) includes an active women's group, hosts regular events including coffee mornings, tennis, dinners, networking events, hikes and a book club. Standard membership is $650 a year.
- The **Swiss Association of Hong Kong** (www.swiss-hk.com) organizes monthly luncheons, Jass, hikes, parties and ladies events. Standard membership is $250 a year.
- The **Canadian Club of Hong Kong** (www.canadianclub.org.hk; tel. 2526 8175) organizes social events, book brunches, trips around Hong Kong and festival dinners. Standard membership is $400 a year.
- **The India Club** (tel. 2388 8184) and the **Indian Association** (tel. 2669 9529).

- The **Japan Society of Hong Kong** (www.japansociety-hk.org; tel. 2537 3797) organizes get-togethers, Japanese courses and a Japan Festival. Standard membership is $120 a year.

UNIVERSITY ALUMNI ASSOCIATIONS

- The **Oxford and Cambridge Society of Hong Kong** (www.oxbridge.org. hk; tel. 2528 4205) holds social and sporting events for members, an annual ball and special event dinners. Standard membership is $220 a year for alumni.

Chapter Twenty-One

Taking Classes

HK Magazine (www.hkmagazine.com) and *Time Out Hong Kong* (www. timeout.com.hk) are two great sources of information on classes and activities in Hong Kong. You can pick up *HK Magazine* on a Friday from the bars and cafes around Wanchai, Central and Soho, from Pacific Coffee, Great, Olivers and some ParknShops. *Time Out* is published every fortnight and is sold at bookshops round the city.

Please note that all clubs and associations listed below cater to English speakers.

GENERAL INTEREST

The **English-Speaking Members' Department** at the **YWCA** (1 MacDonnell Road, Central; www.esmdywca.com; tel. 2524 0639) produces a schedule of eclectic classes every quarter. Classes include cookery (such as Japanese, Thai and Indian), jewellery design, life drawing, candle-making, foot reflexology, belly dancing, Pilates, tennis, golf, and mother and baby classes.

The **YMCA** (1 Salisbury Road, Tsimshatsui; www.ymcahk.org.hk; tel. 2369 2211) runs a wide variety of fitness courses for adults and children, most of which are in Cantonese supplemented with English. Sports classes include wall climbing, badminton, martial arts and table tennis.

Art-Tastic Hobbies Centre (G/F, 4–8 Arbuthnot Road, Central; www.art-tastichobbiescentre.com; tel. 2234 0319) offers classes such as soap-making, painting, wood-working and candles.

People U (http://peopleu.hk) offers classes in business skills, computing, digital video editing, photography and food.

ANTIQUES

Free antiques appreciation classes are offered via the Hong Kong Tourism Board's **Cultural Kaleidoscope** programme of events for visitors (www.

51. Hong Kong Museum of Tea Ware
Photograph taken by Stanley Ng

discoverhongkong.com; tel. 2508 1234). **HKU SPACE** (www.hku.hk/space/; tel. 2559 9771) also offers courses when demand is sufficient.

COOKING

Towngas Cooking Centre (Basement, Leighton Centre, Leighton Road, Causeway Bay; www.towngas.com; tel. 2576 1535) offers bilingual daytime practical cooking courses from $280 and demonstration courses for around $120 from Monday to Saturday. Courses on offer include the chance to learn the art of 'Advanced French Cakes' and 'Popular Cantonese Roasting'. It's worth joining their Cuisine Club, which is $100 for two years' membership, to get discounts on courses and other benefits.

The Home Management Centre (Hong Kong Electric Co., 10/F, Electric Center, 28 City Garden Road, North Point; tel. 2510 2828) teaches Cantonese cooking from Monday to Saturday. The **Chinese Cuisine Training Institute** in Pokfulam (www.ccti.vtc.edu.hk; tel. 2538 2200) offers accredited full- and part-time courses in Chinese cuisine.

Complete Deelite (www.completedeelite.com) offers courses in cake baking and decorating, whilst **6 Senses** (www.s6nses.com) takes food allergies into account when designing recipes for students.

Besides the **YWCA** (details above), five-star hotels in the city also advertise occasional Asian cooking courses.

COSMETICS-MAKING

Ophelia Chan at the shop **Herbal Bliss** (Unit 11A, 128 Wellington Street, Central and Room 702, Workingport Commercial Building, 3 Hau Fook Street, TST; www.herbalbliss.com.hk; tel. 2676 2885) runs occasional English language courses in holistic cosmetics-making, aromatherapy and DIY detox, etc. Call her to register your interest at the Central shop – both shops are open between midday and 7:00 pm.

DANCE

Whatever type of dancing you're into, you'll be guaranteed to find it in Hong Kong. Many nightclubs, such as ClubIng at The Renaissance Harbour View

Hotel, Wanchai, offer early evening salsa dance classes before the night really gets going. A directory of dance studios in Hong Kong is available at www. mai.com.hk/dance/dirhk_studio_e.htm.

Below is a selection of major dance studios and popular classes:

- the **Herman Lam Dance Studio** (1/F, 13 Wyndham Street, Central; www. hermandance.com; tel. 2320 3605) teaches salsa, jazz, hip-hop and ballroom;
- the **Dansinn Dance Studio** near Sheung Wan MTR station (www. dansinn.com; tel. 2581 1151) specializes in ballroom and Latin. Group classes start from $80 a class, but they also offer private individual classes and wedding classes;
- the **Oasis Dance Centre**, Wanchai (www.oasis-dance-centre.com) offers belly-dancing at $200 a lesson and other ethnic dance classes, including flamenco and hula;
- **Tango Tang, The Hong Kong Tango Club** (www.tangotang.com; tel. 8209 0520) offers weekly *practica*, workshops and special events such as *milongas* and movie evenings. Discounts are available for members;
- The **Hong Kong Academy for Performing Arts** (www.hkapa.edu) **EXCEL** programme offers evening classes in ballet, Chinese dance, modern dance, ballroom, Latin and jazz dance, etc.;
- **The Fringe Club** (tel. 2521 9126) offers salsa classes costing $800 for eight one-hour lessons and modern dance classes, which cost $880 for eight one-and-a-half-hour classes; and
- **Pole Divas** (www.poledivas-hk.com). Pole dancing and lap-dancing for the gym-leery.

FLOWER ARRANGING

The Hong Kong Academy of Flower Arrangement (www.hkafa.com.hk; tel. 2882 1832) offers IAF-approved (International Academy of Floristry) certificate courses for those who would like to become trained florists, as well as short courses such as 'Bridal Bouquets and Wedding Flower Arrangements' and 'Dried Flowers'. Individual classes are also available.

JEWELLERY AND GLASS

Asimi College of Jewellery (7B Wing Lok Street Trade Center, 235 Wing Lok Street, Sheung Wan; www.asimiart.com; tel. 2157 1970) runs foundation design courses, beading and silver clay design and enamelling.

Short courses and certificate/diploma courses in gemmology – using pearls, diamonds and jade – are offered by the **YMCA** (see above for address). Free pearl and jade appreciation classes are offered via the **Hong Kong Tourism Board** (www.discoverhongkong.com).

Selling point in Lamma (www.sellingpoint.com.hk; tel. 2982 4050) has a one-day glass studio session.

LANGUAGES

A full list of language courses is given in Chapter Sixteen, 'Professional Development'.

PAINTING AND FINE ARTS

Colour My World (Room 108, Aberdeen Marina Tower, 8 Shun Wan Road, Aberdeen; tel. 2541 8816) runs classes and creative workshops for adults in sculpture, watercolour and oil painting, fabric printing, lino block printing and photography. Art classes are usually held in the mornings, costing $420 for a one-and-a-half-hour session, although there are also art evenings designed for fun and relaxation.

Art Jamming (G/F, 123 Wellington Street, Central; www.artjamming.com; tel. 2541 8816) is open from 3:00 pm until late for art jams at special weekday night rates, art jam parties on-site and off-site. Prices vary.

The **State of the Arts Gallery** (2/F–3/F, 78 Queen's Road, Central; www.sotagallery.com.hk; tel. 2526 1133) hosts exhibitions in their upstairs gallery, and supports emerging artists and art students. Glasswork, chocolate sculpture, wood sculpture, polished stone and work by contemporary Austrian artists have featured prominently in recent exhibitions.

Cecilia Ho's Art Club (www.artamaze.com) offers Fine Art classes for adults and art camps for kids.

The **Hong Kong Academy of Fine Arts** (tel. 2385 9929) offers serious learners classes in drawing, watercolour, oil and Chinese painting.

The **5 o.p.t Studio/Gallery** (5 Prince's Terrace, Mid-Levels; www.5opt.com. hk; tel. 2536 9818) runs adult life drawing classes at $500 per two-hour session and drawing classes for children and adults, which cost $350 per two-hour session. Classes are available during the daytime and evenings.

The **Porcelain Painting Workshop** (Unit C, 26th Floor, Eastern Commercial Centre, 83 Nam On Street, Shaukeiwan; www.porcelainpainting.com; tel. 2513 7687) runs daytime group courses at $200 a lesson. Beginners are welcome. Opening times are from 10:00 am to 1:00 pm on Tuesday, Thursday and Saturday, and from 6:00 to 9:00 pm on Tuesdays.

A part-time artist offers the following advice for newcomers to the city's art scene: 'HKU Space offers some good drawing/painting classes, and the Art School (part of art centre). There are many private groups offering classes around Hong Kong too. Not all arts courses are in English though. At the moment I am also working at the Hong Kong Open Printshop, a printmaking workshop at the Jockey Club Creative Arts Centre in Shek Kip Mei. There are some people offering classes at the JCCAC. HKOP offers printmaking courses, too. I tend to look online for courses, or get info from friends, but local magazines usually also have information. There are quite a lot of people working in the arts in Hong Kong these days, and lots of workshops/gallery spaces (commercial and alternative) in old factories in different parts of town, e.g. Fotan, Chaiwan.'

POTTERY

The **Pottery Workshop** (2 Lower Albert Road, Central; www.ceramics.com. hk; tel. 2525 7949) is a professional studio, offering classes every day during the daytime and some evenings. Besides 'basic pottery', 'intermediate throwing' and other clay-making classes – all of which are priced at about $1,700 for seven three-hour sessions – they also offer special master workshops with visiting artists. Nearby, the **Klei Pottery Studio** (2/F, 24 Hollywood Road; tel. 2526 8567) offers small-group classes between Thursday and Saturday with dogs for company! Eight lessons cost $2,000.

At **Hong Kong Claycraft** (19/F, Cameron Commercial Centre, 468 Hennessy Road, Causeway Bay; tel. 2838 0086) you can learn how to use airdry clay to make doll's house furniture and other clay crafts. They also offer jewellery-making. Classes start from $120 for two hours.

The **Cobo Ceramic Workshop** (1/F, Fortune Court, 33 Morrison Hill Road, Causeway Bay; tel. 2528 0672) runs an open workshop where you can call in once a week for a two-and-a-half-hour session. Basic clay techniques, throwing and decorating are taught for $800 a month.

Another ceramics studio serving professional artists in Shatin is **i-kiln studio** (www.i-kiln.org.hk). Beginners can attend ceramics, throwing and raku-firing courses Saturday afternoons and Wednesday evenings.

MUSIC

Music teachers can best be found through recommendations by musicians at the **Hong Kong Philharmonic Orchestra**: call the general office on 2721 2030 and ask if you can put a note up on the noticeboard. Leonard Wong at the music school of the **Hong Kong Academy for Performing Arts** (tel. 2584 8517) can refer graduates or go to the teacher database at www.hongkongstrings.com or **Tom Lee** (www.tomleemusic.com).

Kumi (www.drumjam.hk; tel. 9750 4212) has a great reputation for drumming and drum jams – or try **GunGoDo World Percussion** (tel. 8202 3814; www.gungodo.com). African drumming and other music classes are also available through **HKAPA EXCEL** (see above). Serious percussion learners can approach the **Hong Kong Percussion Centre** (tel. 2153 1566).

PHOTOGRAPHY

Craig Norris offers a thorough-going photography workshop for beginners (www.camerahongkong.com; tel. 9810 4265).

The Hong Kong Arts Centre (see above) and the Hong Kong Institute of Professional Photography also offer classes. Photography exhibitions are regularly held at the Fringe Club.

SINGING

Bethan Greaves (bethan@katterwall.com; tel. 2575 3931) provides one-to-one tuition and coaching for adults and children aged 11 and over, with songs drawn from a classical repertoire. The company also runs men's, women's and youth choirs. Leonard Wong at the music school of the **Hong Kong Academy for Performing Arts** (tel. 2584 8517) can refer graduates who now teach adults and children (mainly classical repertoire).

SPORTS

Details of sports classes and training courses are given in Chapter Nineteen, 'Sports'.

WINE APPRECIATION AND TASTING

The **International Wine Centre** (20C Right Emperor Center, 122–6 Wellington Street; www.iwinecentre.com; tel. 2549 0282) holds wine appreciation classes from beginner to advanced. Courses for 2010 include 'The Complete Wine Tasting Course' and 'Blend your own Bordeaux Challenge'. The Open University also offers a Foundation Course in Wine Tasting. Informal tastings are often held at outlets of **Watsons Wine Cellar** on Friday, Saturday and Sunday afternoons (tel. 3151 7628).

Class Act (www.classact-online.com; tel. 2911 7997) provides training in 'Entertainments and Protocol of Business and Social Occasions', including invitation preparation, pairing food and wine, setting tables and choosing glasses.

Chapter Twenty-Two

Visiting Places of Interest

The suggestions below are good to do by yourself or when you have visitors. Tours are offered by Gray Line (www.grayline.com.hk, or visit their booths inside selected MTR stations, e.g. Admiralty) and via the government's tourism website www.discoverhongkong.com.

PEACE AND TRANQUILLITY

- Getaway islands for day-trips or camping out include:
  - **Tai Long Wan Bay** and **Tap Mun** on Grass Island, both of which are accessible by ferry from Wong Shek pier in Sai Kung;
  - **Hap Mun Bay** on Sharp Island – take a sampan for about $40–50 per person from Sai Kung; and
  - **Tung Ping Chau** – weekend-only ferries run from Ma Liu Shui Pier. Visit http://parks.afcd.gov.hk for more information. There's more on best beaches in Chapter Eight, 'Having and Raising Children'.
- Visit the **Mai Po Nature Reserve** far up in the New Territories with your binoculars. It's a 380-hectare wetland area home to birds such as storks, egrets and endangered black-faced spoonbills migrating between Australia and East Asia. Join a tour with the YWCA or the World Wildlife Fund (tel. 3193 7701), or try calling 2526 4473 two weeks in advance of your visit to arrange a one-day permit.
- Visit the **cemeteries in Happy Valley** to learn more about Hong Kong's Parsi and Catholic history. Browse the plant nursery inside and why not visit Moon House Chinese dessert cafe, near the tram terminus?
- Walk along the leafy **Bowen Road** from Mid-Levels to the top of Happy Valley and get a fabulous scope of the city. Stop off at the police museum en route or drop down to Wanchai if you've had enough.
- Visit **Kadoorie Farm and Botanic Garden** (www.kfbg.org.hk; tel. 2483 7200) for a tranquil day out.
- Get off the beaten track on **Lamma, Lantau, Peng Chau** and **Cheng Chau**. Midweek is better, as the islands get busy at weekends and on public

52. Cheng Chau Temple
Photograph taken by the author

holidays. For details on where to find maps, see Chapter Twenty-Three, 'The Great Outdoors'.

■ Take the bus to **Shek O**, at the tip of the south-east finger of Hong Kong Island, or walk the **Dragon's Back** trail down to the village. Enjoy the dramatic rocky scenery and admire the houses in this exclusive location.

■ **Go on retreat**. Stay overnight at one of Lantau's 100-plus monasteries and nunneries, or join a weekend yoga retreat – visit www.holisticasia.com for details.

■ **Yuen Yuen Institute, Tsuen Wan** – a ten-acre religious park of decorative gardens and ponds, strewn with temples, pavilions, monasteries and prayer halls dedicated to Confucian, Buddhist and Taoist beliefs.

■ Browse **Aberdeen Harbour** and see one of the few surviving boat communities in Hong Kong.

URBAN BUSTLE

■ Witness a little bit of history: the **noonday gun** immortalized in Noel Coward's song 'Mad Dogs and Englishmen' is still fired at midday every day. Access is via the car park in the basement of the **World Trade Centre** (280 Gloucester Road, Causeway Bay). If you can't wangle an invite to lunch at the nearby **Royal Hong Kong Yacht Club**, console yourself with pillow toast and banana custard at **Pokka Café** (9 Kingston Street).

■ The **Hong Kong Tourism Board's Visitor Information and Service Centre** (tel. 2508 1234) runs guided **architecture tours** of Central every Saturday morning. Local historian and author **Jason Wordie** also runs acclaimed walking talks in Hong Kong and Macau for the YWCA, AWA and other organizations.

■ A day at **the races**: place your bets for as little as $10 on Wednesday nights and Saturday afternoons in Happy Valley or Shatin, which is also open on Sundays. Check the **Hong Kong Jockey Club**'s website for details of upcoming races at www.hkjc.org.hk. Soak up the atmosphere in the public stands or persuade a member to take you for dinner in the Member's Lounge, where you can enjoy a superb view of the action. The Tourism Board also organizes racing packages that allow you into usually restricted areas. Please note, however, that there is no racing in July and August.

■ Visit **Wong Tai Sin Temple** and have your face or palm read by the fortune tellers in the booths behind the temple.

- **Mongkok day markets**: take your pick from **Goldfish Market** (Tung Choi Street), **Bird Garden** (Yuen Po Street), **Flower Market** (Prince Edward MTR) or **Jade Market** (Jordan MTR). Refer to Figure 4.6 for the locations of these markets.
- **Kowloon night markets**: **Temple Street Night Market** (Yaumatei) is open between 5:30 pm and midnight, and is a ragbag mix of clothes, toys, electronics, luggage, opera singers, fortune tellers and food stalls. **Ladies Street Market** (Mongkok) keeps similar hours – go there for T-shirts, watches, copy bags, belts, scarves, etc. and lots of atmosphere. Again, refer to Figure 4.6 for the locations of these markets.
- **Stanley Market**: every visitor's favourite. When you're footsore and shopped out, wander over to Murray House for tapas or relax on the beach behind the bus station.
- **Peak Galleria Market**: third Sunday of each month. 10 am to 5 pm on Level 3 of Peak Galleria. See live animals including spiders, snakes and tortoises.

HISTORICAL SIGHTSEEING

For opening times and directions to the places below, visit www.discover hongkong.com. For a complete listing of declared monuments by location, visit the Antiquities and Monuments Office's website, www.amo.gov.hk.

Chinese buildings and monuments

In Hong Kong, there is nothing on the same scale as the Chinese architecture you may have seen on the mainland. The historical buildings here are often either of religious significance – temples built to honour local deities such as Tin Hau – or they are ancestral halls or yamens with clan or political importance. The list below is by no means comprehensive but meant to act as a taster. Most are free admission:

- **Po Lin Monastery**, on Lantau Island: the famous 'Big Buddha', airlifted into place in 1993, is a must-see for visitors.
- **Man Mo Temple** (Hollywood Road) was built in 1847 and is one of the most famous temples in Hong Kong. The **Sun Yat-Sen Historical Trail** is nearby.
- **Sam Tung Uk Museum** (Tsuen Wan) is a well-preserved collection of historic Hakka village buildings dating from 1786, including an entrance hall, ancestral hall and assembly hall.

- Make a wish and throw it into the **Lam Tsuen Wishing Tree**, something traditionally done at Chinese New Year (Lam Tsuen, near Tai Po). A Tin Hau temple is nearby.
- The **Lung Yeuk Tau Heritage Trail** (Fan Ling) winds past watch towers and entrance gates through walled villages connected to the powerful Tang clan. Buildings of significance include the Tang Chung Ling Ancestral Hall, dating from 1525.
- The **Kowloon Walled City Park** (Kowloon City). Built on the site of the Kowloon Walled City, this attractive park of fountains, pavilions and grassy knolls preserves the memory of the famed Walled City and its antecedents, including a well-preserved nineteenth-century yamen building.
- **Chi Lin Nunnery** (Diamond Hill). A functioning nunnery built in the Tang dynasty style and completed in 2000, the compound includes 16 halls of wood built without a single nail and pleasant gardens for taking a stroll in.
- The **Ping Shan Heritage Trail** (Yuen Long) takes in the oldest pagoda in Hong Kong, the Tsui Shing Lau pagoda dating from 1486, the Tang Ancestral Hall and Kun Ting Study Hall.
- **Law Uk Hakka House** (14 Kut Shing Street, Chai Wan). Over 200 years old, this folk museum has an interesting display of furniture, farm tools and implements used by the minority Hakka ('guest') people.
- **Tai O Village** (Lantau Island) – not strictly speaking a monument, but unlike the walled villages of the New Territories, this one's built on stilts.
- **Golden Bauhinia Square**, outside the Hong Kong Convention and Exhibition Centre in Wanchai. Catch the flag-raising ceremony (daily), enhanced on the first of the month, to relive some of the pomp which accompanied the '97 Handover to China.

Colonial buildings and monuments

Not all of the buildings listed below are open to the public; this selection reflects my personal favourites.

- **Old Supreme Court**, next to Statue Square in Central, which dates from 1912. Part of the iconic architecture of the city, this two-storey granite building is in the neoclassical style with Ionic columns and the Greek goddess Themis regal on the pediment.
- **Court of Final Appeal** (formerly the French Mission Building). Nestling behind the skyscrapers of Central, this three-storey red brick and granite

building was built in 1843, sold to French missionaries (who added the chapel) in 1915 and returned to the government in 1953.

- **Flagstaff House** (Hong Kong Park). The oldest surviving original colonial house in Hong Kong, it was built in 1846 for Major General George D'Aguilar. The building now houses a tea museum – the **Flagstaff House Museum of Tea Ware** (http://hk.art.museum).
- **The Helena May** (35 Garden Road, Central). This pretty building dates from 1916 and still retains its original function as a ladies club. Inside, the Main Lounge and Blue Room retain some classic Art Deco features. Please note that it is closed on Sundays.
- **The Fringe Club** – a great example of a 'living' old building – is a stylish cold storage warehouse built in 1913 that now serves as an important hub for the arts community. Other attractive colonial buildings nearby include the **Foreign Correspondents' Club, Central Police Station** and **Government House**, formerly home to the British governors.
- **Western Market**, dating from 1906. I still enjoy this architectural surprise in Sheung Wan, even though it has seen better days. Inside are small boutiques, cloth sellers and a Chinese restaurant on the top floor.
- **Former Kowloon–Canton Railway Terminus Clock Tower** (TST promenade). Completed in 1921, this is the only surviving part of what used to be a railway terminus for the train line linking Hong Kong to China. It is open on Sundays between 10:00 am and 6:00 pm.
- **The Peninsula Hotel**, Salisbury Road, TST, dating from 1928. The opulent and highly decorated lobby must be the most beautiful hotel interior in Hong Kong.
- **Old Stanley Police Station** built in 1859 is, bizarrely, now home to a Wellcome supermarket.

Jason Wordie (www.jasonswalks.com) is a knowledgeable author and local historian who conducts well-received walking tours.

For more on routes to take which encompass important monuments, visit www.hongkongextras.,com ('Central and Western Heritage').

MUSEUMS

Hong Kong is not famous for its museums, and blockbusting international exhibitions are few and far between. However, for an appreciation of Hong

Kong and Chinese history and culture, the **Hong Kong Museum of History** (http://hk.history.museum) and the massive **Hong Kong Heritage Museum in Shatin** (http://hk.heritage.museum) – which boasts interesting collections of Chinese comics and fashions, among other things – are definitely worth a visit. The boutique university art museums at **Hong Kong University** and **Chinese University** have some beautiful pieces for those interested in Chinese art.

The Hong Kong Museum of Coastal Defence in Shau Kei Wan (http://hk.heritage.museum) is a personal favourite, partly because of the peace and quiet of the location and the beauty of the surrounding landscape, and also for the fascinating video footage documenting the invasion of Hong Kong by the Japanese during the Second World War and the Communist Party's mobilization in China. Family/children programmes are offered at various times through the year.

The Hong Kong Museum of Medical Sciences (2 Caine Road, Mid-Levels) is another interesting museum, housed in a red brick Edwardian building that served as Hong Kong's first Pathological Institute. The Museum has galleries devoted to the history of Chinese and Western medicine in Hong Kong and the personalities who played a part in its development, as well as gory exhibits such as a 'lotus' foot.

More on museums is included in Chapter Eight, 'Having and Raising Children'.

53. Taipa Houses-Museum
Photograph taken by the author

Chapter Twenty-Three

Exploring the Great Outdoors

As well as admiring the fantastic views and getting some fresh air, outdoor explorers may be lucky enough to come across some interesting flora and fauna. Hong Kong provides a habitat for leopard cats, barking deer, pangolins, civets, mongooses, dolphins, ferret badgers, porcupines, bamboo snakes (bright green and very dangerous), pythons, cobras, water buffalo, macaques, brown kites, bats, butterflies and several endangered species of fish, coral and birdlife.

There are altogether 23 country parks in Hong Kong and five marine parks and reserves. Information on all parks can be found at **www.afcd.gov.hk**. Most country parks are equipped with barbecue pits and some also have visitor centres. Several areas of Hong Kong, such as **Tung Ping Chau** and **Mau Shi Chau**, are rich in fossils and of significant geological interest and have recently been designated part of **Hong Kong Geopark** (www.geopark.gov.hk).

HIKING

Hiking at the weekend is a great antidote to the stress of the working week. For those who like their hiking in small and manageable doses, there are the green, shady walks above Central and Wanchai, spanning the **Peak** and **Bowen Road**: for instance, Black's Link and Lady Clementi's Ride. For others who are happy to hike for five to six hours or more, Hong Kong's efficient public transport means it's easy to get out of the city to the beautiful scenery of the New Territories for the day.

The YWCA and YMCA run hikes where you follow the leader, but there are also informal hiking get-togethers organized by the **Hong Kong Trampers** (www.hktrampers.com) who tramp every Sunday and the **Saturday Hikers Club** (http://groups.yahoo.com/group/saturdayhikers/facebook). See also www.hiking.com.hk.

Other informative websites include Martin Williams' **www.hkoutdoors.com**, which has postings on different walks and eco-tours in Hong Kong, forums

54. Lin Au Village, Tai Po
Photograph taken by Stanley Ng

and logistical information on how to get out to the farther reaches of the territory. Information on Country Parks, Hiking Trails and Family Walks can be found by clicking through on the Leisure & Sports link at www.gov.hk. A selection of fitness, tree and family walks are given on the website www.**afcd. gov.hk**. There are several excellent hiking trail books in print, including the laminated cards *Hong Kong Hikes* by Christian Wright.

Maps

Government countryside maps are available for purchase at Map Publications Centres in North Point and Yaumatei, major post offices, selected bookshops or online at the government bookstore (**www.gov.hk**). Information on how to get to the country parks is provided at **www.afcd.gov.hk**.

Safety

The best time of the year for hiking is from September to May, when the sun is not as fierce and the humidity is less stultifying – typically, year-round humidity is 75–90%. Hikers should take plenty of water and cover up to avoid mosquito bites and sunburn. Heatstroke claims several lives every year, so take precautions. Although hiking is generally safe, there have been more than a few muggings attributed to illegal Chinese immigrants in recent years, including on the Peak and in Tai Tam Country Park, where victims were tied up and robbed of their ATM and credit cards.

The only other nuisance to watch out for are the bands of macaques that roam Lion Rock, Kam Sham and Shing Mun Country Parks. The monkeys have become used to being fed, which is illegal, and have been known to harass strollers and even their dogs in pursuit of food.

Major trails

- **Hong Kong Trail**, which goes through Pok Fu Lam, Aberdeen, Tai Tam and Shek O Country Parks.
- **Wilson Trail**, encompassing Violet Hill, Stanley Mound on Hong Kong Island, and Shing Mun and Pat Sin Leng Country Parks in the northern New Territories.
- **Maclehose Trail**, used for November's Trailwalker charity race (www.trailwalker.com), Hong Kong's longest trail stretches the width of the New Territories.
- **Lantau Trail**, which runs from Mui Wo down through Lantau North and South Country Parks past Sunset and Lantau Peaks.

Other popular trails
- Dragon's Back (Shek O).
- High Junk Peak Trail (Clearwater Bay).
- Clearwater Bay Peninsula.
- Pat Sin Leng Nature Trail and Bride's Pool waterfalls (Plover Cove Country Park, near Tai Po Market).
- Discovery Bay to Mui Wo.

CAMPING

There are 38 campsites in country parks around Hong Kong. For more information on campsite locations and facilities, as well as a camping guide, visit **www.afcd.gov.hk**. It's also possible to camp at many of the HK Youth Hostels Association hostels (**www.yha.org.hk**). Camping at public beaches is not allowed, nor is nude bathing.

CYCLING

Areas of the New Territories and Outlying Islands provide a perfect environment for cycling – bikes can be hired quite cheaply at about $40 for the day. Cycle paths in the New Territories – for example, starting at Tai Wai and cycling up to Shatin – can be found around the **Tolo Harbour** area.

OUTDOOR ADVENTURES

A number of local private companies offer outdoor adventure trips and courses. Paul Etherington at **www.kayak-and-hike.com** (tel. 9300 5197) runs a selection of hiking, kayaking, snorkelling and exploration trips, including transport by power boats. For a minimum of four to six people, prices start at around $600 per person including equipment, instructors, guides, safety gear, drinks on board and lunch.

Outward Bound Hong Kong offers adult and youth courses, including sailing programmes with offshore voyages to Taiwan and the Philippines, rock climbing, kayaking and hiking in remote parts of the countryside.

JUNKS

Companies that hire out junks for the day include **Pana Oceans** (www. panaoceans.com; tel. 2815 8235), **Viking's Charters** (tel. 2814 9899) and **Traway Travel** (tel. 2527 2513). Junks, which are usually licensed to carry 30 people or more depending on their size, cost from about $1,800 for weekday hire and $2,600 or more for weekend hire. Buffet lunch can usually be provided for around $80-plus per person. **Jaspa's** provides a one-stop junk and party catering service that costs $600 per person (tel. 2792 6001).

BIRD- AND ANIMAL-WATCHING

The **Hong Kong Bird Watching Society** (www.hkbws.org.hk) runs regular field outings around Hong Kong. Their website features a map of prime birding spots. A key bird-watching territory is the **Mai Po Nature Reserve**, a 380-hectare wetland area home to birds such as storks, egrets and endangered black-faced spoonbills. More information on the Reserve is available at **www.wwf.org.hk.** The website **www.drmartinwilliams.com** has photo galleries, as well as information on bird-watching in China and regional conservation issues.

Hong Kong Dolphin Watch (1528A Star House, 3 Salisbury Road, TST; www.hkdolphinwatch.com; tel. 2984 1414) organizes half-day boat trips out to the sea off north Lantau to see Hong Kong's pink dolphins (*Sousa chinensis*). Coach pick-up is available from Tsim Sha Tsui.

55. Panda
Photograph taken by Mimi Mori

Chapter Twenty-Four

Travelling

Hong Kong has traditionally been a very expensive place to fly out of because of the monopoly held by a few airlines over routes into and out of Hong Kong and the high airport taxes. This is starting to change, with low-cost airlines such as Orient Thai, Bangkok Airways, Cebu Pacific Air and JetStar Asia picking up regional traffic with several flights per day.

Expect to pay a hefty premium on flights out of Hong Kong during the major holidays – that's if you can get a flight – especially at Chinese New Year, Christmas, Easter and during the summer. The airlines do not have identical high season dates, though, so check with your travel agent when booking tickets to get the best deal possible. If you've committed to going home for Christmas, book your flight well in advance – in September, say – even though prices have not yet been confirmed. You only have to pay for your ticket(s) in early December.

POPULAR ASIAN DESTINATIONS

The most popular Asian destinations from Hong Kong include Borracay, Vietnam, Bali and Thailand. Sri Lanka is also a big seller for agents. Langkawi (Malaysia) is very popular with those who want to go upmarket and enjoy five-star resort luxury. For many Hong Kongers, a two- or three-day package abroad is common. A holiday of five days or more is considered extravagant (time-wise)!

CHINESE TRAVEL

If you plan to visit Beijing or other destinations in China, it can be significantly cheaper to fly from Shenzhen Airport rather than Hong Kong. An example is provided by Ben Pearce, an English teacher who ran a travel agency for eight years in Hong Kong:

> My aunt lives in Kunming. She came to Hong Kong last week, en route
> for LA. The flight from Kunming to Hong Kong costs about $1,600. The

56. Shing Mun Reservoir

Photograph taken by Stanley Ng

flight from Kunming to Shenzhen costs $540. Plus the cost of the ferry from Shenzhen Aiport to Hong Kong Airport [$178–185] … you're still saving.

Ferries between the airports run about every 90 minutes (see **www.hong kongairport.com/eng/aguide/skypier.html**), or you can take a coach, which costs about $180. Other ferry and coach services connect Hong Kong Airport to Macau, Guangzhou, Shekou, etc.

To get to Shenzhen Airport from Hong Kong city centre, passengers can take the ferry from the China Ferry Pier in TST (www.ctshk.com; tel. 2998 7888). The fare is about $200 and ferries run every 90 minutes or so. Alternatively, you can take the train from Hung Hom to Lowu, which costs $33 and then pick up a taxi to Shenzhen Airport – a further $110.

Useful phone numbers for ferry services from Hong Kong International Airport:

- Sky Pier, tel. 2215 3232;
- CKS (to Shenzhen, Shekou, Fuyong, Dongguan, Humen, Zhongshu, Zhu-hai, Jiuzhou), tel. 2858 3876;
- TurboJET (to Macau, Guangzhou, Nansha), tel. 2859 3333.

Many Hong Kong agents sell domestic air tickets for mainland China but add a $50 handling charge. **China Southern Airlines** has an English website through which you can book (www.cs-air.com/en/).

VISAS

Visas are not required by many nationalities traveling to Macau, but do take your passport. However, visas are required for travel to Shenzhen and else-where in China. It is possible for some nationalities, though not the British, to apply for a visa at the Shenzhen border – check with the **PRC Visa Office** (7/F, Lower Block, China Resources Building, 26 Harbor Road, Wanchai; tel. 3413 2424; e-mail visa@mail.fmcoprc.gov.hk).

Your travel agent can arrange a visa (usually the cheapest option), or you can apply in person at a branch of the China Travel Service (one is conveniently located in the Hong Kong International Airport). For regular trips to China, consider getting a multi-entry visa for six months. **CTS** (www.ctshk.com) sells tour packages to China as well as train, coach and air tickets. The largest branch is at G/F, CTS House, 78–83 Connaught Road, Central; tel. 2853 3531.

TRAVEL AGENTS

In Hong Kong, as elsewhere, it's worth cultivating a good relationship with a travel agent who is knowledgeable about the most popular places to go for a short break, the best-value resorts in each price range and the cheapest flights. Expats usually share information by word of mouth. You need to know what package you're after and then go through your chosen agent. Do your homework via travel agents such as **Aero International** (www.aerohkg.com) or **Tiglion** (www.tiglion.com).

Local Chinese travel agencies such as **Hong Thai Travel** and **Wing On Travel** can provide good package tour prices, as long as you don't mind staying at a Chinese-style hotel serving Chinese food, etc. Branches of these agents exist all round the city, but a concentration of them can be found in places such as **Star House** (TST) and **3/F–4/F, Bank Centre Building** (Mongkok MTR station Exit E2). An extensive list of registered travel agents is provided at the **Hong Kong Association of Travel Agents** (www.hata.org. hk).

When buying an air ticket or package:

- check that the quotation you are given includes taxes;
- check how much these taxes are; and
- make sure that the amount of tax paid is shown on the tickets.

Always get a franked receipt for a tour package. E-tickets are common here and perfectly safe.

Web-based travel agents

It's worth checking out **www.lastminute.com.hk** for attractively priced short-break packages in Asia and cheap international flights. You can offer your own price at **www.priceline.com** and the company also gives you the option of choosing your preferred airline and dates: they then match your offer with an airline willing to accommodate it. Singapore-based **www.zuji. com** can sometimes offer better seat availability, although prices are similar to www.priceline.com.

Group travel

Groups such as the AWA and the Royal Asiatic Society organize regular trips in Asia.

57. Hiking through the forests near Shing Mun
Photograph taken by Stanley Ng

Chapter Twenty-Five

Enjoying the Night Life

'I have a social life on the Mid-Levels Escalator – where else in the world can you do this?' So says Lynda Aurora, one of several life coaches working in the city.

If you were to sit in Pacific Coffee on Hollywood Road or Kosmo café on D'Aguilar Street for any length of time, shop in Great or Olivers, or visit Pacific Place cinema, then sooner or later you'd see someone you know. Besides building your network of friends and acquaintances through professional organizations (see Chapter Thirteen, 'Work') and interest groups (see Chapter Twenty), expats of all ages enjoy soaking up the atmosphere at the many bars, restaurants and clubs in the three main expat hangouts – **Lan Kwai Fong** (LKF), **Soho** and **Wanchai**.

To find out what's hot and happening on the scene, check the pages of *HK Magazine* or visit the monthly events calendar at **www.hkclubbing. com**. The website also has reviews, club and bar search functions, and chat forums.

Bars and clubs live a precarious existence in this city of high rents and intense competition, so the scene is constantly evolving. Incentives such as happy hours (usually between 6:00 and 9:00 pm), ladies' nights, live music and special guest DJ nights are common. Some bars even run a happy hour all night: drinks are expensive in Hong Kong, so it's worth shopping round for the best deal. Most bars also serve food in a separate restaurant area.

EXPAT DISTRICTS FOR SOCIALIZING

LKF

LKF – which, when used loosely, includes D'Aguilar Street and Wing Wah Lane – is where tourists head to sample Hong Kong's nightlife, although it is also popular with long-termers and is a convenient watering hole for city executives. It is home to a bright array of stylish and glitzy restaurants and bars – mostly in the 'expensive to very expensive' category – and things get

58. Lan Kwai Fong
Photograph taken by the author

very busy on Thursday–Sunday nights, when the crowds spill out onto the pavement and the atmosphere is very jovial. Below is a selection of popular bars and clubs. To see their location, visit **www.lankwaifong.com**.

Bars

- **C bar** (G/F, 30–32 D'Aguilar Street; tel. 2530 3695) – a swish, rose-tinted bar furnished with a stainless steel cocktail counter.
- **Insomnia** (G/F, 38–44 D'Aguilar Street; tel. 2525 0957) – longer-than-average happy hours, free snacks and an open-fronted bar on the main drag attracts the punters.
- **La Bodega** (42 D'Aguilar Street, tel. 2524 7790). Cocktails such as caipirinhas and mojitos are the speciality at this Catalonian-style bar.
- **Lux** (UG/F, 30-32 D'Aguilar Street, tel. 2868 9538). A hip bar and restaurant with house DJs.
- **La Dolce Vita** (9 Lan Kwai Fong; tel. 2810 8098) – this small bar attracts a huge crowd, which fills the street outside.
- **Post 97** (UG/F 9 Lan Kwai Fong; tel. 2810 9333) – comfortable for a quiet drink and the food's good too.
- **Stormies** (G/F and 1/F, 46–50 D'Aguilar Street; tel. 2845 5533) – this three-level nautical-themed venue includes a bar and restaurant, and attracts large crowds.

Nightclubs

- **Mooch** (G/F, 30–32 D'Aguilar Street; tel. 2521 8001).
- **Club 97** (G/F, 9 Lan Kwai Fong, tel. 2816 1897).
- **Beijing Club** (2/F–5/F Wellington Plaza, Wellington Street; tel. 2525 8298.

Soho

Trendier than LKF, Soho has a cool vibe and the clubs only really get going after 10:00 pm and may stay open till 3:00 or 4:00 am. Many are discretely hidden down backstreets or have inconspicuous entrances. Below is a selection of popular bars and clubs.

Bars

- **Backroom** (Veda, 8 Arbuthnot Road; tel. 2868 5885) and **Bombay Dreams** (1/F, Carfield Commercial Building, 75–77 Wyndham Street) play host to Indian/'Bollywood' nights.

- **Boca Tapas & Wine** (65 Peel Street, tel. 2548 1717) – stylish and beautiful; not cheap.
- **Fringe Club** (2 Lower Albert Rd; tel. 2521 7485) – must be one of the cheapest venues in town for a drink. The Japanese Big Jazz Band plays the last Saturday of every month; other rock and jazz bands play regular gigs.
- **Gecko** (LG/F, Ezra Lane, Lower Hollywood Rd; tel. 2537 4680) – live music on Tuesday and Wednesday nights after 9:30 pm.
- **RACKS MDB** (7/F, 2–8 Wellington Street; tel. 2868 3762). Music, drinks and billiards.
- **Staunton's** (G/F, 10–12 Staunton Street; tel. 2973 6611) – positioned near the escalator, this bar is one of the most popular in Soho; great for people-watching.

Nightclubs
- **Chapter Three** (B/F, 22 Hollywood Road; tel. 2526 5566).
- **Dragon-I** (UG/F, The Centrium, 60 Wyndham Street, Central; tel. 3110 1222) – rather exclusive.
- **Drop** (B/F, On Lok Mansion, 39–43 Hollywood Road; tel. 2543 8856).
- **Nu** (1 Elgin Street; tel. 2549 8380).
- **The Edge** (G/F, The Centrium, 60 Wyndham Street, Central; tel. 2523 6690) – live music daily.

Wanchai
Concentrated in the Lockhart Road/Jaffe Road area, the bars of Wanchai run the gamut of sports pubs, themed bars and dancing-on-the-bar or pole-dancing venues. Many bars have widescreen TVs broadcasting sports matches. The erotic dancing establishments and shabby hotels that share the neighbourhood combined with an over-abundance of scantily clad south-east Asian women create a seedy feel to the place. The American Navy dock at nearby Fenwick Pier when they're in town.

Men frequenting 'girlie' bars, or hostess bars, should be aware of the system. The customer pays for the attentions of his hostess by buying her drinks, often at inflated prices. Bills should be settled on the spot, preferably with cash. Avoid going to cashpoints with hostesses.

Below is a selection of popular bars and clubs where the patrons are clothed.

Bars

- **Spicy Fingers** (78–82 Lockhart Road; tel. 2861 3588).
- **Coyote Bar and Grill** (114–120 Lockhart Road; tel. 2861 2221) – this Mexican-themed bar and restaurant serves up a comprehensive menu of exotic margaritas; a salsa band plays Saturday nights.
- **Delaney's** (2/F, One Capital Place,18 Luard Road; tel. 2804 2880) – Irish pub ambience.
- **Devil's Advocate** (G/F, 48–50 Lockhart Road; tel. 2865 7271).
- **Carnegie's** (G/F, 53–55 Lockhart Road; tel. 2866 6289).
- **Mes Amis** (G/F, 81–85 Lockhart Road; tel. 2527 6680) – a part-open venue on a busy street corner that is great for people-watching. A DJ plays on Wednesdays, Fridays and Saturdays after 10:30 pm.

Nightclubs

- **De Fenwick** (B/F, 42–50 Lockhart Road; tel. 2528 2560).
- **Dusk Till Dawn** (G/F, 76 Jaffe Road; tel. 2528 4689) – live music at the weekends.
- **Joe Bananas** (23 Luard Road; tel. 2529 1811) – live music from Monday to Saturday between 8:00 pm and midnight.
- **JJs** (Grand Hyatt Hotel, 1 Harbour Road; tel. 2588 1234).
- **Tribeca** (4/F Renaissance Harbour View Hotel, Harbour Road; tel. 2836 3690).
- **Neptune Disco II** (98–108 Jaffe Road, tel. 2865 2238).
- **1/5** (Starcrest, 9 Star Street; tel. 2520 2515) – dark, glam and svelte.
- **Strawberry Cafe Disco** (B/F, 48 Hennessy Road; tel. 2866 1031).
- **The Wanch** (54 Jaffe Road; tel. 2861 1621) – live band music a few times per week.
- **Yu Club** (13/F Luk Yu Building, 24–6 Stanley Street). Members only.

Other bars

- **Aqua Spirit** (1 Peking Road; tel. 3427 2288) – the bar is on the mezzanine floor of an Italian/Japanese restaurant and has a stunning view of the harbour.
- **Champagne Bar** (Grand Hyatt Hotel, 1 Harbour Road; tel. 2588 1234).
- **Felix** (28/F, Peninsula Hotel; tel. 2315 3188) – a Philippe Starck-designed venue with stunning harbour views – and you've probably already heard about the men's toilets.

- **Lobster Bar & Grill** (Lobby Level, Island Shangri-la Hotel; tel. 2820 8560).
- **The Captain's Bar** (G/F, Mandarin Oriental Hotel; tel. 2522 0111) – popular with bankers after work. A jazz band plays on Sunday evenings and there is music every night.

TEA DANCES

Tea dances – disco-type scenarios – are often held on Sundays between 6:00 and 11:00 pm at different nightclubs around the Soho area.

LATIN AMERICAN DANCING

Latin rhythms are popular in Hong Kong and clubs or restaurants offer salsa dancing lessons at midweek salsa nights. Check *HK Magazine* for details of upcoming events.

KARAOKE

Although karaoke was a worldwide fad in the 1980s and 1990s, it has been a more enduring phenomenon in Asia. In Hong Kong, it is still a popular form of entertainment with locals. The karaoke bars are quite lavish, with individual soundproofed rooms, food and drink menus, a full microphone system and video. Many karaoke establishments can be found in TST and Causeway Bay, including **V-Mix Karaoke** (2–8 Sugar Street, Causeway Bay; tel. 2137 9888) and **Big Echo Karaoke Box** (92 Granville Square, Energy Plaza, TST; tel. 2732 7000).

MASSAGE PARLOURS

Along with karaoke, the massage parlour is another Hong Kong late-night standard that is particularly popular with Hong Kong men and businessmen visiting Hong Kong. Parlours are open until 2:00 or 3:00 am and offer straight body and foot massage services. Massage parlours and saunas offering sexual services usually advertise the nationalities of their female masseurs. Gay saunas are altogether another ball game.

THE GAY SCENE

Although homosexuality is variously considered by China to be a mental illness or a nasty Western import, Hong Kong is a tolerant society and gay expat men generally find Hong Kong a great place to live and socialize. The community is vibrant, partying and freewheeling, with occasional police raids on private parties (ostensibly for drugs) the only drawback.

Since homosexuality was legalized in Hong Kong in 1991, gay support groups such as **Horizons** (www.horizons.org.hk; tel. 2815 9268) have been battling to get equal rights for gays. Horizons offers a gay advisory service and organized events. There are also gay bookshops, a gay art gallery and even a supposedly gay beach – Middle Beach. Lesbians are also tolerated and it's common to see couples on the MTR fondling or holding hands. For expat lesbians, the scene is rather dry.

Local lingo

Duck – male prostitute
Chicken – female prostitute
Dau fu ('beancurd') – lesbian
Sticky rice – gay Chinese men who prefer Chinese partners
Potato queen – gay Chinese men who prefer Western partners

Gay bars and clubs

Most of the bars in the Soho area are gay-friendly and some have gay happy hours – a long-standing one is at **Post 97** on Friday nights. Clubs and bars that have established themselves as primarily gay hangouts include:

- **Mei Lang Fang** (14 On Wo Lane, Sheung Wan; tel. 2152 2121);
- **Propaganda** (L/G, 1 Hollywood Road, Central; tel. 2868 1316);
- **Volume** (LG/F, 83–85 Hollywood Road, Central; tel. 2857 7683);

- **Wally Matt Lounge** (3A, G/F, Granville Circuit, TST; tel. 2367–6874) and **New Wally Matt Lounge** (G/F, 5A Humphrey's Avenue, TST; tel. 2721 2568);
- **Works** (1/F, 30–32 Wyndham Street, Central; tel. 2868 6102); and
- **Zoo** (33 Jervois Street, Sheung Wan; tel. 2851 4800) – features a monthly 'Womyn Mixxer'.

For information on other gay-friendly bars and venues, visit **http://sqzm14. ust.hk/hkgay.htm**, **www.gayhk.com** or pick up the magazine *DS*, free in bars (www.dimsum-hk.com).

Chapter Twenty-Six

Dating

Although the demographics of Hong Kong are officially about 52% women and 48% men, it feels as though there are a lot more women around. FDHs from the Philippines and Indonesia, many of them women, make up almost 3% of the total Hong Kong population. On Sunday, the streets of Central are literally paved with women.

Over the Chinese border in Shenzhen, it was common in the 1990s for Hong Kong men to install a Chinese mistress in her own apartment, purportedly at a cost of about $2,000 a month, for weekend visits. The collection of enclaves where these women lived was nicknamed 'Er Nai Cun', or 'Second Breast Village'. Unfortunately, like everything in Hong Kong, modern-day concubinage is subject to economic climates and the depression in 1997 saw many mistresses abandoned by their sugar daddies. As a consequence, sex is cheaper than ever. A recent report in a local newspaper quoted $70 as the going rate outside the cross-border railway station of Lowu.

Never one to be outdone, the sensationalist *Apple Daily*, a popular Chinese tabloid owned by media mogul Jimmy Lai, until recently, used to advertise the 'best' brothels in Hong Kong. Now it's Macan that gets the listings. But go up to Ladies Street Market in Mongkok and you can see boards advertising hourly prices for girls from around the world. Those on a budget head to Sham Shui Po. The Chinese women dressed in their house clothes lounging around on the street in the middle of the day are all busy plying their trade. One-woman brothels, where women who are typically in their 30s or older operate out of their own apartment, are fairly common. Prostitution is not illegal in Hong Kong, but living off the income of a prostitute and soliciting are.

Meanwhile, poll after poll finds married Hong Kongers dissatisfied with sex, blaming the living environment, work stress and financial pressure. The average age for marriage here is 28 for women and 31 for men. Increasingly, as elsewhere in the developed world, women are marrying later. Because Hong

59. Lovers
Photograph taken by Stanley Ng

Kong women expect to marry above their education level and earning power, tying the knot is becoming increasingly difficult. Divorce is also common.

Sex shops

(Information drawn from *HK Magazine*'s Mr Know-It-All column.)
Night Shanghai (G41–42A Peninsula Centre, 67 Mody Road, TST; tel. 2723 7172).
Fetish Fashion (M/F, Merlin Building, 32 Cochrane Street, Central; www. fetishfashion.com.hk; tel. 2544 1155).
Joy Gift Shops (Shop 39, Presidents Shopping Centre, Causeway Bay; tel. 2836 0581).

HONG KONG: GRAVEYARD OF EXPAT MARRIAGES?

Hong Kong's tolerance means that mixed couples flourish here, particularly Western men with Asian partners. Unfortunately, not all expat marriages survive the strain of what one friend dubs 'the rising executive in the oriental sweetie shop syndrome', or what's commonly referred to here as 'yellow fever'. The combination of long work hours (often involving business travel outside Hong Kong on a weekly or monthly basis), available and attractive young women, and the absence of a social index of criticism that could make a straying partner think twice back home, can play havoc with long-term domestic partnerships. One Australian boss I met over drinks explained how he flies back to see his wife and four sons in Perth every seven to ten days. They returned to Australia eight years ago while he stayed in Hong Kong. He does this to protect his relationship with his wife, as he'd heard that if you are away for more than 16 days, a wife develops her own life and the couple drift apart.

Hong Kongers insist that racism does not exist in Hong Kong, but Filipinas will be the first to take issue with that. Expats with Filipina or south-east Asian partners may encounter some level of ignorance or prejudice, although it is unlikely to manifest itself in the aggressive way found in Western societies. Laws aimed at curbing racial discrimination are currently in process; sex and disability discrimination acts were passed in the 1990s.

Dating expats

Either I have very unfortunate girlfriends or they are representative. T speaks for many when she describes the expat dating scene as 'in a word: difficult'. Like other women friends of mine, T was asked out by married expat men or men with no intention except having a good time. One-night stands are common and a casual relationship is virtually the norm. Compared with Asian women, Western women have a reputation as being difficult to please and uninterested in home-making and child-rearing. Financially independent single women here are acutely aware of the fact that they are competing for partners with younger, attractive Asian women who, for many men who plan to stay in Asia, are the ideal route into the culture.

Comments from expat men published in the *South China Morning Post* reflect a stereotypical view of Asian women:

- 'I just love their boutique size. My Chinese girlfriend makes me feel ten feet tall';
- 'They are skinny and cute'; and
- 'They know the rules of love affairs – which is to follow wherever your man goes'.

Another said:

> *Maybe all Western men look the same to them. Or maybe they just don't care. Because, let's face it, an ugly guy like me would never get such a beautiful girlfriend back in the USA.*

Many expat women are not interested in dating Chinese men, either because they don't find them physically attractive or because of cultural differences.

Once you've cut out the local men, the gay men, the married men and the men only interested in Asian women, you've pared down the field quite a bit. M, 46, has been in Hong Kong for the past ten years. According to her, it's a numbers game. She says:

> *A couple of my friends have asked me how I expect to meet a man in Hong Kong. My answer was that I didn't come to Hong Kong to meet a*

man – I came to experience Hong Kong and develop aspects of my life
... But one of the greatest things about Hong Kong is there are lots of
intelligent and interesting men. ... I've dated lots of men during my time
in Hong Kong for varying periods. In one year, I think, the youngest was
32 and the oldest was 61.

In spite of the apparent difficulties, several good expat women friends of mine
met and married expat men here.

Dating Hong Kongers

Hong Kong men tend to get a bad press – unfairly, I think – when the topics
of 'dating' and 'relationships' come up in conversation or in lifestyle news reporting. Although generally speaking shorter and thinner than their Western
counterparts, many Hong Kong men are cute, good-looking, have nice skin
and are well-groomed. They make the most of their appearance with trendy
hairstyles, are fashion-savvy, well-dressed and smart. They often have an
admirable commitment to working hard and making money, and by and large
are not heavy drinkers.

However, Hong Kong women often complain about the fact that Hong
Kong men are shallow, selfish, boring, uncultured, lack a sense of humour
and think drinking red wine is the height of sophistication. This dissatisfac-
tion is reflected in the growing trend for Hong Kong women to seek mates
over the border. Mainland men are gaining a reputation for being responsible, well-informed, broad-minded and egalitarian when it comes to sharing
housework. The traditional Chinese view of wifely obedience – expressed
in the adage 'husband sings and wife accompanies' – seems well past its sell-
by date in contemporary Hong Kong.

Hong Kong men in their turn accuse Hong Kong women of being mercenary
and status-seeking. The fact of the matter is that, although a small percent-
age of Hong Kong's economic elite are extremely wealthy, the vast majority
are lower-middle-class urbanites looking to improve their standard of living.
When the starting salary for a graduate is roughly $7,000–10,000 and more
than 80% of Hong Kong's population don't pay salary tax because their earn-
ings fall below the tax threshold, there is a powerful incentive for both sexes
to concentrate on making money.

Single men and women in their twenties and thirties and even older tend to live in the same house as their parents until they get married. This can cause problems with regard to privacy when you are visiting. Depending on your partner's family set-up, the amount of time you spend with his relatives may vary considerably. If your partner's parents are divorced, or the relationship between the parents and children is not close, contact can be minimal. In situations where families are closer, you may be invited over for Sunday lunch or to *dim sum* on a regular basis.

Most Hong Kongers feel it is their duty to provide for their parents. This can range from giving them an allowance every month for food, entertainment and so on to buying them an apartment – even when the parents have sufficient money of their own.

I once read a letter published in the *South China Morning Post* written by an expat man who was about to marry a local Cantonese girl he had been dating for some time. He was upset because his girlfriend's family were not going to contribute to the cost of the wedding, which his parents were willing to do. In addition, they were expecting him to pay a dowry on marrying his girlfriend – part of the culture here for traditional families.

As a girlfriend, you will not be expected to pay a dowry should you marry a Cantonese man. Cantonese parents, like Asian parents in general, are also less strict with regard to a foreign woman (or *gweipo*) dating, sleeping or living with their son than a foreign man (*gweilo*) doing the same with their daughter.

Hong Kong dating etiquette dictates that when a man takes a girl out on a date he will pay. Further along the line, a more Western-style approach to paying the bill may be adopted, such as turn-taking. Going Dutch is considered a bit uncouth by Hong Kongers in any situation. Valentine's Day is observed religiously!

DATING WEBSITES, ORGANIZATIONS AND PERSONALS

Recently in Hong Kong the trend has been away from official matchmaking agencies and more towards informal networking evenings or speed-dating with other add-ons, such as wine-tasting. Organizations setting up such events include **HK Speed Date** (www.hkspeeddate.com and **Coffee Matching Club** (www.coffeematching.com). A free online dating service is provided by **www.wheresmydate.com.hk**. Other dating services and websites include **www.asiafriendfinder.com**. SMS services include **Chat Pals** (www.findnchat. com.hk; tel. 2880 2788). *HK Magazine* and the *South China Morning Post* have Personals sections, and free posting of personals is available at **www. asiaxpat.com**.

Tertiary Institutions

- The University of Hong Kong, Mid-Levels, Hong Kong Island (www.hku. hk).
- The Chinese University of Hong Kong, Shatin, New Territories (www. cuhk.hk).
- The Hong Kong University of Science and Technology, Clearwater Bay, New Territories (www.ust.hk).
- City University of Hong Kong, Kowloon Tong, Kowloon (www.cityu.edu. hk).
- Hong Kong Baptist University, Kowloon Tong, Kowloon (www.hkbu.edu. hk).
- Hong Kong Polytechnic University, Hung Hom, Kowloon (www.polyu. edu.hk).
- Lingnan University, Tuen Mun, New Territories (www.ln.edu.hk).
- Hong Kong Institute of Education, Tai Po, New Territories (www.ied.edu. hk).
- The Hong Kong Academy for Performing Arts, Wanchai, Hong Kong Island (www.hkapa.edu).
- Shue Yan University (private university).

Airlines

Airlines	Reservations	Flight information
Air Canada	2867 8111	2867 8111
Air China	3102 3090	2216 1088
Air France	2501 9433	2180 2180
Air India	2522 1176	2216 1088
Air New Zealand	2862 8988	2862 8988
All Nippon Airways	2810 7100	2810 7100
American Airlines	3678 8500	3678 8500
Asiana Airlines	2523 8585	2180 2180
Australian Airlines	2822 9070	2822 9070
British Airways	2822 9000	2216 1088
Cathay Pacific	2747 1888	2747 1888
China Airlines	2868 2299	2769 8391
Delta Airlines	2117 7488	2117 7488
Dragonair	3193 3888	2180 2180
Emirates	2801 8777	2216 1088
Gulf Air	2882 2892	2882 2892
Japan Airlines	2523 0081	2847 4567
KLM Royal Dutch Airlines	2808 2111	2808 2111
Korean Air	2366 2001	2868 2313
Lufthansa	2868 2313	2916 0066
Malaysia Airlines	2916 0088	2769 7345
Northwest Airlines	2810 4288	2116 8730
Orient Thai	2366 6869	2116 8730
Pakistan International Airlines	2366 4770	2366 4770
Philippine Airlines	2301 9300	2216 1088
Qantas Airways	2822 9000	2822 9938
Scandinavia Airlines System	2865 1370	2865 1370
Singapore Airlines	2520 2233	2520 2233
South African Airways	2877 3277	2877 3277
Swiss International Air Lines	3002 1330	3002 1330
Thai Airways International	2876 6888	2876 6888
United Airlines	2810 4888	2122 8256
Vietnam Airlines	2810 6680	2810 6680
Virgin Atlantic	2532 6060	2532 6060

Consulates

Consulate	Phone number
Australia	2827 8881
Austria	2522 8086
Canada	3719 4700
Denmark	2827 8101
France	3196 6100
Germany	2105 8788
Great Britain	2901 3000
Greece	2774 1682
India	3164 6188
Indonesia	2890 4421
Ireland	2527 4897
Israel	2821 7500
Italy	2522 0033
Japan	2522 1184
Korea	2529 4141
Malaysia	2527 8016
Netherlands	2522 5127
New Zealand	2525 5044
Norway	2587 9953
Pakistan	2827 0681
Philippines	2823 8500
Portugal	2802 2587
Russia	2877 7188
Singapore	2527 2212
South Africa	2577 3279
Spain	2525 3041
Sweden	2521 1212
Switzerland	2522 7147
Taiwan (trade commission)	2525 8315
Thailand	2521 6481
USA	2523 9011
Vietnam	2591 4517

Useful Telephone Numbers

EMERGENCY SERVICES

Police/fire/ambulance	999
Locate nearest police station	2860 2000

LOCATING TELEPHONE NUMBERS

Directory enquiries	1081
International directory enquiries	10013

UTILITIES AND TELECOMMUNICATIONS

Phone service (PCCW)	1000
Hongkong Electric	2887 3411
China Light and Power	2728 8333
Report a gas leak	2880 6999
Gas maintenance enquiry	2880 6988
Water Supplies Department	2824 5000

REPORTING LOST CREDIT CARDS

American Express	2811 6122
Visa	2810 8033
MasterCard	2511 6387

Calendar of Annual Festivals and Events in Hong Kong

Please note that the dates of the Chinese festivals vary slightly year to year, following the lunar calendar.

January
1st – **New Year's Day**.
Chinese New Year Festival: a three-day public holiday; flower markets in Victoria Park; family celebrations – the most important dinner is held on Chinese New Year's Eve; streets are deserted and shops closed; firework displays over Victoria Harbour.

February
Hong Kong Arts Festival: concerts, dance, opera, theatre and multimedia performances by international companies.

March
Rugby Sevens: a three-day competition at the Queen Elizabeth Stadium.
Hong Kong International Film Festival: watch movies all day long at cinemas around the territory.

April
Ching Ming Festival: sweeping the graves and honouring the ancestors.
Easter: a three-day public holiday.

May
1st – **Labour Day**: a one-day holiday.
Cheung Chau Bun Festival: a pageant and bun grab on Cheung Chau Island.
Le French May: films, concerts and shows featuring French performers.
Buddha's Birthday: thousands make a pilgrimage to Buddhist temples such as Po Lin (Lantau) and Wong Tai Sin; Buddhist-related exhibitions.

June
Dragon Boat Festival (Tuen Ng): racing off Discovery Bay, Stanley, etc.

July
1st – **HKSAR Establishment Day**: fireworks and parades.

September
Mid-Autumn Festival: moon-viewing on the Peak; lantern parades in Victoria Park and lots of mooncakes; family dinner.
Tai Hang Fire Dragon Dance: takes place on the streets of Tin Hau.

October
1st – **National Day**: celebrated all over China.
Cheung Yeung Festival: climbing mountains and sweeping the graves.
Hallowe'en: in recent years, Hong Kongers have taken this festival to heart and come out onto the streets to see each other's fancy dress. Lan Kwai Fong is the hotspot (restaurants and clubs are decorated) and gets very busy, so be prepared for crowds.

November
Hong Kong Youth Arts Festival: art exhibitions and performances by students from around the city.

December
Christmas Day and **Boxing Day**.

Index

restaurants (vegetarian), 80–1
roast meats, 68
rock climbing, 258
rowing, 232
Royal Hong Kong Yacht Club, 32, 254
rubbish, 139–40
rugby, 232
rugs and carpets, 104
running, 232–3

Sai Kung, 45
sailing, 233
salary tax, 181
Sam Tung Uk Museum, 255
Samaritans, 148, 216
sandwiches, 67
SARS, 137, 143
savings, 161
schools, 119–24
seafood, 78
second-hand clothes, 92
Securities and Futures Commission (SFC), 160
serviced apartments, 50–1
serviced offices, 186
setting up a company, 182
sex, 281
sex shops, 282
Sham Shui Po, 93
Shatin, 45
Shek O, 254
Sheung Wan, 41
shoes, 90
shooting, 233
shopping malls, 83, 133
Shouson Hill, 43
side-line employment, 189
sight-seeing, 253
singing, 251
ski-ing and snowboarding equipment, 108
skiing, 233
SME tips, 191
Snoopy's World, 133
snowboarding, 233
soccer, 233
social clubs, 235
society, 165

softball, 233
Soho, 28, 41, 274
South Horizons, 43
spas, 151
SPCA, 215
special needs schools, 120, 123
sports, 230, 279
sports clubs, 229, 235
sports equipment, 107–8
sports for kids, 124
Sports Market, 33
sportswear, 93
squash, 233, 260
St John's Cathedral, 222
St John's College Chorale, 240
St John's Counselling Service, 148
stamp duty, 49
Stanley Market, 86, 91, 254
Stanley, 43
Star Ferry, 25, 29, 32
State of the Arts Gallery, 226, 248
street snacks, 70
stress, 147–8
studying, 209–12
Sun Yat-Sen Historical Trail, 255
supermarkets, 98
surfing, 234
swimming, 234

tai chi, 151
Tai Long Wan, 253
Tai O Village, 256
Tai Tam, 43
Taikoo Shing, 42
tailors, 93
Taipo, 45
Tap Mun (Grass Island), 253
tax, 181
tax reserve certificates, 181
taxi complaints hotline, 29
taxis, 17–18, 26–9
TDC Business Information Centre, 186–7
tea (afternoon), 69
tea buffet, 69
tea dances, 277
tea shops, 72
Teddy Bear Kingdom, 32, 133

4716184R00177

Printed in Great Britain
by Amazon.co.uk, Ltd.,
Marston Gate.